IMMIGRATION AND AMERICAN DIVERSITY

Problems in American History

Series editor: Jack P. Greene

Each volume focuses on a central theme in American history and provides greater analytical depth and historiographic coverage than standard textbook discussions normally allow. The intent of the series is to present in highly interpretive texts the unresolved questions of American history that are central to current debates and concerns. The texts will be concise enough to be supplemented with primary readings or core textbooks and are intended to provide brief syntheses of large subjects.

1	Jacqueline Jones	*A Social History of the Laboring Classes*
2	Robert Buzzanco	*Vietnam and the Transformation of American Life*
3	Ronald Edsforth	*The New Deal*
4	Frank Ninkovich	*The United States and Imperialism*
5	Peter S. Onuf & Leonard J. Sadosky	*Jeffersonian America*
6	Fraser J. Harbutt	*The Cold War Era*
7	Donna R. Gabaccia	*Immigration and American Diversity*

IMMIGRATION AND AMERICAN DIVERSITY

A Social and Cultural History

Donna R. Gabaccia
University of North Carolina

BLACKWELL
Publishers

First published 2002

2 4 6 8 10 9 7 5 3 1

Blackwell Publishers Inc.
350 Main Street
Malden, Massachusetts 02148
USA

Blackwell Publishers Ltd
108 Cowley Road
Oxford OX4 1JF
UK

Library of Congress Cataloging-in-Publication Data has been applied for.

ISBN 0–631–22032–1 (hardback); 0–631–22033–X (paperback)

British Library Cataloguing in Publication Data

A CIP catalogue record for this book is available from the British Library.

Typeset in 11 on 13 pt Sabon
by Ace Filmsetting Ltd, Frome, Somerset

This book is printed on acid-free paper.

Contents

Figure and Tables

Preface and Acknowledgments

Short books produce large debts. *Immigration and American Diversity* was written as a book that undergraduate students could profitably read in conjunction with many fine collections, which gather "immigrant voices" past and present. As a teacher, I know how much students enjoy hearing those voices, and as a writer, I appreciate the authors who make them accessible. Without collections of documents and personal narratives edited by Colin Calloway, Thomas Dublin, Jon Gjerde, Gordon Hutner, Thomas Kessner, Betty Boyd Caroli, Dale Steiner, and Al Santoli, mine would have been a very different book.

For years, I have labored happily in the multilingual world of interdisciplinary and transnational studies of migration while teaching world history. The experience has alerted me to the distinctive characteristics of immigration and ethnic histories of the USA. The rest of the world does not think about race, mobility, ethnicity, religion, or history and chronology in quite the ways Americans do. This awareness pushed me to respond positively when Blackwell editor Susan Rabinowitz first encouraged me to consider a small interpretive book on a grand, important theme.

I took seriously the goal of Blackwell's Problems in American History series to "present in highly interpretive texts the unresolved questions of American history." *Immigration and*

American Diversity does not aim to document in all their rich detail the histories all of the immigrant and ethnic groups of the USA. Others have done that well. But doing it well has diverted attention from social and cultural interactions among immigrants and Americans of diverse backgrounds.

My goals were straightforward. I wanted students to consider how immigration shaped social interactions *across* cultural boundaries. I wanted to trace the resulting changes in group and individual identities, among newcomers and diverse Americans alike. Finally, I wanted them to face the unresolved issue of American national culture. To write briefly about four centuries of ethnic interaction, I drew on my experience teaching world history, and organized the material thematically rather than offering the tight chronology appropriate for histories of politics, policy, and demography.

A year-long sabbatical from the University of North Carolina at Charlotte allowed me to revise a very rough draft of this manuscript during the early months of my tenure as a Fellow at the Charles Warren Center at Harvard University. There I benefited from good advice delivered by my fellow Warren Fellows in its 2000–2001 seminar "Global America." Jim Campbell, Jona Hansen, and Jessica Gienow-Hecht were particularly helpful, perhaps without fully realizing how.

Jim Barrett, Peter D'Agostino, Dirk Hoerder, Cindy Kierner, and Lea Zuyderhoudt were kind enough to read drafts of some of the chapters of this book. I thank them for it, as I do the three anonymous readers who saved me from some errors and sharpened my interpretation in countless ways.

More personally, I again thank both Thomas Kozaks, Jeffrey Pilcher, Jeanne Chiang, Dorothy Kachouh, and my mother, Marjorie Gabaccia, for their unfailing love. It sustains me in all I do.

Donna R. Gabaccia
Cambridge, MA

Introduction

If you are like me, and are an American living in the USA, then your ancestors – like mine – lived on other continents before coming to North America. But while I think of myself as a descendant of immigrants, you very well may not. Why should that be so? Since World War II, the United States has often proudly proclaimed itself, in the words of John F. Kennedy, "a nation of immigrants."[1] In his book, Kennedy acknowledged the importance of American diversity. But even when he wrote in 1959, the word "immigrants" – understood to mean those who had left Europe voluntarily between 1820 and 1920 in search of liberty – excluded many Americans. If your ancestors arrived in America before 1492, came from Spain, England, or France before 1776, or traveled unwillingly as slaves from Africa, it's unlikely you considered them part of Kennedy's nation of immigrants. If you arrived more recently, leave the USA to go home on vacations, or don't possess a green card, you may not think of yourself as an immigrant even today.

Immigration and American Diversity aims to broaden your understanding of the USA as a culturally diverse nation by portraying immigration as just one of many important migrations transforming American life. It offers a short survey of a long sweep of American history, beginning with the arrival in North America of migrants from Asia, Africa, and Europe and ending with a discussion of the USA at the turn of the twenty-first century. It identifies the places where mobile peoples have met and describes the American communities – including those we today call "ethnic groups" – that emerged from their encounters. It shows how these encounters produced individual identities and regional cultures that are uniquely American in combining elements from diverse traditions.

Immigration and American Diversity shows you how discussions of newcomers have also been central to Americans' efforts to define their nation. Could anyone who chose American citizenship and espoused its civic ideals become an American? Or were Americans themselves a racial or a cultural group willing to exclude other peoples they deemed too different? While urging you to ponder these unresolved questions, *Immigration and American Diversity* ultimately argues that migration helped make Americans of newcomers and natives alike.

Who is an Immigrant?

If you have traveled abroad as a tourist or moved from one US city or state to another, you already know that all people on the move are not considered immigrants, nor do they consider themselves to be immigrants. National governments define immigrants by identifying foreigners who are eligible to join their nations. To do this, they must first draw boundaries around their national territories, embrace the residents of that territory as national citizens or subjects, and legislate which foreigners may enter. They must distinguish immigrants from both their own mobile citizens and from other foreigners who – as students, temporary workers, businesspeople, or tourists – will again quickly leave. Many distinguish immigrants from foreign "denizens" who live permanently on their territory without joining their nation.

Because governments define immigration, it is problematic to speak of American immigrants before the USA became an independent country. Many newcomers in the seventeenth and eighteenth centuries came as conquerors and viewed the natives as enemies to be vanquished if not totally eliminated. Many were slaves captured in Africa. Although different from later immigrants, these early migrants established and institutionalized forms of human interaction with which Americans would long grapple.

Nor did migrations of conquerors end in 1776. When the USA defeated Mexico in 1848, and when it obtained Spain's remaining colonies in the Caribbean and the Philippines in a war in 1898, neither the natives nor the newcomers in these encounters are best understood as immigrants. Many Americans migrated westward as rulers; Mexican residents of Arizona and the colonials of Puerto Rico became subjects and, eventually, citizens, of the USA without leaving home. Puerto Ricans who then moved to New York as citizens crossed no national boundary and no inspector counted them as immigrants.

And they had plenty of company. Contrary to popular belief, there was no golden time in the past when Americans were immobilized by strong attachments to their home places in the USA. Even during the nineteenth century's peak eras of immigration, larger numbers of people moved about within the USA than across its national borders. Yet, surely, to leave rural Alabama for Chicago's "promised land" in 1910 was a cultural journey almost as long as the one from Poland to Cleveland.[2]

Immigration itself has ebbed and flowed considerably since the USA began counting foreign newcomers in 1820, as Figure I.1 shows. Yet immigration, somewhat like the westward "frontier" migrations, has nevertheless generated a controversial interpretation of US history. While the latter emphasized the nation's destiny to expand and conquer, portraits of the USA as a "nation of immigrants" have celebrated the American nation's ability to incorporate outsiders peaceably and to unify peoples of diverse backgrounds.

This celebration of immigration as a foundation for national unity is quite recent, however. Americans did not even label foreigners as immigrants until a full century after the USA became a nation. Until 1820, they called the newest arrivals

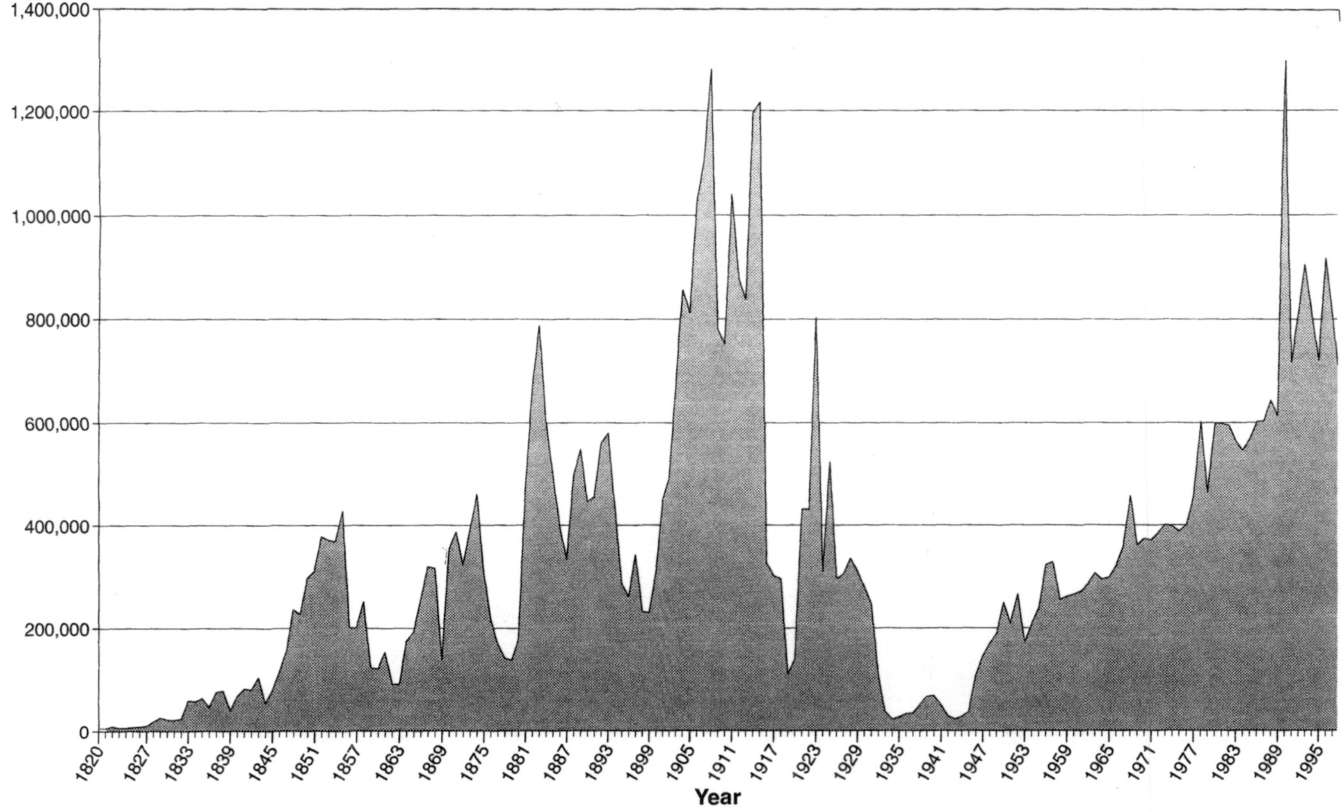

Figure I.1 Immigration as an influence on American life

"aliens": citizenship defined Americans, aliens lacked it. When aliens obtained citizenship they "became American." For a half century after 1830, natives increasingly questioned this easy transformation of aliens into citizens; they began calling newcomers "emigrants," to emphasize their flight from a backward and intolerant "Old World." In the 1880s and 1890s, natives hostile to newcomers (we now call such people nativists) became the first Americans to popularize the term "immigrant." Efforts to diminish immigration from abroad date from this era.

Celebrations of the USA as a nation of immigrants, and of the transformation of immigrants into Americans, developed only after immigration was, in fact, sharply restricted between 1882 and 1924. Only then did immigration seem to provide a satisfying illustration of the national motto of making "out of many, one," and even that illustration failed to satisfy the many mobile Americans who felt little connection to immigration. Since 1965, historians of immigration have increasingly questioned the unifying power of immigration, emphasizing instead its contributions to American diversity.[3] Both popular and scholarly accounts have also catalogued the experiences of "the many" – Native-Americans, women, Asian immigrants, and African-Americans – excluded from the "one" during the years when European immigrants could easily acquire citizenship.

One of the purposes of this book is to bridge the chasm between an upbeat image of the USA as a nation of immigrants and more critical accounts of American multiculturalism written in the past three decades. While both recognize diversity as a central theme in American life, each interprets national unity differently. Viewing the USA as a nation of immigrants has the advantage of focusing our attention on the transformations of cultures and identities that inevitably occur as people move about, recognize their differences and try to live together despite them. But to view all these transformations as a direct path to national homogeneity might be inaccurate. Most Native- and African-Americans have deep roots in North America but maintain distinct identities; some of the most important influences on newly arrived foreigners have been mobile natives, many of them racial minorities, and they, too, changed during their encounters with each other and with the newcomers.

Immigration, Ethnicity, and American Diversity

Diversity is too obvious to ignore in the USA; we see it in personal identities, physical appearances, cultural and religious values, and group affiliations. Newcomers to the USA generate some of this diversity although immigration is by no means its only source. People in the USA vary in religious faith, language, and geographic origins; around 1930, scholars began labeling such differences "ethnic."[4] Americans with darker skin colors have developed distinctive cultures through their long histories of exclusion and discrimination; Americans typically call these differences "racial" or "racial ethnic."[5] Immigration and ethnic history are thus best analyzed together – the former for its focus on mobility as a source of transformation and the latter for its attention to cultural groups.

Even among immigrants and their immediate descendants, cultural diversity is never exclusively the product of mobility. Historical memories of conquest and abuse define important elements of group solidarity and identity for Jewish-Americans, Native-Americans, Black-Americans, Asian-Americans (especially in the west), Mexican-Americans in the southwest, and many white southerners, too. For immigrants and natives with distant or recent origins in Asia and Africa, racial discrimination encourages ethnic group formation. Religious practices are important in defining ethnicity among immigrant Catholics, Jews, and Moslems and among long-time American Mormons and Black members of the Nation of Islam while spoken accents are salient to southerners, Latinos, Blacks, and most foreigners.

Ethnic groups, with their distinctive cultures, have considerable significance in American history. Religious faith has generated local churches, mosques, and synagogues and large nation-wide and even international associations of the faithful. The southern states did secede in 1860 to form an independent country based on regional loyalties. Many immigrants and racial minorities in 1900 married, socialized, and worked mainly with people of their "own kind," and their newspapers, associations, and leaders spoke for them as separate groups. The American government has traditionally treated ethnicity and race as real and sometimes even as scientific ways of categorizing diversity. American law labeled and limited the legal rights of enslaved Africans, Native-American nations, and foreign aliens, and treated individuals first and foremost as members of these groups, determining who could marry or vote, what schools children attended, what kind of jobs adults took, and which political opinions they expressed.

Nevertheless, ethnic groups, like nations, are also to some degree "imagined communities," and they are imagined by both insiders and outsiders to possess an ethnic culture.[6] People on the move have especially strong incentives to choose to identify with and thus to imagine themselves as members of distinct ethnic groups. But they also have better-than-average opportunities to escape group constraints. This means that group life usually reflects some element of choice among insiders. Leaders of the Catholic Church may speak for all the faithful but many Catholics do not attend services or support the church financially. Many migrants change their religion, not just their residence. And Jewish- and Chinese-Americans may prefer their children to marry within their groups, but they do not always do so.

Powerful outsiders can also play a powerful role in imagining cultural communities, and for this reason, many theorists argue that physical appearance, especially color, provided such a firm indicator of cultural difference that racial groups differed from ethnic groups in being imposed rather than chosen. It is certainly true that white outsiders imposed racial identities on Americans with roots in Africa and Asia and that, over the centuries, black Americans encountered the especially thick boundaries whites drew between themselves and those of darker skin. Nevertheless even their identities changed over time from "Africans" in the early eighteenth century to "Colored" or "Afro-Americans" and later to "Negroes" and "Blacks" or "African-Americans."

Whenever possible, *Immigration and American Diversity* employs the ethnic and racial labels used by the people of the era under study. This may very well have a jarring or even upsetting effect on you as reader. That sense of discomfort should serve to remind you that because ethnic groups are imagined, imposed, and chosen, they are also always evolving. And one of the reasons they evolve, is that people move about, meeting new neighbors and highlighting new elements of their cultures, histories, and identities in the process.

However important, ethnic groups are also not monolithic; even those who participate voluntarily in their activities, and embrace ethnic and racial identities, are diverse as individuals. Immigrants from Italy speak differing dialects; Jews are culturally Sephardim or Askenazim and follow Orthodox, Conservative, or Reform rituals. An Irish mill girl in 1880 could join the multi-ethnic Knights of Labor, confess to an Irish priest, join an ethnic society led by wealthy, "lace curtain," Irish men and women or seek "sisterhood" with American suffragists. Southerners are Baptists or Catholics, who think of themselves as black or white, and who are often fiercely loyal to their home state or to a local community. Black Americans can be Catholic or Protestant, northerners or southerners, natives or newcomers speaking British-accented English, Spanish, French, Portuguese, or Arabic.

As a result, most Americans can and do claim loyalties to more than one cultural group. (See the Student Exercise at the end of this Introduction.) And race, color, and ethnicity may or may not be the most salient elements in their individual identities. In fact, a recent survey revealed that only a third of Americans agreed that "race played a big role" in making them who they are. Instead, fully 60 percent of black Americans and almost half of white Americans felt religion played that role.[7]

Language, religious beliefs, food habits, gender conventions, family relations, and music also mark boundaries between ethnic groups in the USA. That is why, for example, Americans sometimes labeled German immigrants as "Krauts" (eaters of sauerkraut). Jazz or the blues can be described as an element of African-American culture just as spaghetti can be said to be Italian-American: African-Americans do listen to jazz, just as Italian-Americans do eat spaghetti. Cultural practices even provide important elements of Americans' individual identities. An orthodox Jewish woman may not feel like herself if she removes the wig or kerchief that covers her natural hair.

But while language, religious beliefs, and family practices can exclude outsiders, other elements of ethnic culture – notably food and music, which can be bought and sold – do not. Today, Americans of many backgrounds enjoy the blues and eat spaghetti. Because many elements of cultural diversity can, and are, exchanged across ethnic boundaries, *Immigration and American Diversity* particularly emphasizes the role of migration in creating the regional cultures of the USA. These regional cultures have been changing mixes of the accents, foods, and everyday customs of the particular migrants that came together in particular times in different parts of the USA.

All these regional cultures are American in being unique to the USA. Yet many Americans today rightly express doubts that centuries of cultural exchanges among mobile individuals have generated a single, homogeneous American culture. No discussion of immigration and American diversity would be complete without taking up this issue. What, if anything, has migration contributed to the making of the national group that people in the USA so easily, and without much reflection, label "American?"

What are Americans?

Building a national identity among mobile people is always a complex matter, but the USA has not been unique in facing this challenge of nation-building. Many countries (including Canada, Australia, France, Argentina, and the United Arab Emirates) are also nations of immigration, and each at times has had far higher proportions of foreigners in their populations than the USA ever did. Indeed, most large countries – India, China, Brazil, South Africa – have culturally diverse populations with sharp variations in language, culture, religion, and physical appearance.

The USA stands out among such nations mainly for its long history of immigrations from so many origins. American identities also stand out for their "hyphens," which link ethnic with national loyalties – "Italian-American," "African-American," "Native-American." While there are also "Italo-Canadians" and "Italo-Australians," people of Italian descent in France or in Latin America regard themselves quite simply as French, Brazilian, or Argentine. Many culturally diverse nations dispense with ethnic identities, while in the USA, the national element often disappears in discussions of diversity, as if it were the insignificant side of the hyphen.

It is not. Ninety-one percent of the people who responded to the survey mentioned above felt that "being an American is a big part of who I am."[8] What makes it such a big part? Is there anything at all that all Americans share?

Foreigners – including newly arrived immigrants – often see the American cultural homogeneity that remains invisible to Americans. One by no means unusually hostile British newspaper recently summed up American national characteristics as "the facile amiability; the ostentatious religiosity . . . the love of guns . . . the all-consuming fetish for material success; the infantile literal-mindedness; and the faith, withal, in America's planetary moral superiority."[9] To translate, Americans are a friendly and god-loving, if sometimes violent, people who don't much respect abstractions but are proud of their country because they believe that, there alone, the poor can become rich, thus proving to the world the moral superiority of political democracy, free enterprise, and individual initiative.

None of these traits are universally shared around the world. They could be labeled American, and as recently as the 1950s, historians of an American "national character" did just that.[10] It seems ironic that today – as Americans celebrate their cultural diversity – Europeans, Asians, Africans, and Latin Americans outside the USA fear "Americanization" will homogenize their diverse cultures into a global commercial culture symbolized by McDonald's hamburgers.

While Europeans and Africans debate the national consequences of purchasing American products, people in the USA, when they discuss their nation, typically focus instead on shared ideas about citizenship, political ideals, and government. Scholars believe Americans share a "civic nationalism" in the form of a political philosophy, not a common culture. In many modern languages other than English, however, the word nation actually means an ethnic group with its own culture; thus scholars distinguish this "ethnic nationalism" from the civic nationalism of the USA. Yet for much of the nineteenth and twentieth centuries, Americans espoused their political principles with such fervor that commentators later referred to their embrace of these ideas as a form of "civic religion."

While it is true that the earliest American nationalists adapted the civic ideals of England, and opened citizenship to men of differing religions and origins, they also, and at the same time, marked a color boundary around a white American nation by excluding slaves and Indians from citizenship as too racially and culturally different from their conquerors to be included in the nation. At least since 1776, tensions between civic nationalism and racial or ethnic nationalism have produced fierce conflicts in the USA; many of these have focused on access to citizenship and its rights. Only in 1965 did the federal government of the USA confirm its commitment to a civic nation of citizens that included all Americans, regardless of race and color. And since 1965 many Americans have also openly worried that civic nationalism – embodied in the simple universalizing principles of "liberty and justice for all" – might be too weak a foundation for unity among the diverse American people.

Ultimately, *Immigration and American Identity* asks you to consider the complex relationship between national solidarity and cultural diversity by considering the lives of individuals on the move and the special place of immigrants in this history of American mobility. It acknowledges the shared

American traits that foreigners and newcomers notice and critique, as well as the diversity that natives of the USA both celebrate and fear. American diversity is not simply a measure of division nor immigration a unifying force. By viewing diversity as a product of mobile people coming together – sometimes in conflict, sometimes in cooperation – we can imagine new answers to the old question of "Who is an American?"

Further Reading

Thomas Archdeacon, *Becoming American: An Ethnic History* (New York: The Free Press, 1983).

John Bodnar, *The Transplanted: A History of Immigrants in Urban America* (Bloomington: Indiana University Press, 1985).

Leonard Dinnerstein, Roger L. Nichols, and David M. Reimers, *Natives and Strangers: A Multicultural History of Americans* (New York: Oxford University Press, 1996).

Lawrence H. Fuchs, *The American Kaleidoscope: Race, Ethnicity, and the Civic Culture* (Hanover: University Press of New England, 1990).

Donna R. Gabaccia, *From the Other Side: Gender, Women, and Immigrant Life in the United States* (Bloomington: Indiana University Press, 1994).

Jon Gjerde, ed., *Major Problems in American Immigration and Ethnic History* (Boston: Houghton Mifflin, 1998).

Oscar Handlin, *The Uprooted*, 2nd edn. (Boston: Little, Brown, 1990).

Alejandro Portes and Rubén G. Rumbaut, *Immigrant America, A Portrait* (Berkeley: University of California Press, 1990).

Ronald L. Takaki, *A Different Mirror: A History of Multicultural America* (Boston: Little, Brown, 1993).

Student Exercise

American Diversity – and Me; American Diversity – and You

In thinking about American diversity and its relationship to immigration, I have always found it helpful to reflect on my own family history and life. I encourage you to do the same.

You'll find my thoughts below. After reading them, write your own short autobiography with thoughts on how moving (including immigrating) and how ethnicity, color, race, religion, region, and nationality have shaped your own identity, social life, and personal values. At the end of the semester, after you've finished reading *Immigration and American Diversity*, re-read your own essay. How have your ideas about yourself, your family, your identity, loyalties, and culture, changed over the course of the semester?

American Diversity – and Me

Like many others, my family has moved around quite a lot in search of work, love, and happiness. In the early twentieth century, my grandparents and great-grandparents came to the USA as immigrants from Germany, Switzerland, and Italy. I was born in Great Barrington, Massachusetts, and grew up in a working-class family – my father was a plumber, my mother a book-keeper – in nearby rural Columbia County, New York. I was the first person in my family to attend college; afterwards I earned a Ph.D. in Michigan, where I also married. Research then took my husband and me to Italy and Germany. In Germany, I took my first academic job and gave birth to my son. After that I worked in the suburbs of New York for 10 years before moving to the "New South" city of Charlotte, North Carolina. I still spend part of each year in Europe. But as I write this, I'm living in Cambridge, Massachusetts, enjoying a sabbatical from teaching while doing research at Harvard University.

During my many moves, my sense of individual identity has definitely evolved. As a child, I felt connected to a remaining, and (to me) somewhat mysterious immigrant grandfather. This was true even though my mother, father, aunts, and uncles demonstrated little interest in their origins. In my childhood, cultural diversity meant differences among Catholics, Protestants, and Jews with Irish, Italian, German, Greek, and eastern European names. A few of my relatives were Catholic or Protestant but my parents were both proud not to go to any church; they pronounced themselves agnostics. I was an Episcopalian for a few adolescent years, then joined the family skeptics. The small town where I lived was overwhelmingly white, and it was the presence of blacks that made "the city" (e.g. New York), where many of my relatives also lived, seem like an exciting but also dangerous place to me.

By the time I finished my studies at Mount Holyoke College (an all-female college), I thought of myself as an Italian-American, was painfully aware of my working-class origins, and felt that my gender was probably the largest single determinant of "who I was." My best friends were two women who had come to college from New Jersey after being born in Ohio and in Hong Kong. One thought of herself as a southerner (and soon left to study in Chapel Hill and quickly to marry there), the other was weighing the advantages of becoming an American citizen before going to Germany to study. I subsequently married a midwesterner from Ohio; two of his grandparents were immigrants from Poland but unlike mine, his parents had already "made it" into the professional middle class in the 1940s and 1950s. He had lived in Europe and thought of himself as a cosmopolitan. In the early 1970s, when I met him, he was vociferously antinationalist and was working as a Conscientious Objector to the military draft.

Because we moved to Europe after graduate school, I sometimes wondered if our dead grandparents would have thought of us as "returning" there. At the same time I definitely felt like an immigrant and an outsider while in Germany. Nevertheless, my husband and I raised our Berlin-born child as a German-speaker, and over the years after I returned again to the USA, I acquired a German-speaking stepmother and a host of German, Italian, and "international" friends and colleagues. Back in the USA, I also joined several Italian-American and other ethnic organizations, participated in quite a few Italian-American events, and made quite a few Italian-American friends and colleagues. But my ethnicity seemed mainly a product of my professional life and my scholarly interests in Italian migration: I'd never lived in an Italian-American neighborhood, and I'm the only person in my family who feels a connection to an Italian-American ethnic group or who still understands the Italian language.

In recent years, I've thought more and more about how my personal identity reflects who others think I am. When I returned from Germany to suburban New York City, I realized that my Irish- and Italian-American neighbors assumed I was Jewish. Why? Because my son – who has a Polish name - was the only neighborhood kid who didn't attend Tuesday afternoon Catholic catechism classes. Clearly, no neighbor could imagine a white ethnic family like ours as Protestants (in our lower-middle class neighborhood, the Protestants were mainly black and Hispanic Pentecostalists and Evangelicals), let alone as atheists. In the south, more predictably, my white neighbors considered me a Yankee but they invited me to join their churches; my black neighbors saw me as white and didn't. (Note, however, that I actually had black neighbors for the first time only in the 1980s and 1990s.) Surrounded by southern Protestants in Charlotte, I also became interested in Catholicism – although only intellectually – for the first time. What surprised me most, however, was a call from my local bank inquiring how well it was serving its Hispanic customers. Recall that "ia" at the end of my name? A computer had selected me as Hispanic. In fact, I rarely have had a business interaction in Charlotte without a question about that last name of mine.

What is my culture? As New Yorkers, my older relatives thought of the "west" – e.g. Michigan, where I did my Ph.D., and where people ate jello, called it salad, and drank coffee with it – as farther away and more mysterious than Europe. Did my relatives eat Italian-American food? If you call polenta and rabbit Italian-American food, then, yes, of course they did. I was certainly aware of my New York accent – and theirs - while in Michigan, although I also lost much of it, if only while living there. For most of the 1970s, I thought of myself culturally as a "child of the 60s," most influenced by the feminist, student, and radical movements of that era. Although I was fascinated by my own ethnicity – and academically interested in the topic, too – I rejected the politics of leading spokesmen for a "white ethnicity" as too conservative and too hostile to feminism and to Black Americans. When I voted (and sometimes I didn't, feeling alienated), I voted for Democrats.

In the 1980s, in Europe, where I learned to speak passably good German and passable but poor Italian, I was always most aware of my national, and American, cultural identity. People often told me "you don't seem American at all," presumably because I could stumble through conversations in languages other than English and because I rather quickly learned the fashion styles and – most surprising for me because it was so easy – "body language" of Italy. And, yes, I could pass as a native in Rome – until I opened my mouth. Nowhere did I feel more culturally American than I did in Italy.

By contrast, in the US, no friend or stranger who met me ever seemed to doubt I was American. Was that because I – like the African-American leader and intellectual W. E. B. DuBois – was born in Great Barrington, Massachusetts and thus a native? Because my blue passport proved I was a citizen? Because I (unlike my Chinese-American best friend) appear unambiguously white? Doubts about my American loyalties always came from inside, not outside. I assume I'll never learn to pass as an American southerner. And I'm generally uncomfortable with nationalism, whether in the form of pledges-of-allegiance to the USA or celebrations of the grandeurs of the Italian renaissance. In that sense, perhaps, I am still a "child of the sixties." It's unlikely that I would respond to any survey by announcing that "being an American is a big part of who I am."

At this point in my life, however, I also believe that the biggest cultural changes I've experienced have been the consequence of social and economic rather than geographic mobility. As a well-paid, white, university professor, with friends who are multicultural and international, I can now live comfortably in a uniformly middle-class, professional, and secular social world – on both sides of the Atlantic. But the world of my childhood – like some of my blue-collar relatives – now seem far away and almost foreign to me. And I feel sad about that. For me, as a scholar, studying ethnicity, labor, and immigration has been a small way of remaining connected to that sense of a lost "home."

1

Creating America; Creating Americans

In the eastern woodlands of North America in the twentieth century Cherokee people still preserved a fairly detailed account of how they arrived in America. Its pragmatic and undramatic language provides a little-known account of what may have been the first migrations to America.

> . . . the old country in which we lived . . . was subject to great floods . . . the tribe held another council and concluded to move out . . . they journeyed for many days and years and finally came to a country that had a good climate . . . The emigration continued for many years, never knowing that they crossed the great waters. In the course of time the old pathway which had been traveled by the clans was cut by the submergence of a portion of the land into the deep sea. This path can be traced to this day by the broken boulders.[1]

Is this how the first people arrived in America? Scientists agree that humans first came to America as migrants from somewhere else. But they puzzle over the date of their arrival (having pushed it back from 10 to 15 and possibly even 50,000 years ago) and they sharply disagree about the origins and pathways the newcomers took.[2]

Still, many scientific findings confirm the details of this Cherokee oral account, identifying the "old country" as Asia and the pathway to America as a tenuous land bridge between Siberia and Alaska. Called "Beringia," this passage opened as the glaciers of the long Ice Age lowered sea levels; it disappeared again with the subsequent warming of the earth's climate.

Unlike scientists, however, and much more like recent immigrants, Cherokees seem less interested in the exact arrival date, or whether or not their ancestors were the first Americans or not. They seem interested instead in their ancestors' motives and in the outcome of their move. Note that the Cherokee story emphasizes a successful, communal search (for a better climate) and satisfaction with their new home (in what is now the southeastern United States).

As the Cherokee account suggests, humans migrated to America centuries before the date that marks the beginning of most American histories, including most histories of American immigration. If, in fact, the ancestors of the Cherokee crossed the land bridge from Siberia into Alaska, they did not enter a land called America. There were no people there calling themselves Americans, and there was, of course , no Ellis Island to record their arrival as immigrants. In all likelihood, the earliest residents of America called themselves simply "humans." And while they gave many names to their home territories, "America" was not one of them. Only in 1507 did a German cartographer affix the first name of a Florentine explorer, Amerigo Vespucci, to a landmass that Columbus (from Genoa) had claimed for the Spanish crown but thought was the Indies, in Asia. When this European cartographer first "imagined America," not a single European lived in what is now the territory of the USA.

The landmass he labeled America was – and it remains today – an enormous expanse of two vast adjoined continents, the home to many peoples. Furthermore, writing America on a map in 1507 did not automatically make anyone "American." For two centuries, Europeans as often called the indigenous peoples of America "Indians" or "heathens" as Americans. Few Europeans in British North America claimed the term American for themselves until the mid-eighteenth century. Then, in 1776, as they created an independent country, the United States of America, the country's new citizens did so with considerable vigor, and attached the broad label

American to their own small nation. Even today, residents of the USA refer to themselves and their history as American; few realize how much this annoys their equally American neighbors in Canada, the Caribbean, and Mexico.

Beginning our examination of migration to America before the arrival of the English and before the revolution that created the USA has many advantages. One is that it broadens our understanding of who Americans are and where they came from. It also helps us to see that the roots of all Americans may very well be in Africa.

From Africa to America

Did "Eve" the common genetic ancestor of all *Homo sapiens* living today die in East Africa some 60,000 years ago? Scientists agree that the earliest humans appeared there as many as two million years ago, and that these earlier human groups migrated in waves into Europe and Asia. Most then died out, and how long it took the migratory *Homo sapiens* to reach America is disputed. But by the time the ancestors of the Cherokees reached Beringia, humans had probably walked more than half way around the world. By the year 10,000 BCE, humans lived from Alaska to the tip of South America. These were small groups, hunting small animals and gathering edible plants; seasonal migrations remained a key feature of their lives, ensuring their survival.

Beginning around 5000 BCE, agriculture transformed human life in America as it did also in Asia, and somewhat later in Africa and Europe. It encouraged people to abandon their seasonal migrations and to build towns and cities near their cultivated fields. In the Old World, the first large-scale agricultural civilizations developed in broad river valleys but in America they appeared first in the central highlands and coasts of Mexico and the mountains of western South America.

In what is now the southwest of the USA, the Anesazi formed the northernmost periphery of Mexico's early agricultural civilizations; they eventually moved from their flatland towns into dense cliff dwellings in order to defend themselves from newly arriving migratory hunters from the north, who preyed on the wealth their agriculture produced. The later Aztec empire of Mexico's central valley – with its large cities, complex religious and state institutions, written language, astronomical science, and sophisticated arts – never conquered territory anywhere near the Rio Grande. Still, the religious rituals and beliefs of southwestern cultures, and the pottery and ceremonial cities of eastern mound-builders in the Mississippi Valley document centuries of long-distance trade exchanges and cultural influence emanating from central Mexico. By 1000, for example, most people living east of the Mississippi River cultivated the corn that had originated there.

Corn cultivation created only a modicum of cultural homogeneity in North America. In the years between 1000 and 1500, over 600 indigenous peoples, speaking variations on 12 mutually incomprehensible languages lived in what would later become the United States and Canada. Sun worshipers prevailed in some areas; corn worshipers in others; elsewhere, animists saw the power of great spirits throughout the natural world.

In the southwest, Hopi and Zuni villages had been cultivating corn for centuries but lived in such a harsh environment they were forced to irrigate in order to grow it. Nomadic hunters later called Apache – recently migrated south from Alaska – also still preyed upon, and traded with, them. Along the Pacific, men and women worked together in small migratory bands to gather acorns or fish for salmon and they took their identities – Yuki, Hupa, Miwok, Makah – from the places they lived. On the central plains, hunter-gatherers were the ancestors of Blackfoot, Sioux, Crow, and Cheyenne peoples. In the northeast, women cultivated corn during the summer months, while men devoted themselves to hunting, warfare, and the creation and maintenance of federations among related groups. Largest of these alliances was the Ganonsyoni ("The Lodge Extended Lengthwise") of Mohawks, Oneidas, Onondagas, Cayugas, and Senecas; their usual enemy were the Algonquians to the north. In the southeast, large corn-raising villages also supported federation among the Cherokee, the distant relatives of the Ganonsyoni.

By 1500, it is possible that more people (estimates range from 8 to 100 million) lived in America than in Europe. Of these, only four or five million resided north of the Rio Grande, however, and only about 700,000 occupied the east-coast regions that would become the 13 British colonies. On the other side of the Atlantic, roughly 84 million Europeans lacked the dependable plant foods of America – notably corn – and their cities were smaller and arguably poorer as a result. What Europeans possessed in abundance were iron, wheels, weaponry, and large domesticated animals, such as horses and oxen. Europeans' discovery of America in 1492 quickly sparked a migration of conquest.

Migration and Empire-building

At least since the advent of agriculture, military campaigns by autocratic empire-builders had been among the most important generators of human migrations. Europe's invasion of America was only the most recent of many eras of empire-building but it was the first in centuries to emerge from Europe. In the years between 1000 and 1300, the soldiers of Catholic Europe, and the monarchs of Portugal, Spain, and France, were pushing earlier Islamic invaders out of the Iberian and Italian peninsulas back into Africa and the eastern Mediterranean. They had launched a crusade against Moslems to capture the Christian "Holy Lands" of Asia. Their expansion into America was an extension of these Old World campaigns.

In going to war with the Moslem world, Catholic empire-builders had unintentionally destroyed their access to highly valued products – notably spices and silks – first introduced into Europe by Arab traders from the older and more advanced civilizations of India and China. Merchants and mariners employed by Portugal and Spain, many of them from Italy, then ventured out into the Atlantic to find a new sea path to

Asia. At first they traveled south, around Africa, then westward. Discovering islands in the Atlantic, they introduced sugar – a food of the Islamic world popular also in Europe – and bought slaves from Africa to cultivate it. And they kept sailing westward.

For 200 years after Columbus's voyages to the Caribbean, America north of Mexico remained as peripheral to Europe's new American empires as it had been to the Aztecs. Spanish and Portuguese campaigns focused on the conquest of the richest, most advanced civilizations of Central and South America, murdering their leaders, soldiers, and people in large numbers. Where populations were dense (Peru and Mexico), the European invaders forced defeated peoples to work in their mines, producing gold and silver for them. Where conquest or disease destroyed sparser local populations (as in Brazil and much of the Caribbean), but where the climate was warm, Spain and Portugal introduced sugar cane. They purchased laborers in Africa from local chiefs and crammed them onto boats for the "Middle Passage." From 1500 to 1760, two-thirds of the 6 to 10 million who crossed the Atlantic were from Africa, en route to the warmest regions of America. They traveled in chains as slaves, the largest forced migration in human history.

Still looking for wealth, Spain's soldiers and missionaries pushed from Florida into the Carolinas and beyond the Rio Grande in the 1540s, and established a first Spanish fort in St. Augustine, Florida in 1565. In 1598, 500 Spanish-speakers from central Mexico invaded the territory they called "New Mexico," but were able to establish only a small string of Catholic missions and forts, scattered around Santa Fe. No gold was found, no sugar could be cultivated: northern America seemed economically useless to the Spanish.

The ambitious but poorer rulers of Protestant England, Sweden, and the Netherlands, and Catholic France sought advantage where their competitor lost interest. Trading with the indigenous peoples for fish, timber, and furs along the Atlantic coast and exploring North America's largest rivers provided the initial incentive for them to claim colonies in northern America. In quick succession, France established trading posts in Port Royal in 1605, Quebec in 1608, and Montreal in 1642; the Dutch in New Amsterdam and Fort Orange (Albany) in 1626, and the English, after failing on Roanoke Island in 1587, established Jamestown in Virginia in 1607 and Plymouth in Massachusetts in 1620. Each explorer from Europe was accompanied by some acculturated servants and sailors from African ports. But with no obvious way to generate wealth, the future of these newer colonies in northern America remained uncertain until 1700.

From Europe and Africa to North America

Far more than Europe's other empire-builders, England's rulers saw in North America a potential "New Europe" where Europeans might settle. By the time English explorers ventured across the Atlantic, England had already conquered Ireland and termed its Catholic residents the "wild Irishmen." They had encouraged Protestants from Scotland (the "Scotch Irish") to resettle its northern districts, consolidating English rule. England had itself also undergone a violent Protestant reformation and was about to enter a wrenching era of rapid urban and industrial growth. In the 1600s, its population of rural poor grew particularly quickly even though religious conflicts among Catholics, Protestant dissenters, and members of the established, church-supported, Church of England still provoked periodic armed conflicts. A civil war initiated by Puritan religious dissenters after 1642 deterred migration temporarily while the restoration in 1660, and the subsequent consolidation of England, Wales, and Scotland into a militantly Protestant "Great" Britain, seemed to open the floodgates.

More important, perhaps, the seventeenth-century English planters' successful experiments with profitable cash crops for export to Europe – tobacco, indigo, and rice – began to generate an insatiable demand for labor. North American ports quickly became important places for trade among the scattered colonies of Britain's expanding American empire. While fewer than 10,000 Frenchmen journeyed to New France 1608–1760 (and migrants to Spanish North America were even fewer), well over half a million newcomers arrived in England's colonies after 1600.

Many of the European migrants who crossed the Atlantic, even in the 1600s, were not conquerors. But neither were they just like later immigrants to the USA; many exercised little control over their individual destinies or destinations. We do not know much of the earliest illiterate slaves and the English indentured servants or about their motives, dreams, or satisfactions, however. The first laborers from Africa were brought to Virginia from the Caribbean in 1619; perhaps as many as 10,000 had been imported by 1700. By 1670, roughly 50,000 men and a few women servants from Europe went to Virginia and the Chesapeake to clear land and cultivate tobacco. Thereafter, the balance changed, as did the experiences of slaves and servants. After 1700, 278,000 slaves outnumbered servants from Europe and new migrant groups – notably 84,000 from Germany, 66,000 from the south of Ireland, and 42,000 from the north of Ireland, outnumbered the 44,000 newcomers arriving from England during the same years. In addition, migrants from Scotland almost equaled the numbers of English newcomers in the eighteenth century.

In the 1700s, new slaves from Africa outnumbered the servants arriving from Scotland, Ireland, and Germany. Fairly typical of those forced out of Africa was a boy, later known as Venture Smith, who was born in 1729 near Dukandarra, Guinea, in West Africa. Raised in a family of sheepherders and farmers, Smith was captured when warriors armed with European guns invaded his homeland from the coast in 1735. After demanding tribute, they pursued the fleeing villagers, killing Venture's father and taking the six-year-old boy, whom they marched along with other captives toward Anamabo, an English fort on the coast. After being stolen by another group of warriors, Smith was then imprisoned in Anamabo before he was put on a boat headed for Barbados along with 260 others – most of them men.

In many respects, Venture Smith's subsequent life as a migrant and slave was unusual – that is why we know his story. For one thing, unlike 60 of his companions, Venture survived; death rates on slave ships often reached 30 percent. Unlike Venture, most slaves destined for North America after 1700 traveled there directly from the west African and Angolan interior. And they went south. By then, European owners of rice plantations in the Charleston area had even learned to purchase slaves from Africa's rice-growing regions. While the majority on his ship from Africa were sold in Barbados, Venture Smith remained onboard to be sold as a servant, first in Rhode Island, and then in Connecticut. Most unusual of all, Venture Smith eventually purchased his own freedom and became a small businessman who himself purchased slaves.[3]

Death rates among migrating servants from Europe were also very high in the 1600s but at least most of these migrants chose to risk the voyage. The German Gottlieb Mittelberger tried unsuccessfully to discourage his poorer compatriots from swarming to the port city of Hamburg, where they heard myths spread by "soul sellers" or "newlanders" of a prosperous New World. These labor recruiters paid for servants' passages and then sold their contracts or indentures to ship captains. Mittelberger warned of the inedible food on shipboard and reported "there are so many lice, especially on the sick people, that they have to be scraped off the bodies." The fate of those who survived was that of Rosina Dorothy Kost, born in Waldenberg in what is now Germany – who was sold in Philadelphia "at public action."[4] Six or seven years of hard labor followed.

By the eighteenth century, the even larger numbers of indentured servants traveling to America typically shared the fate of Venture Smith, and gained release from the bondage ("indenture") they had entered temporarily in exchange for passage across the Atlantic. Those who survived diseases endemic in hot, humid climates like those of the Carolinas and Virginia commonly became laborers in port cities; others tried to acquire land and transform themselves into farmers. While most servants were young and male, more people now also traveled as "redemptioners" (people borrowing smaller sums for their passage) and in family groups. Still, the Scottish John Harrower, a particularly well-educated servant who arrived shortly before the American Revolution, observed that in Virginia traders called "soul drivers" still purchased servants to "drive them through the country like a parcell of Sheep untill they can sell them to advantage."[5]

In the 1600s, religious refugees more often chose their own destinations and more often traveled as parts of organized communities. Wishing to separate from the state-supported Church of England, the fabled Pilgrims arrived in Massachusetts in 1620 after a temporary sojourn as a community of exiles in Holland. Prior to the English Civil War, North America also offered English Puritans their best hope to "purify" English Protestant practices, free of the harassment of the Church of England. In the 1630s, 21,000 Puritan dissenters from England also settled together in Massachusetts during their own "great migration." And in 1634, a small group of English Catholics followed Lord Baltimore to Maryland where he had received royal permission to establish a colony. After 1685, Protestant Huguenots from France passed through England before settling in and around the coastal cities of Charleston and New York. And small numbers of Jews fleeing the anti-Semitism of Catholic reformation in the Spanish and Portuguese colonies made New Amsterdam, Charleston, and Philadelphia their new homes.

Although religious conflict declined after the formation of Great Britain in the 1700s, the country's Protestant rulers nevertheless remained eager to expand the wedge they had created between the Catholic empires of Spain and France in America. To attract settlers, they welcomed Protestants regardless of national origin and allowed them to acquire British nationality through a process called naturalization; their children were British if born on colonial soil. Simultaneously, colonial law sought to prevent settlement by Catholics from New France, Ireland, or Germany. Nevertheless, religious diversity among Protestant newcomers in the eighteenth century remained impressive. Many of the new English arrivals were Quakers; German-speaking Pietists shared the Quakers' opposition to established religions and viewed faith as a private, not public, matter. Scottish Presbyterians (from both Scotland and from Northern Ireland) and Anglicans were also numerous among seventeenth-century migrants.

New migrations from Africa and Europe thus augmented the diversity of North America as Europeans killed or pushed out natives and carved their lands into colonies. On the eve of the American Revolution, the new arrivals and their children constituted roughly half the European-origin population, a proportion never to be reached later in the USA. Already home to diverse indigenous populations, divided into several competing empires, and attracting newcomers from many cultures and two continents, North America was to become, and it has long remained, a land of sharp regional contrasts.

American Regions: Encounters and Transformations

On the east coast in 1633, a hopeful Wicomesse spokesman reminded the new English governor of Maryland "since that you are heere strangers and come into our Countrey, you should rather confine yourselves to the Customes of our Countrey, then impose yours upon us."[6] In a way, his comment was prescient: Europeans would not annihilate local cultures and instead adopted some of their habits. But further west, a Lakota proverb – "our tradition is a tradition of change" – offered a better recipe for all the peoples involved in colonial encounters.[7] The result was "new worlds for all." First obvious in New Spain, cross-cultural exchanges nevertheless followed distinctive regional paths in the Catholic and Protestant empires.

The Catholic empires

For many indigenous peoples of North America, the first cross-cultural encounters were not with the European conquerors themselves but with the germs they carried. The Spanish invaders of Mexico in the sixteenth century were surely cruel. But they were also few in numbers, and their diseases – smallpox and influenza – had already decimated the Aztecs of Mexico, ensuring their eventual conquest. European diseases then spread as the Spanish explored northwest and northeast Mexico. They traveled still farther north and inland into North America along local trade routes and with the native survivors who fled from spreading epidemic outbreaks.

Although weakened by disease, indigenous peoples met invaders from Europe on relatively equal terms in both Spanish and French North America. With the onset of European expansion, Pope Paul III in Rome had proclaimed the worthiness of the souls of the human "heathens" of the world and charged Europe's Catholic monarchs with their conversion. Catholic missionaries – "Black Robes" or Jesuits in New France, Franciscans in Florida and New Mexico – succeeded in building missions but faced an uphill struggle to attract local converts. In both empires, soldiers built forts to dominate and defend lands claimed by distant rulers. Often they did not so much defeat local peoples or occupy their lands as try to force or lure them into delivering food, tribute, and trade goods to sustain the few Europeans among them.

As this suggests, most of the migrants in both Catholic empires were men. While missionary brothers sought converts, traders and soldiers had more earthly concerns, and wanted wives and consorts. Having left a Mediterranean world where people from Asia, Europe, and Africa had long traded and intermarried, the Spanish found indigenous women to be desirable partners. Spain's and France's rulers hoped, furthermore, that the European men who married local women facilitated their conversion. Just as often, however, influence traveled in the opposite direction with fur traders from France becoming adopted members of the indigenous communities of their wives.

Indigenous populations were especially large and powerful in the southwest where small numbers of Spanish-speaking missionaries, farmers, and soldiers lived far from the center of

Spanish imperial and military power in Mexico City. There, agriculturalists exhausted by decades of forced labor to raise food for the Catholic missions and tribute for Spain's soldiers and enraged with pressure to abandon their own religious rituals for Catholicism actually forced Hispano (Spanish-speaking but American-born) soldiers and European missionaries to flee temporarily in 1680.

Despite these conflicts and within a century, however, the residents of New Mexico also idiosyncratically blended the cultural traits of two worlds. Hispano soldiers, missionaries, and farmers had learned to eat the corn dishes and peppers of the locals, while abandoning the use of olive oil; they had also adopted adobe-building techniques. Local people adopted the pigs and lard as well as the fruit trees, wheaten baked goods, and horses introduced by the Spanish. A few became Catholics and learned Spanish. Others, like the Navajo, maintained their autonomy and languages but abandoned their lives as migratory hunters to become herders of new European animals and weavers of woolen blankets; they learned even to drink milk and make cheese – foods unknown to the indigenous peoples of America.

In Quebec, along the St. Lawrence River and especially in the Great Lakes and Mississippi Valley, French traders, missionaries, and farmers were also outnumbered, for example by the politically well-organized Algonquian peoples. Algonquians were rarely much impressed with the newcomers, and wondered why they had made such long journeys if, as they claimed, France was so superior. In New France, a Micmac announced himself "astonished that the French have so little cleverness," and asked why French men measuring five feet needed the tall houses they boasted about in France. Lecturing a French listener, he summed up the superiority of his tribal ways, for "Indians . . . carry their houses and wigwams with them so that they may lodge wheresoever they please, independently of any seignior whatsoever."[8]

Conflict and accommodation in British North America

Relations between natives and newcomers seemed distinctive from the very onset in British North America. A Powhatan living near Jamestown in 1609 concluded "we perceive and well know you intend to destroy us."[9] The English intention to settle made conflicts over land – communally used by the eastern woodlands peoples but privately owned by the British – inevitable and violent, even though 90 percent of North America's original population may already have been dead by the time the English arrived. In the Chesapeake in 1622, five groups united under the chief Opechancanough attacked English newcomers; another war followed in the 1640s, shortly after the Pequot War wracked New England. Battles with local peoples moved westward and inland with European settlement in the eighteenth century. Warfare was the most feared interaction between Europeans and local peoples, and the two groups continuously borrowed weaponry, battle strategies, and styles of combat from each other, seeking to gain advantage.

Trade provided a more peaceful, and common, form of intercourse. The peoples of North America had long been trading among themselves; they treated only their earliest exchanges with the newly arrived English as gifts, and they quite rapidly set prices for food, furs, and hides. While they acknowledged, "We want Powder and Shot & Clothing," (along with the beads and iron cooking pots of the Europeans), they also complained, that the Europeans "first give us a large cup of Rum."[10] Seventeenth-century English and Dutch traders did exchange large quantities of alcohol for furs and skins. As the men of the Carolinas specialized in delivering these export products to Europe's traders, local women also cultivated more corn to sell to them.

Ultimately, the exchange of food and furs for alcohol and iron pots most benefited the newcomers. By 1700, 225,000 people with roots in Europe and another 25,000 originating in Africa outnumbered the 100,000 remaining indigenous peoples. Ninety thousand Puritans had created a "New England," in the north. A roughly equal number of poorer and richer English and about 10,000 slaves from Africa, lived around the Chesapeake, in the south. The remaining 60,000 – mainly English, Dutch, and Swedes, with small numbers from Africa – lived strung along rivers connecting port cities to agricultural hinterlands. The subsequent explosion of migration across the Atlantic in the 1700s further complicated these nascent regional differences.

New England

Table 1.1 reveals the considerable diversity of British North America in the eighteenth century while also pointing to the uniquely homogeneous population of New England – the only region where settlers of English descent actually predominated.

Table 1.1 The population of the new USA, by region, in 1790

	*New England**	*Middle states***	*Inland south****	*Coastal south*****
Black	2%	6%	24%	40%
English	71%	41%	49%	39%
Scotch	4%	7%	10%	6%
Northern Irish	3%	7%	5%	4%
Southern Irish	2%	3%	4%	3%
German	–	18%	4%	5%
Other White	18%	18%	4%	3%
TOTAL	1,009,371	1,017,226	504,096	1,398,959

* New Hampshire, Massachusetts, Rhode Island, Connecticut, Vermont
** New York, New Jersey, Pennsylvania, Delaware
*** North Carolina, Kentucky, Tennessee
**** Virginia, Maryland, South Carolina, Georgia

Source: Calculated from data in Thomas J. Archdeacon, *Becoming American: An Ethnic History* (New York: Free Press, 1983), p. 25.

Not only had New England's earliest settlers believed, conveniently, that "God is English," they had also assumed he was a Puritan. Near Boston, where an English newcomer reported that the natives had "died on heapes as they lay in their houses," Puritans often concluded their God was clearing out the heathens to make room for them.[11] Settlers had quickly "established" their Puritan church and required all residents of the colony to support it financially. They excluded English Quakers who refused and they banished Protestant dissidents like Roger Williams to Rhode Island (which after 1663 became the only British colony apart from Maryland officially tolerating religious practice by Catholics).

In the 1630s, Puritan settlers such as John Winthrop had believed that "the eyes of all people are upon us" as they sought to build the model community in Boston that he called a "city upon a hill."[12] But it was mainly Puritans that found New England attractive even in the seventeenth century. With few exports and poor land, New England became important mainly as a center for imperial trade and shipping. Despite its relative prosperity, it attracted relatively few newcomers after 1700.

Until the Revolution, the settlers of Massachusetts persisted in their exceptional and self-conscious traditionalism and in their devotion to reproducing European ways rather than adopting local customs. Populations of the original inhabitants continued to fall and intermarriage between natives and newcomers was exceedingly rare. Europeans adopted local place names, learned to cultivate Indian corn (but prepared it, European-style, as pudding or bread), and to enjoy pumpkin (which they baked into pies). Overall, however, they preferred the roasted meats, along with the rye and wheat breads and bean pottages of Europe, and they adopted many fewer features of local housing or dress than their counterparts in the Spanish southwest. New England seemed a completely appropriate name for their new homeland.

The coastal south

Elsewhere in British North America, the English were politically and economically powerful, but a numerical minority. In the coastal south, a relatively small planter class dominated a large population of slave and indentured laborers from Africa and Europe, supplying indigo, rice, and tobacco to Europe and sending food, lumber, and hides to British sugar colonies in the Caribbean. Compared to the spiritually oriented and self-consciously English settlers of New England, the settlers of the Chesapeake glorified material gain but pursued it by exploiting the labors of others.

Forbidden in Great Britain, slavery was legal throughout colonial North America. But the presence of large numbers of slaves from Africa literally made visible the regional distinctiveness of the coastal, plantation south. Within 40 years after the first Africans arrived in Virginia, the planter owners of large tracts of land were writing laws that institutionalized slavery and differentiated it from European servitude by making it permanent and heritable across the generations. Slavery shaped the English planters' relations even with natives. In the Carolinas, planters unconsciously emulated the many competing rulers of Africa, and sought to intensify rivalries among local groups by offering to purchase men and women captured and enslaved in their wars with each other. And a vigorous slave trade, along with the institution of slavery, structured every interaction of migrants from Africa and Europe.

It was a violent encounter. Although his family had owned slaves in Nigeria, Olaudah Equiano's first meeting with long-haired and light-skinned European slave traders in Africa nevertheless evoked great fear on his part. Once captured and sold to a European trader, he assumed he would be killed, and he wished only to die. Upon arrival in the Caribbean, he feared he would be eaten until told otherwise by slaves speaking a language that he understood. Equiano's story highlights the beatings and physical violence European planters used to force labor from the demoralized servants and slaves who outnumbered them.[13] Even in Rhode Island and Connecticut, where Venture Smith was transported and eventually earned money to purchase his freedom, his owner had smashed him in the head with a huge club and the two had battled physically, resulting in the shackling of the slave.[14]

Surprisingly, migrants from Europe also seemed to fear those they enslaved and dominated. Unlike the Spanish and Portuguese, the English confronted dark-skinned people for the first time during the slave trade. Comparing them to devils and animals, they associated their physical darkness with dirt, disease, and sin, and they feared contamination by them.[15] The Scottish indentured servant John Harrower wrote of meeting "a Black" only two weeks after his arrival in Virginia. Because he worked as a tutor, Harrower lived apart from field laborers, and reported to his wife in a letter "how many blacks young and old the Lord only knows for I belive there is about thirty". Within a year he had observed an overseer strip an enslaved blacksmith and give him "39 laches with Hickry switches that being the highest the Law allows at one Wheeping."[16]

By 1700, the institutionalization of slavery prevented even heavily unbalanced gender ratios from facilitating intermarriage in the coastal south. Around the Chesapeake and in Virginia, the earliest English planters had used first physical violence and then law to monopolize their access to scarce women, regardless of skin color, while blocking competition from male slaves and servants. British colonial law soon forbade the marriage of Europeans to Africans (although not to indigenous peoples) and even religiously sanctioned marriages between slaves had no legal standing whatsoever. Slavery guaranteed that the child of a slave mother remained a slave, while pregnancy lengthened a European servant woman's term of servitude. Masters thus had every incentive to force enslaved and indentured women to submit to their passions while denying their offspring any access to their privileges.

Yet despite slavery, cultural transformations were far more extensive among the peoples of the coastal south than in New England. While Europeans in the plantation south began to raise and eat Indian corn and to cook it as natives did – as hominy, grits, meal, bread, and mush – their most important exchanges were with the enslaved migrants from Africa who outnumbered them. Servants and planters adopted the work routine – beginning early and working at a measured pace – of African laborers long accustomed to tropical climates. In the Carolinas, slaves not only knew how to cultivate and irrigate rice, they also taught planters from Europe how to prepare, process, and eat it. They introduced the peppery flavors, fishing nets, basketry, and building styles of Africa. West African herding techniques also soon spread through coastal Carolina. And in Virginia, John Harrower reported his master playing a fiddle and then inviting a "Niger come and play on an Instrument call'd a Barrafou."[17]

Migrants from Africa changed too, although perhaps more in response to each other than to their masters from Europe. Planters pressured slaves to learn enough English to follow orders but they were ambivalent toward slaves' conversion to Christianity, fearing it created grounds for slaves to claim their freedom. Where migrants from Africa were the majority, slaves from a wide variety of origins developed their own pidgin languages and religious practices. Gullah, a mixture of African and English languages developed in coastal Carolina; throughout the south, slaves blended their diverse oral traditions and religious practices into a new slave culture even as they adopted elements of European everyday life.

The upland south and middle colonies

A particularly diverse group of migrants from Europe had arrived in the middle colonies and the upland areas of Virginia and the Carolinas. Slavery existed in both places, and only in the 1760s would the Quakers of Pennsylvania become the first among Europeans to oppose the institution, yet slaves remained everywhere a small minority. Together these two regions became the "best poor man's country" for servants and redemptioners only by constantly pushing natives farther west; free from the competition of enslaved labor, humble Europeans sought modest economic improvements. The independent, small-scale, yeoman farmers so common in these regions lived far more simply than planters; at most they exported grain and imported a few finished products (cloth, iron goods, and rum). With no established churches, the middle colonies and upland south also provided a better "American asylum" than New England for religious dissenters.

Scottish, German, and Scotch-Irish newcomers feared but also learned from the natives among whom they lived in both regions. Visitors from the coast often expressed astonishment at finding "indianized" European frontiersmen with skin clothes, living by hunting and fishing, eating corn dishes like hominy grits and hoecake, and dosing themselves with local herbs and barks. At the same time, however, the Cherokees of the southern mountains adapted many elements of European agriculture and animal husbandry, developed a written alphabet for their language, and even purchased slaves. Groups that fled inland to escape settlers from Europe generally took along their iron cooking pots, rifles, and pigs. Slaves escaping from the plantations of the coastal south joined the retreating natives on the inland frontiers (when they did not head for Spanish Florida). There, in "maroon" communities, they intermarried equally with runaway indentured servants and with indigenous peoples.

If interactions between newcomers from Africa and Europe marked the south as distinctive, the middle colonies and upland south instead brought together Europeans of sharply differing cultures. Port cities were particularly cosmopolitan places; in New Amsterdam, Dutch had jostled Swedes, English, Africans, and Germans, and a dozen languages were heard on the streets. Capturing the city from the Dutch in 1664, and renaming it New York, the British soon ate Dutch cookies and built gable-ended buildings on Dutch models but their campaigns to anglicize the language and political habits of New Yorkers were otherwise surprisingly successful.

A diverse population of religiously dissident newcomers also especially welcomed the religious toleration promised by William Penn, the Quaker founder of a colony in Pennsylvania in 1681. (Pennsylvania's religious toleration extended even to natives: Tuscaroras from the south also relocated to Pennsylvania after warring with other settlers from Europe.) By 1744, in one Philadelphia tavern, Dr. Alexander Hamilton would report finding Scots, English, Dutch, Germans, and Irish; religiously their company included Roman Catholics, Anglicans, Presbyterians, Quakers, "Newlightmen," Methodists, "Seventh day men," Moravians, Anabaptists, and a Jew.

Religious diversity did not prevent men in cities from drinking and eating together. But in the countryside it often limited intermarriage among newcomers, even though colonial law nowhere prohibited it. In fact, the Frenchman Hector St. John de Crèvecoeur seemed fascinated when he discovered a New York family "whose grandfather was an Englishman, whose wife was Dutch, whose son married a French woman, and whose present four sons have now four wives of different nations."[18] In this family, de Crèvecoeur claimed to find the first real Americans, dismissing any claims Indians might make to the term as natives of the land. To most residents of the middle colonies, however, such intermarriage remained invisible and uncelebrated. Even migrants from Europe instead more typically feared each other and they avoided conflict with each other by separating in private even as they became culturally more alike.

Groups in Formation; Colonial Identities

In 1492, the residents of Africa, North America, and Europe had scarcely known of each other's existence. Over the next three centuries, they learned of and emphasized differences among themselves. To a surprising degree, colonial laws and assumptions shaped the formation of new groups and group identities. By 1776, there were "reds," "blacks," and "whites," "heathens" and "Christians," and "Indians," "Britons," "Natives," "Pennsylvania Dutch," "Virginians," and "Africans" all living in North America. Few resembled modern ethnic groups, yet they created the diversity the USA would inherit from Britain even as it separated from it.

Native nations

The indigenous peoples of North America were neither subjects, colonists nor citizens of British North America. Completely unlike modern ethnic groups in the USA, they were independent nations with their own governments. And the European invaders generally saw them as that, too. Great Britain and France repeatedly signed (and also repeatedly violated) treaties with Indian representatives, detailing land ownership and use and alliances of mutual defense. If, in 1492, the identities of indigenous peoples had reflected their trade, wars, and differences with each other, over the next centuries they increasingly emphasized their differences from newcomers, defining themselves as natives of the land. While Europeans sometimes called them Americans, they rarely called themselves that.

Newcomers and natives alike saw physical traits (notably skin color), gender and family relations, and religious practices as important markers of their differences. Natives commented on the pale skin, eyes, and hair of some Europeans; Europeans saw the natives as "tawny" or "red." Natives laughed when Christians' prayers failed to work but British settlers like the Reverend Thomas Mayhew went further in describing natives as the opposite of the Protestant settlers – heathens were "mighty zealous and earnest in the Worship of False gods and Devils . . . abounding with sins."[19] Cotton Mather also attributed to the natives the traits he most feared in his fellow Protestants, insisting "They are lying wretches, they are very lazy wretches; and they are out of measure indulgent unto their children." Spanish, Dutch, and English alike deemed Indian men lazy because women were the main cultivators among them; to native eyes the European men who worked in the fields seemed effeminate. For Europeans, the ease of divorce and matrilineal customs of the Iroquois seemed telling proof of their inferiority and Mather even concluded, "there is no family government among them."[20]

To Dutch, English, and French explorers, diplomats, and

generals, indigenous people were not so much a single group of natives but "heathens," "savages," "Indians." With time, the Spanish learned to distinguish settled agriculturists (whose names they translated as Pueblo, "the people") from migratory hunters. In the east, the English began to call the Ganonsyoni the "Iroquois" – the name used by their traditional enemies. For their part, the Iroquois quickly recognized the French, English, and Dutch as imperial competitors, and they negotiated with all three empires to gain any possible advantage for themselves.

Responding to precipitous population declines and constant pressure from settlers from Europe, natives also increasingly united as natives. Their hostility to the newcomers made them North America's first nativists, opposing migration of more newcomers. By 1750, the British in North America faced not hundreds of separate independent nations but five pan-tribal alliances or federations – Iroquois, western Delaware, Shawnee, Cherokee, Creek, and Choctaw. Each federation negotiated independently with the European empires, but within each group voices called for unity of all to end Europeans' incursions. Thus in 1723, Antoine Le Page du Pratz appealed "Before they came, did we not live better than we do, seeing we deprive ourselves of a part of our corn, our game, and fish, to give a part to them?"[21] For Pratz "we" were the nations of Natives, "they" were the European newcomers, and the interests of the two groups could not be reconciled.

Blacks or Africans?

Unlike the natives of America, slaves transported to North America became the property of, and thus the most subordinate of subjects of the British Empire. Denied most of the rights even indentured servants took for granted, slaves turned to each other for support and sustenance – Olaudah Equiano, for example, expressed discomfort when forced to work in Virginia among indentured servants from Europe. From simple preferences like his, a sense of shared community emerged among slaves. But it did so only gradually because slaves had to bridge considerable divisions – among Moslems, Christians, and animists and among Yoruba, Edo, Bantu, Igbo, and Mandingare. Fear of slave revolts, such as the Stono rebellion in South Carolina in 1739, indicate that planters recognized their slaves' developing sense of community without understanding how their violence and ostracism toward slaves contributed to its strength.

In English eyes, physical difference eventually trumped religion as the boundary dividing slaves from themselves, especially as slaves became Christians in the 1700s. But while John Harrower called slaves "blacks," he never referred to himself as white, and slaves too more often called men like Harrower "Boccarora" or "Buckra" than white. Just as Mather attributed to Indians the sins he most feared in his Protestant neighbors, planters in the south claimed special horror at the "boisterous passions" of their slaves. Women hardened by fieldwork symbolized to planters the absence of female virtue and delicacy – traits attributed instead to their wives and daughters – among the slave women they had themselves often violated.

Europeans lumped together all slaves, regardless of cultural background, language, or religion, as "blacks" but they failed to impose that identity on them. Newcomers from Africa instead disparaged the English-speaking culturally assimilated "salt-water Negroes" they first encountered in America while increasingly calling themselves Africans. In coastal cities as far north as New York, the free descendants of the first arrivals from Africa confirmed their choice, naming their first segregated cemeteries and churches not Black but African. Venture Smith too also regularly referred to himself as an African, distinguishing himself from white "gentlemen."

European cultural diversity

Unlike natives, Protestant migrants from Europe were all subjects of the British Empire; unlike slaves, they either were or could become naturalized as British Colonials. Until the 1760s and 1770s, few of the newest arrivals recognized this commonality as important, however. Cultural difference, not racial or cultural unity, characterized group life among recent arrivals from Europe in British North America.

Newcomers from Europe were divided by sharp class and cultural differences. John Harrower saw indentured servants from the British Isles shackled, beaten, and in chains during his own far more comfortable passage to Virginia. In Pennsylvania, the English-speaking Benjamin Franklin, fearing that a colony founded by the English would become a "Germanized" colony of "aliens," castigated his German neighbors for their "tawny" skins. But the difference newcomers most feared among their European neighbors was religious. Franklin's outburst was fuelled in part by Pietist Germans' opposition in the Pennsylvania colonial assembly to requirements for political oaths and militia service among voters. Armed conflict over religious differences were fresh in the memories of many recent migrants from Europe; separation in private life and religious liberty in public life provided an American solution to European religious battles. But it also provided the basis for group formation, and considerable segregation, among Europeans.

Group formation along religious lines was especially evident in the countryside of the middle colonies and upland south where families spoke differing languages, and where German Moravians, Mennonites, Dunkards, Schwenkfelders (or other Anabaptists), Reformed Calvinists, and Lutherans settled apart from English and Scottish Presbyterians, Quakers, and Anglicans. Any traveler could see cultural differences in the barns, houses, and crops of British, Dutch, and German settlements. While the English roasted meats on an open fire, the Germans ground their meats, ate sausage, or cooked meats in "dutch ovens." Migrants from Germany spoke their own dialects at church and at home; they also published and purchased newspapers and books in German.

In their private lives, too, newcomers separated along cultural lines. Thus, even the cosmopolitan cities of British North

America were in some ways religious mosaics. In Charleston, French Huguenots and German, Scotch-Irish, and English Protestants built their own churches and burial grounds, separating themselves even more firmly in death than in life. Sephardic Jews formed their own communities and burial societies, even where they did not build synagogues. The earliest ethnic societies also appeared in port cities, usually to provide aid to newcomers and to widows and orphans. Scots formed the first in Boston in 1657; in the eighteenth century "Die Deutsche Gesellschaft," the "Friendly Sons of St. Patrick," "La Société Française de Bienfaisance de Philadelphie" also appeared. In Philadelphia, where they were a minority, even the English formed a mutual aid society. Much like churches in colonies with no established religion, membership in mutual aid societies was voluntary and many newcomers chose to ignore them.

The formation of distinct but voluntary cultural groups suggests that among migrants from Europe, too, new identities, unique to America, were replacing those of the past. There was no country of Germany in Europe in the 1700s, but there were already "deitch" (Deutsch, usually written by English-speakers as "Dutch") in Pennsylvania. For their part, the Pennsylvania Dutch (like the newcomers from the Netherlands in New York) usually referred to all English-speakers, regardless of origin, culture, or religion – including the Scots and even the Irish – as "Englishmen" rather than as Britons.

Still, settlers from Europe – regardless of religion or origin – also rather quickly adopted common identities defined by colonial governance. Colonial assemblies were an important place where Europeans of many backgrounds met; slaves and Natives had no place there. Already in the early seventeenth century, newcomers from Europe regularly referred to themselves as Colonials or – taking the British name for their colonies – as New Yorkers, Pennsylvanians, Virginians, and Carolinians. New England instead generated a powerful regional colonial identity; to this day, residents of Massachusetts call themselves New Englanders, not Massachusettians. Even in the realm of identity, then, politics and governance molded European diversity into a broadly shared "Colonial" identity. That the new identities of British North America – Colonials, Africans, and Natives – differed so sharply from those of New Spain and New France suggests the considerable influence of imperial policies and governing institutions on the formation of all American identities.

"In-between" peoples: the Catholic alternative

With their expectations of conversion and intermarriage, New France and New Spain also generated new identities in North America. But these usually bridged or confused rather than highlighted skin color or physical differences between peoples from Africa, Europe, and America, creating a multitude of racially "in-between" peoples. In New France, the children of French traders and Indian women were called "metis" ("halfs"). In New Spain and French Louisiana, people of European descent but born in America were "criollos" (creoles) or "hispanos," distinguishing them from mestizo ("mixed") persons born to Spanish or creole men and native (india) women. Spain's rulers even created a complex legal system of classification and registration for the products of intermarriages among Spanish or creole, Indian and African (called moros or negros) and those of mixed (mestizo) blood – mulatos, moriscos, chinos, lobos, and cribaros.

British North America apparently feared "in-between" identities such as these. Among newcomers from Europe there, cultural and even religious variation was no barrier to Colonial status. But identities distinguishing cultural difference among Africans – "saltwater Negroes," for example – disappeared, just as sharp cultural differences among the local residents seemed increasingly irrelevant. Divisions among Natives, Colonials, and Africans became sharper as these three pan-cultural identities, reflecting the very different status of each group in the British empire, and their distinctive physical characteristics – notably skin color – solidified in law and in perception.

Thus, in British North America the term "mulatto" (for the

child of African and European parentage), while used, remained highly pejorative because it linked an individual socially and sometimes legally to slave origins. Perception of African physical characteristics could do the same. Meanwhile, the few native converts to Protestantism in New England, called "praying Indians," lived segregated in farming villages, apart from their European neighbors, and settlers often feared the "white Indians" who had gone to live among them and to adopt their customs. In the south, too, planters regarded the maroon communities formed by servants, run-away slaves, and Indians as places of rebellion and even treason (since racial mixing was more common in the territory of their Spanish enemies in Florida).

Over the course of 200 years, ethnic groups, regional cultures, and new identities unique to America had emerged from the cross-cultural encounters that followed Europe's invasion of America. These new identities obscured some differences that had mattered in Africa, Europe, or North America while emphasizing new differences among settlers or Colonials, Natives, and the enslaved Africans.

In British North America, Iroquois and Choctaw became Natives and nativists or (in Europeans' eyes) Indians; Swabians became Germans (or, in the eyes of their English-speaking neighbors, Dutch); English and Scots became British Colonials and Ibos became African or, in the eyes of whites, blacks. For those newly arrived from Europe, encounters with natives and with Africans encouraged them to think of themselves as morally superior Christians. Among Europeans, cultural diversity persisted but their legal status as members of the new British nation also increasingly united them as Colonials.

As subjects of Great Britain, those with recent origins in Europe faced troubling questions about their identities in the years after 1750. Were they to remain Colonials – as "British in America"? It would take a revolution to answer this question, and that revolution created a nation of Americans of European descent in North America. The American Revolution in turn forced these new Americans to define what distinguished them as a nation from Britain, from their American neighbors in New Spain, from the increasingly hostile and nativist Natives who lived among them, and from new waves of newcomers they would soon call the "aliens."

Further Reading

Bernard Bailyn, *The Peopling of British North America: An Introduction* (New York: Vintage Books, 1988).

Marilyn C. Baseler, *"Asylum for Mankind": America, 1607–1800* (Ithaca: Cornell University Press, 1998).

Ira Berlin, *Many Thousands Gone: The First Two Centuries of Slavery in North America* (Cambridge, MA: The Belknap Press of Harvard University Press, 1998).

Colin G. Calloway, *New Worlds for All: Indians, Europeans, and the Remaking of Early America* (Baltimore and London: The Johns Hopkins University Press, 1997).

Alfred W. Crosby, *The Columbian Exchange: Biological and Cultural Consequences of 1492* (Westport: Greenwood, 1972).

Jack P. Greene, *Pursuits of Happiness: The Social Development of Early Modern British Colonies and the Formation of American Culture* (Chapel Hill: University of North Carolina Press, 1988).

Martha Hodes, ed., *Sex, Love, Race: Crossing Boundaries in North American History* (New York: New York University Press, 1999).

Francis Jennings, *The Invasion of America: Indians, Colonialism and the Cant of Conquest* (New York: W.W. Norton & Co., 1976).

Allan Kulikoff, *From British Peasants to Colonial American Farmers* (Chapel Hill: University of North Carolina Press, 2000).

Gary Nash, *Red, White, and Black: The Peoples of Early North America* (Upper Saddle River: Prentice Hall, 2000).

David Northrup, ed., *The Atlantic Slave Trade* (Lexington: D.C. Heath, 1994).

Tzvetan Todorov, *The Conquest of America: The Question of the Other* (Norman: University of Oklahoma Press, 1999).

David Weber, *The Spanish Frontier in North America* (New Haven: Yale University Press, 1992).

Marianne S. Wokeck, *Trade in Strangers: The Beginnings of Mass Migration to North America* (University Park: The Pennsylvania State University Press, 1999).

2

Americans and Aliens, 1750–1835

The man who has most influenced historians' understanding of the new American nation was an alien, not a citizen of the USA. Born in France in 1735 of a father he described as an "off-cast," Hector St. John de Crèvecoeur migrated to New France only to find its residents at war with the British and their Native allies. Fleeing Quebec to the Great Lakes and then to New York, he acquired British nationality through naturalization in 1765, and married a woman whose family sided with Britain during the Americans' Revolution. Although Crèvecoeur himself supported the revolutionaries, he fled when patriots burned his farm, and after brief imprisonment by the British army, recrossed the Atlantic. In the 1780s, France appointed him consul to the USA and he was reunited with his children before returning in 1801 to live in France and Germany until his death 12 years later.[1]

Crèvecoeur was living in London in the early 1780s when he published his subsequently much-quoted "Letters From an American Farmer." Posing the question "What, then is the American, this new man?" Crèvecoeur offered a complex first description of the American nation. "He is an American," he wrote, "who, leaving behind him all his ancient prejudices and manners, receives new ones from the new mode of life he has embraced, the new government he obeys, and the new rank he holds . . ."[2]

With his focus on ideological transformation, Crèvecoeur seemed to describe the civic nationalism American patriots were proclaiming. The civic nationalism of revolutionaries Thomas Jefferson, Thomas Paine, and James Madison was so powerful that these men rarely even used the word nation except to describe a consensual relation between a republican government and its citizens, whose liberty it guaranteed. They could easily agree with Crèvecoeur that economic liberty in a new country would also appeal to a foreigner by promising, "If thou wilt work, I have bread for thee" and that the result would be "the most perfect society now existing in the world."

To the "founding fathers" of the USA, membership in the American nation required individuals to choose republican political ideology. Citizenship was to be voluntary, and race, color, geographic origin, religious, regional, or family loyalties scarcely appeared in their writings. But culture and race were much more important to Crèvecoeur, who – like most Europeans of his era – viewed nations not merely as compacts between governments and their citizens but as organic groups that, like races (a word they used interchangeably for nations) reproduced themselves culturally and biologically after emerging from their native soil.

"Men are like plants," Crèvecoeur noted, and, in the USA, "individuals of all nations are melted into a new race of men." Crèvecoeur openly admitted that it was the nations of Europe that "melted" into a new race in the USA, and that melting occurred biologically in the intermarried families that had so fascinated him in New York (see p. 38). Crèvecoeur was confident as well that the new race of Americans was producing a distinctive American culture or civilization and that it was openly imperial, and on a moral mission westward. "Americans are the western pilgrims who are carrying along with them that great mass of arts, sciences, vigour, and industry which began long since in the East; they will finish the great circle." Far better than the patriots and American nationalists who were his contemporaries, then, the alien Crèvecoeur had identified tensions between civic and ethnic nationalism that would plague American nation-building for almost two centuries.

Revival, War, and Nation-building

In 1740, the prospects for a new or unified nation emerging in North America seemed slight. Three empires – Spain, France, and Great Britain – still vied for continental domination and had been at war with each other and with Native nations for much of the eighteenth century. Even within the relatively compact eastern colonies of British North America, regional differences were sharp and firmly rooted in everyday habits of life. Colonial identities provided some unity among newcomers from Europe but separated them from the slaves and Natives among them. Over the next half-century, cultural and religious revivals, imperial war, and anti-imperial revolution combined to produce national, American, identities that pitted Natives against Colonials and Colonials against Britain.

Beginning in the 1740s, an incredible series of religious revivals swept through British North America. Together with circulating newspapers, this first "Great Awakening" created a new sense of connection across colonial boundaries. Men and women of many regions experienced conversion during this Protestant revival; converts included not only Colonials but Natives and Africans, too. Much as the Middle Colonies had treated religious persuasion as a private matter, the Great Awakening emphasized the importance of individual choice in matters of faith; for converts, belief was no longer a product of birth into a particular family, community, or nation but an intensely personal commitment to God.

Religious revivals would remain a recurring feature of American life from the 1740s until the 1850s, repeatedly generating new churches and Protestant identities. Prior to the American Revolution, the popular fiery speakers of the first Great Awakening – notably Jonathan Edwards and George Whitefield – preached their message of individual commitment to moral regeneration up and down the east coast. Whether in New York or Virginia, converts often called themselves "New Lights." Many were children and grandchildren of newcomers from Europe.

Especially in the upland and coastal south in the 1740s, the growth of new Methodist and Baptist churches resulted in the decline, if not always death, of older Protestant sects founded on communal and European foundations. Conversion in turn facilitated intermarriage among the converted, further helping to weaken churches that had preserved cultural difference among newcomers from Europe. Since this first awakening remained Calvinist in its theology, it provided converts with a newer vision of the mission once characteristic mainly of New England's first settlers. That is why Crèvecoeur called the new American race "pilgrims."

Religious revival appealed to indigenous peoples and slaves in the south, too. Samson Occom – who described himself as "born a Heathen and Brought up in Heathenism" among "wandering Indians" near New London, Connecticut – was "awakened & converted" at a meeting at a white Church. He subsequently learned English in order to read the Bible, and he committed himself to a life of teaching Indian children to read and write while vowing "frequently to talk with our Indians Concerning Religion."[3]

Awakening worked a more contradictory effect on Africans. Under its impact, both free Africans and plantation masters devoted more attention to spreading Christian beliefs among slaves. Slaves may have viewed the emotionally vivid mass revival meetings typical of the Awakening as revelations of a Holy Spirit that resembled the spiritualism of African animist religions. Protestant evangelicalism carried complex messages, however. While slave owners hoped conversion to Christianity would encourage docility among their slaves, generations of enslaved preachers quickly seized instead on the Bible's story of Israelites' delivery from servitude in Egypt. And outside the south, some "New Lights" joined Pennsylvania's Quakers in demanding a new sense of Christian brotherhood, pointing to slavery as a "moral blot" on British North America. As a product of American life, the first Great Awakening created spiritual grounds for slaves, Natives, and Colonials to claim a shared cultural identity, at least in the realm of faith.

The 1754 outbreak of the Seven Years' War between Britain and France (called the French and Indian War in North America) heightened nation-building in other ways by pitting Natives against Colonials. With increased migrations from Europe and Africa in the eighteenth century, many native peoples had withdrawn westward, causing pressure on groups living in the Appalachian Mountains and beyond. At the same time, growing populations of Colonials in Pennsylvania and New York looked to French lands in the Mississippi and Ohio valleys and saw tempting new homesteads. In fact, settlers' incursions into New France helped trigger the Seven Years' War, and most Colonials enthusiastically supported the British campaign to drive the Catholic French Empire out of North America.

Natives were understandably ambivalent about the war. As in past conflicts, the Iroquois, Cherokee, and Creek confederacies formed alliances with the warring French and British, hoping to gain trade and territorial advantages. But they were not, as allies, invited to the negotiations that produced the Peace of Paris of 1763 and resulted in the expulsion of the French from North America. Natives of the Great Lakes region thus did not accept the treaty's surrender of their lands to Britain; they had not in fact surrendered. The British called the ensuing 1763 Native war with them Pontiac's rebellion. But heavily in debt from war with France, the British could not risk Native opposition. Hoping to buy peace, they closed the lands between the Appalachian Mountains and the Mississippi River (where Spanish territory now began) to settlement by Colonials, reserving them for Indians. In doing so, Great Britain claimed to protect Indians against Colonial incursions rather than to treat them strictly as conquered nations.

The proclamation pleased neither Colonials nor Natives. Natives continued to view themselves as independent nations, unconquered by Britain. Among them, nativist voices hostile to British and Colonials alike moved beyond calls for military cooperation to appeals for cultural revival. The Delaware prophet Neolin, for example, urged natives to return to "their original state that they were in before the white people found out their country," reversing the cultural transformations of previous centuries and giving Natives the will to continue to resist.[4] West of the Appalachians, Native cultural revivals thus left little room for "New Light" converts such as Samson Occom.

Colonial identities also evolved in response to the wars. Colonials had fought under the leadership of British generals they regarded as incompetent, fostering new solidarity among soldiers otherwise divided by regional or religious identities. With the war's end, the Catholic, French enemy that had inspired cooperation of Colonials and British imperialists disappeared. Worse, Colonials remained frustrated by British imperial policy and could not settle Indians' lands in what they increasingly called their "northwest." British efforts to pay off the costs of war by having Parliament impose new taxes and fees in the colonies heightened Colonials' frustrations, as every standard account of the American Revolution emphasizes. Increasingly, Colonials differentiated themselves not from the Spanish Catholics to the west and south but from their British rulers in faraway Europe.

Colonials saw Britain's prohibition of settlement in the northwest as a symptom of increasingly authoritarian governance. The evolution of Colonials into American revolutionaries thus linked population growth and expansion, just government, and individual virtue. Benjamin Franklin, along with many others, commented on the healthful climate of North America and noted that "Marriages in America are more general, and more generally early than in Europe . . . and if in Europe they have but four Births to a marriage . . . we may here reckon eight . . ."[5] An expansive people needed new lands, he suggested. Franklin soon also symbolized the virtues fostered by a healthful American environment; in his later autobiography, he described himself as typically American in being practical and self-taught, hard-working, frugal, and full of energetic initiative.

By contrast, in the words of Scottish clergyman Robert Wallace, Britain was becoming instead, a "debauched nation, addicted to sensuality and irregular amours . . ."[6] By 1776, in

North America, Colonial writers concurred, arguing that independence would result in many benefits, not least of all "a vast influx of foreigners, encouraged by the mildness of a free, equal, and tolerating government . . . ; an astonishing encrease of our people from the present stock."[7] The fact that the British parliament after 1709 had prohibited Colonial assemblies from naturalizing newcomers seemed proof that a Britain in moral decline could prosper only at the expense of its virtuous American colonies. External enemies – in the form of decadent and authoritarian British "Tories" and "savage heathens" – provided the mirrors in which Colonials would first identify themselves, rather than the native "Indians," as Americans.

Revolutionary Americans

Revolutions often occur when rulers are preoccupied with external conflicts, and the American Revolution was one of many rebellions that broke out before Great Britain's century-long wars with France ended in 1815. In 1776, the disgruntled French – having lost their North American colonies – proved natural allies for the American revolutionaries who called themselves "patriots." A republican revolution then followed in France in 1789. Between 1789 and 1815, intermittent war between revolutionary and Napoleonic France and Britain again opened possibilities for revolution and political transformation in Europe and the Americas, with rebellions in Haiti (1793), Ireland (1798), and in much of central and South America (beginning in 1808).

Far from being a multi-cultural movement, the American Revolution was to a large degree a revolt of Colonials of English origin against British rule. Overall, about one-fifth of the population of the 13 colonies, like Crèvecoeur's in-laws, remained loyal to Britain. Among "loyalists," newcomers and the non-English were numerous – for example, many Germans in Pennsylvania and almost all newcomers from Scotland.

Among patriots – about two-fifths of the population – persons of English origin like Sam Adams were especially prominent as leaders from New England and from the coastal south (Thomas Jefferson, James Madison). Revolutionaries were of diverse religious convictions, however; if the majority were Protestants, and a few Catholic, passionate converts and New Lights were relatively few among the military and political leaders Americans called the founding fathers. By contrast, New Lights were exceedingly well represented among ordinary soldiers and supporters of the revolution.

The remaining two-fifths of the white population, like Crèvecoeur, tried to remain as neutral as possible. They, too, were a multi-cultural mix, with perhaps a preponderance of recent arrivals. Their motives varied from pacifism (the case for English Quakers and German Pietists) to indifference or a desire for isolation (the case of the many Scotch Irish settlers in the inland south). In Virginia, the recently arrived Scottish servant John Harrower recorded the mustering of patriot soldiers in his diary with detached indifference and remained focused on his work as tutor and teacher.

Although Harrower reported finding a "real Indian" from Ohio among the patriot soldiers near his town (and reported him as being "of a Yelow couler short brod faced and rather flat nosed, and long course black quite streight [hair,] He spoke very good English,") this soldier was one of a very small group of Indian patriots.[8] Natives rightly recognized that the revolutionaries wanted not just independence from Britain and a more representative form of government, but also their lands in the northwest. The long-standing six-nation confederation of Iroquois broke up during the revolution, but most within it subsequently supported the British. Many Natives of the interior also sided with the British, who had prohibited Colonials from settling on their lands. Even though most indigenous Americans ultimately remained neutral, no other groups would lose as much in the revolution.

For those of African descent, revolution opened small opportunities to exploit the competition of Colonials and British for allies, soldiers, and supplies. Already in 1775 a group of free, southern Africans had petitioned British general Thomas Gage to free slaves, and many slaves ran away when Lord

Dunmore, the governor of Virginia, promised freedom to those joining the British forces. It seems likely that a majority of enslaved Africans hoped for British success, especially where their masters were revolutionaries, as many were in the coastal south. In response, the revolutionaries' army – that had initially excluded Africans from service – welcomed free volunteers, at least in the north, where about 5000 free Africans and a few slaves served in integrated regiments, and were rewarded with freedom or pensions. In the north, most Africans enthusiastically supported the revolutionaries. But their acceptance as Americans would prove short-lived in the new republic.

Creating Civic Nationalism

The formation of an independent government, the United States of America, created a new framework for American diversity, different from that of either British North America or New Spain. Together, the Declaration of Independence, Articles of Confederation, and US Constitution offered preliminary definitions of civic nationalism in a nation of consenting American citizens. In them, we find few celebrations of diversity. The founding fathers firmly believed instead that internal division – factionalism, they called it – had undermined all earlier republics. Distinguishing "aliens" from American "citizens," all three documents anticipated aliens from Europe would become citizens but they also drew firm boundaries around American citizenship, excluding both Indians and slaves from the new nation.

Aliens

The men who wrote the Declaration of Independence, Articles of Confederation, and US Constitution imagined the American nation as a voluntary association of citizens represented by a republican government. Their concept of consensual citizenship built on the British custom of allowing naturalization of aliens, as foreigners like Crèvecoeur were called. All three documents thus described freedom of movement as a form of liberty governments should protect. And all three also affirmed aliens' right to choose American citizenship through naturalization once they had moved to the USA. Until the 1840s, US census takers routinely distinguished "aliens" or "foreigners not naturalized" from American citizens.

In listing Colonials' grievances against the British King in 1776, Thomas Jefferson reminded readers how Parliament had prohibited aliens from naturalizing in the colonies, and he complained that Britain had blocked free migration by preventing Colonials from moving to the northwest. The Articles of Confederation stipulated further that American citizens could move freely across all state borders; it prohibited states from imposing duties exclusively on aliens. By 1789, however, the Constitution expressed some ambivalence about aliens as a possible source of division. While it granted the national Congress the power to naturalize them, it also modestly limited their access to elected office as congressional representatives and as President.

Diverse American citizens

Between the signing of the Declaration of Independence and the ratification of the US Constitution and its "Bill of Rights," Colonials became first revolutionaries, then, Americans. In 1776, the Declaration described Colonials as settlers of a new land still closely tied to Britain. It appealed to their "British brethren" to understand their discontentment. Even in separating from Britain, the rebels did so as "these united Colonies." In naming their "continental Congress" and "continental Army" the revolutionaries emphasized their separation from Britain and from Europe, but also proclaimed their ambitions to re-unite all of America under new government. In fact, the Articles provided for the immediate admission of Canada to the confederacy – a dream shattered by the loyalists who flocked there. Nevertheless, the Constitution, too, assumed the USA would expand, and it permitted Congress to admit new states in the future.

The Articles of Confederation and the US Constitution both reflected the republican revolutionaries' fear of factions or divisions and offered different proposals to minimize the dangers of diversity in an expanding country. The Articles acknowledged the likelihood of discord over religion but left each state to find its own solution. Religious toleration was by no means universal at the time of the revolution. In Virginia, where the Church of England (Anglican) had been established as a state religion, and where Baptists had been jailed as recently as 1771, Jefferson's Statute of Religious Freedom was approved only in 1786. The Constitution went farther than the Articles to prohibit the imposition of religious tests on holders of any public office anywhere. In the bill of individual rights amended to the Constitution before its ratification, state support of any church was also prohibited and liberty of conscience extended to all religious faiths, not merely (as in the British Empire) to Protestants. In its official censuses and other public records, the USA ever thereafter refused to collect information or to categorize Americans by their religious choices. Isolating religious diversity in the private realm, and making it a matter of individual choice, of no interest to the nation, the Constitution sought to diminish its power to divide citizens.

Defusing the divisive power of regional diversity through a multi-layered or federal system of governance was more controversial. The Articles, like many Indian alliances, provided for confederation, or a "firm league of friendship" among the colonies or provinces (more often thereafter called states) where shared Colonial loyalties had first developed. Citizens chose representatives to their state assemblies, and the Articles sought to protect these states, and their citizens, from the tyranny of the central legislature or Congress they formed by enumerating its responsibilities narrowly and providing it with no power to tax.

In the 1780s, James Madison and others arguing for a new

Constitution sought instead to strengthen the central government and to encourage a stronger sense of national over state or regional loyalty. The preamble to the Constitution thus declared the "people" sovereign in the USA; it created a national government directly responsible to, and in part elected by, citizens rather than to the individual states. The national motto "Out of Many, One" later symbolized this effort to unify the 13 states, and their regional cultures, more firmly. But conflicts between those who feared centralizing government and those who feared regional divisions also quickly generated the first American political parties, or factions. Federalists – mainly in New England, New York, and the northeast – advocated a stronger central government, dominated by wealthy men, that would provide national support for commercial and industrial development. Democratic Republicans – many of them living in the south and west – instead preferred local and state autonomy where the interests of agriculture – from wealthy planters to humble farmers – could prevail.

Concerned mainly with regional and religious conflicts, the founding fathers said little about other social or cultural differences. Children, women, servants, and slaves were of little interest to them since they could not consent to citizenship; they were subordinate to their parents, husbands, and masters. Male aliens became citizens by renouncing their loyalty to the sovereign to whom they were previously subject. Until the 1830s, some states prevented men without property from voting since they too were considered dependent on others for their income. Concerns about the subservience of Catholics, women, workers, and freed slaves as citizens would linger well into the twentieth century. For the Africans and Natives of the late eighteenth century, however, exclusion from citizenship reflected more than their subordination. Civic nationalism was for consenting white men only; acknowledged or not, a sharp color boundary excluded non-whites from the American nation in all its early definitions of civic nationalism and itself.

The Boundaries of Civic Nationalism

While white Colonial men and male aliens could become American citizens, Natives and Africans could not. The treatment of both groups in the three foundational documents of American nationalism clearly established the racial limits to the founding fathers' universalizing language of liberty, equality, and voluntary citizenship. But from the time of the Revolution, Natives and slaves also had strikingly different relations to the new American nation and its white citizens.

Already in 1776, Jefferson's Declaration of Independence blamed Britain's policies for America's "domestic insurrections" when it described Colonials under attack by the "merciless Indian savages" Britain sought to protect. The Articles of Confederation then placed Indians firmly outside the nation, ignoring their status as natives of America, and granting the "united states in congress assembled" the responsibility to "regulate trade and manage all affairs with the Indians" as it did also with foreign countries. Natives' status as separate nations in America continued under the Constitution, with Congress regulating commerce with Indians as with all foreign countries. Unlike other countries, however, Indians did not occupy a territory outside the USA; nor were their governments formally elected, allowing Americans to disparage them as "tribes," rather than treat them as independent "states." In determining Congressional representation for the new USA, the Constitution explicitly prohibited census takers from counting "Indians not taxed" as part of the nation. Although the Constitution (and many states) ignored the issue, Congress would soon specify that Indians, unlike white aliens, had no right to naturalization as American citizens.

The status of Africans was left more ambiguous. Jefferson's initial draft of the Declaration of Independence had contained a clause that blamed Britain for introducing slavery to its colonies. Once expunged, the Declaration's silence on slavery provided a model for the Articles and the Constitution, which also directly mentioned neither Africans nor slaves. The

Articles acknowledged the presence of non-whites only by basing militia musters on the numbers of whites residing in a state. To determine congressional representation, the Constitution in turn counted "the whole number of free persons, including those bound to service for a term of years" (e.g. indentured servants), but only three-fifths of "all other persons" – presumably slaves. In an equally indirect and convoluted reference, the Constitution prevented Congress from prohibiting the migration or importation of "such persons as any of the States now existing shall think proper to admit" before 1808, while allowing Congress to impose an import duty on each "such person." It also prohibited states from releasing anyone from "service or labor" in another state and provided for the return of fugitives. If slaves were different from other forms of property – they could not be killed, for example – neither were they free men and women or citizens. Census takers counted slaves, beginning with the first federal census of 1790, as a separate category.

That the founding fathers drew a color boundary around the nation and its citizens becomes more obvious when comparing the USA to countries gaining their independence from Spain after 1810. In Latin America, republican revolutionaries not only abolished slavery immediately, they also eliminated Spain's elaborate racial classifications for children of mixed unions. Mexico's early ethnic nationalists posited their culture, rooted in Spain, as a European civilization superior to that of the Indians. But they also accepted as voters all men born on Mexican soil who spoke Spanish or who possessed property; even men without property could fight as soldiers to defend the nation from foreign invasion. The descendant of Creoles and Indians, Benito Juárez, and a man with African ancestry, Vicente Guerrero, later served as presidents of Mexico. That was unthinkable in the USA, which had adopted not only Great Britain's concept of voluntary membership in the nation but also its abhorrence of racial amalgamation.

In contrast to Latin American nations, the USA limited citizenship to white builders of an American civilization deemed superior to Europe's; it categorically excluded Indians as savages by birth and subordinated slaves, by birth, to white citizens. Tolerating slavery as an inherited status, civic nationalists could view freed slaves or African freedmen only as dangerously anomalous. Between 1790 and 1820, census takers were asked to distinguish free whites from "all other free persons." In 1798 the new Navy and Marines of the USA, unlike those of Mexico and Argentina, banned enlistment of free Africans. And even states without slavery, like Ohio in 1804, would enact "black laws" to limit the rights of free people of African descent to marry whites or to participate in politics, limiting the rights of citizenship even of those few Africans who could try to claim them.

Mobile Americans, 1776–1835

There can be little doubt that the founding fathers' successful efforts to create a nationalist "civic religion" of republican ideology and to unite white men as citizens around it was facilitated by a sharp drop in transatlantic crossings at the onset of Revolution. Of course, some Hessian soldiers recruited in Germany by the British army did remain to settle in the USA after independence. And perhaps 10,000 newcomers arrived yearly from Europe between 1780 and 1800, making a total of 91,000 aliens by 1810. Among these were between 10 and 20,000 political exiles fleeing France's 1789 revolution. Still, this was a very sharp reduction in international migration from the first half of the seventeenth century.

Reduced transatlantic migration reflected both the depressed and fragile economy of the new USA and the suspicion aliens faced there. In the early 1800s, European wars further reduced migration to about 4,000 a year, and a second war between Great Britain and the USA in 1812 did nothing to encourage potential migrants. The USA began publishing the information it collected from ships' captains about newcomers only in 1819 as its economy recovered and as Europe entered a long century of relative peace. Migration increased slowly at first. In the 1820s, the USA counted 152,000 new arrivals. Only after 1830 did migrations to the USA again rise toward mass dimensions.

The aliens who came to the USA in the early nineteenth century originated mainly in the British Isles, whose ships completely dominated transatlantic trade. These newcomers sought much the same religious freedom and economic opportunity that had made North America attractive before the Revolution. In 1818, the boy John Hughes, from Ulster in northern Ireland, joined his father and brother in rural Pennsylvania. Only a few years before, John, a Catholic born in 1797, had been seized by Protestants and threatened with bayonets. After working as a gardener in the USA, he enrolled in a seminary and eventually became a priest.[9] Slightly later, in 1824, Joseph Pickering arrived in Baltimore, after losing his English farm and suffering recurring unemployment in London. He initially looked for a situation as a superintendent or overseer of a farm, but confided to his diary, "I am not prepared for the latter because I do not understand the management of Blacks;" like many dissatisfied aliens, he soon left Baltimore.[10] More fortunate were John and Jabez Hollingworth, textile mill workers who departed Huddersfield in the north of England, and quickly found work in the young textile industry of New England in 1827. Their parents George and Betsey Hollingworth and their brothers and sisters, along with John's wife and children, soon followed them.[11]

With so many aliens arriving in the USA from an enemy country, Britain, and from lands torn by revolution (Ireland, France), many American citizens viewed the aliens of the 1790s and early 1800s with considerable hostility. A naturalization law passed by Congress in 1790 had allowed for the swift naturalization of white aliens. But already in 1798, the passage of the Alien and Sedition acts by Congress, a product of factional battles between Federalists and Republicans, revealed how voluntary citizenship could encourage nativism. The Alien acts briefly required newcomers to wait 15 years before naturalizing; they also provided for their detention and deportation in times of war. The war of 1812 between the USA and Britain only reinforced nativist fears of aliens from abroad.

Although they were not eligible for citizenship, Africans' forced migrations to the USA also dropped sharply after independence: about 51,000 arrived between 1770 and 1860. Most African slaves in the nineteenth century were shipped instead to Brazil and to a few remaining Spanish colonies in the Caribbean, where death rates among sugar cultivators remained high. In the USA, by contrast, a rising birthrate among acculturated slave women now guaranteed planters a growing supply of laborers. Then, in 1808, the American Congress prohibited the slave trade as the Constitution had permitted. A clandestine trade persisted but newly arrived Africans nevertheless formed a tiny part of the more than million and a half enslaved men and women living in the southern states of the USA in 1820.

Practically unnoticed by American record-keepers were the sizeable numbers leaving the USA as emigrants in the uncertain years just after independence. The American Revolution itself drove as many as 100,000 loyalists to British Canada, to British colonies in the Caribbean and – like Crèvecoeur – to Great Britain itself. Africans escaping from slavery emigrated to Canada, avoiding the Caribbean colonies and their slave economies. Along with white loyalists, they soon formed a substantial part of the English-speaking populations of Nova Scotia and Ontario. Natives allied with the British, such as the Iroquois and Anishnabeg of the Great Lakes, also fled north, even when they risked conflict with their traditional Algonquian enemies by doing so. Some of the emigrants who left the USA were dissatisfied British newcomers like Joseph Pickering. Having originally discounted Canada as a frozen wasteland, Pickering left Baltimore first for Philadelphia and New England, and only then for Ontario. There, he found a society, and way of life without slavery, more compatible with his sensibilities.

In the aftermath of the Revolution, Thomas Jefferson sometimes wrote hopefully of emigration, too. But as a troubled slave-owner, he was concerned mainly with the threat Africans might pose for the progress of the new republic. Jefferson speculated that the 60,000 children born yearly to slave mothers in the USA could be freed and sent to Africa or to the Caribbean for education, thus releasing the republic at relatively low cost from the dangers he perceived in racial diversity. A small group of Africans were in fact resettled in Liberia in 1816. Early emigration schemes like these were almost always white initiatives, however, and unpopular with free Africans.

Overall, migrations within America, and especially within the new USA, dwarfed the numbers of newcomers and emigrants combined. As many as 10,000 planters and their slaves had entered the USA after fleeing the Haitian revolution in Santo Domingo in 1793 and an undetermined number of loyalists from Canada also returned to try, as did Crèvecoeur, to reclaim their property in the USA. But the most numerous migrants of this era crossed no political borders; they were American citizens.

Already, in 1799, Isaac Weld, a British traveler, seemed impressed with the mobility of the white Americans. He reported them as "restless and discontented with what they possess, they are for ever changing. It is scarcely possible in any part of the continent to find a man, amongst the middling and lower classes of Americans, who has not changed his farm and his residence many different times." Jacques Pierre Brissot de Warville, a visitor from France, concurred, noting "apparently for Americans a migration to a place several hundred miles away is no more serious than moving from one house to another and is taken in the spirit of a pleasure party."[12]

While they surely exaggerated, both Weld and Warville were correct that the revolution had unleashed the pent-up desires of Colonials living on the east coast to cross the forbidden Appalachians, into Tennessee, Kentucky, and the northwest. As many as 50,000 had already crossed the mountains illegally before the Revolution began, mainly into the northwest territories above the Ohio River. Below the river lived about 12,000 new settlers in 1783; by 1790 their numbers had reached 100,000 in Kentucky and Tennessee alone. The purchase of Louisiana from France in 1803 then promised to open a vast new western territory stretching from the Gulf of Mexico to Minnesota. The physical size of the new nation had doubled, and as Crèvecoeur had predicted, the new "pilgrims" of the USA were soon "completing the great circle" by again moving westward. But as they did so, they again encountered independent nations of indigenous people determined to defend the territories as their own.

In the late eighteenth and early nineteenth centuries, at least five percent of Americans changed their place of residence in any given year. As Weld noted, some moved many times and over quite long distances. Among these many migrants was a future president of the USA, Andrew Jackson. Jackson had first moved from North Carolina to Nashville in 1787. In Tennessee, he began a law practice while operating a store. Then, in 1814, he negotiated purchase of lands from the local Chickasaw Indians and opened the Chickasaw Bluffs on the Mississippi River to white settlers. When he sold his remaining lands there in 1818, Jackson became a wealthy man, theoretically able to imitate the life-style of the slave-owning planter class of the coastal south.[13] Despite his wealth, however, Jackson – called "Old Hickory" by his followers – instead exemplified to many new Americans the ideal man of a new era: like Ben Franklin he was self-made, practical, and self-educated. But unlike Franklin, Jackson was also a frontiersman and an Indian fighter.

Jackson had left North Carolina with no slaves in tow. In the same year, Congress had prohibited slavery in the northwest territories. In the past, small numbers of slaves had seen the frontier as a beckoning refuge, inspiring them to escape. To prevent that, Congress in 1793 passed a fugitive slave act to underscore the Constitution's intention that no state or territory should become an easy refuge for runaway slaves. By 1810, 100,000 slaves lived west of the Appalachians, but they lived there under the firm control of their white owners. The vast majority were not new arrivals from Africa but rather – like their owners – former residents of Virginia and the Chesapeake.

Determined to expand the cultivation of cotton, for which industrialization in Britain and the USA was beginning to create an almost insatiable demand, many white southerners traveling west had brought their slaves with them, transplanting the plantation economy and slavery to the west. Planters remaining in the east faced exhausted soils and a competitive market for tobacco. To prevent economic collapse, many sold even more slaves west and to New Orleans, which became the center of an important and internal new market for human chattel after the 1808 prohibition against importing new slaves.

In 1819, contemplating the future of slavery, James Madison toyed with the idea of creating a separate western homeland to which freed slaves could be transported. But the 1820 Missouri Compromise, drawing a line through the Louisiana Purchase to delineate territories open and closed to the institution of slavery ended such schemes. Instead of offering a promised land to freed Africans, the slave child, sister or mother sold away from her family to the west by a slave trader from New Orleans came to symbolize slavery's worst abuses to its growing band of critics.

Nor were slaves the only migrants forced west. Between 1776 and 1840, many new Americans – like Andrew Jackson – wanted Indians removed from national territory. Like Britain in 1763, the newly independent USA had not negotiated with the Native confederacies allied with Britain when it proclaimed victory in 1783. Those negotiations began only in 1784. Thus, when Congress unilaterally passed the Northwest Ordinance in 1787, it simply ignored Indians' claims to their western lands. The result was a violent military confrontation between Americans and Natives at Fallen Timbers, in Ohio; more extensive negotiations followed in which the USA again recognized Indians as sovereign over the lands they still claimed.

Westward migration and settlement inevitably sharpened conflicts between mobile Americans and Natives. And war between Britain and the USA in 1812 again made Britain's Indian allies the focus of American ire. During this war, Andrew Jackson had established his reputation as a fearless frontier Indian fighter, willing to defy agreements made by representatives of the national government in far-off Washington. Once again, Indians were not represented at negotiations that ended the war, this time in Ghent, and armed resistance to American expansion south and west continued as the Seminole Wars until 1818.

Americans' hatred and resentment of Indians mounted in frontier regions. Already in the 1820s, Georgians refused to tolerate even the presence of the Cherokees, demanding their removal. The Cherokees were by then settled agriculturalists with a formal republican government, a written language and newspapers, and an 1827 constitution modeled on that of the USA. They otherwise so resembled their southern neighbors that some even owned slaves. Their leader John Ross – himself a man of mixed descent – brought the Cherokee case for remaining in Georgia to the Supreme Court in 1831, where John Marshall firmly declared them protected in their sovereignty over their lands within the USA.

But to no avail. A year earlier, Congress had already passed its first Indian Removal Act, building on state laws, like those of Mississippi, that unilaterally revoked Indian sovereignty over lands within their boundaries. The election of Andrew Jackson in 1828, reflecting the growing power of western voters, had sealed the Indians' fate. The "trail of tears" to the west – forced migrations of nearly 100,000 Choctaws, Cherokees, and Chickasaws, under army supervision – had already begun. A small group of Seminoles actively resisted removal; nearly one-quarter of the forced migrants died on their way west. In Oklahoma, where they were resettled, the native peoples of the east were neither native nor sovereign. They faced an environment completely unlike that of their woodland homelands as well as intense hostility from the hunting peoples native to these territories.

By 1835, only a few scattered remnants of the natives of America remained in the eastern USA. Their migrations confirmed the sharp limits ethnic nationalism had imposed on the revolutionary civic nationalism of the founding fathers. Newcomers from Europe might be distrusted aliens but it was expected they would become citizens. By contrast, most of the earliest natives of America, having first been denied citizenship and transformed into aliens, were now driven physically out of the USA itself. Free Africans lived in constant fear that they too could be excluded at any time.

Old Interactions; New Identities

The American nation had emerged during a temporary lull in international migrations across the Atlantic, relieving it of the worst burdens of cross-cultural exchange and complex loyalties among white citizens and potential citizens. While few revolutionary changes occurred in the interactions of Natives, Africans, and Europeans after independence, the creation of a new government for the USA did transform the cultural and regional identities of the colonial era. Regionalism and party politics eclipsed religion and national origins in Europe as sources of diversity among white citizens. Slaves and Indians were excluded from the nation even though both otherwise had firm cultural claims as longtime residents to being Americans, too.

For both Natives and Africans, the independence of the USA posed new choices. Should they demand inclusion, and integration as Americans into the new civic nation, or should they instead seek to maintain (in the case of Natives) or to gain (in the case of Africans) autonomy as ethnic nationalists and separatists, apart from the nation of white American citizens? For acculturated natives, such as Samuel Occom, who could speak English and who had become a "New Light" in New England, or for the Indian John Harrower had found fighting with patriot soldiers in 1776, integration may have seemed possible. Men like Occom sometimes even found that in their home counties and towns whites accepted them as fellow citizens and allowed them to vote.

Cherokee acculturation – and removal farther west – taught a different lesson, however. In the south and west, preference for autonomy and sovereignty remained pronounced. In the first decade of the century the Shawnee leaders Tecumseh and Prophet had again attempted to build a pan-native confederacy to exploit growing tensions between the USA and Britain. Like the nativists of the northwest before him, Prophet had urged natives to abandon Europeans' culture – even their bread, domestic animals, and guns – to achieve spiritual renewal and, with it, to regain their ancient strengths as independent nations. The removal of Cherokees and Choctaws may have temporarily ended nativists' dreams of driving Americans out of their lands, but it did not eliminate the attraction of independence or the hatred of the American conquerors.

For Africans, who had long lived in much closer proximity to whites, the promise of inclusion in the civic nation was more often appealing. The first abolitionist organizations – like the "Society for the Relief of Free Negroes Unlawfully Held in Bondage," founded by Benjamin Rush and Benjamin Franklin in 1775 in Philadelphia – were formed by white patriots. Indeed, all northern states abolished slavery in the aftermath of the Revolution, although most did so gradually, beginning with Pennsylvania in 1780 and Massachusetts in 1783 and ending with New York in 1799 and New Jersey in 1804. Because civic nationalism highlighted the distinction between Africans who were slaves and those who were free, it also provoked a new round of group formation among free Africans. Their numbers growing with abolition and their thinking shaped by service in the Revolutionary War and conversion to a religious faith that demanded moral action, free African patriots and "New Lights" would eventually claim the principles of the Declaration and Constitution for themselves.

Yet even the pursuit of inclusion by free Africans usually required organization along racial lines. Thus the former slave, Richard Allen, born in 1760 in Philadelphia and awakened as a Methodist in the early 1770s in Delaware, stopped preaching in a white Methodist church after purchasing his freedom in 1783 and organized the Free African Society in 1787. (It then inspired sister societies in New York, Boston, and Newport). In 1790, Allen founded the African Methodist Episcopal (AME) Church, in his words "the first African Church in America." By 1830 the church had congregations throughout the north and some 10,000 members. Through evangelical work, the AME Church expanded its influence among slaves in the south – whom Allen's replacement as leader in the 1830s noted were "like ripe fruit, waiting to be plucked."[14] But the AME Church hesitated to organize for abolition; secular groups would more often press for the end of the slavery beginning in the 1820s.

The organizations and churches of free Africans reflected both their desire for autonomy and white citizens' distaste for racial mixing in public or private. In fact, more than one historian has argued that the exclusion of Indians and Africans from the American nation served mainly to unify citizens of diverse European backgrounds as white supremacists. Certainly white Americans in 1830 were more unified than they had been in 1750. They had successfully claimed the term American for themselves, differentiating themselves from indigenous peoples and from Spanish Catholics alike. Evangelical Protestantism had become popular throughout the country, diminishing religious tensions; new arrivals from Europe were few in number; the patriots had succeeded in separating from Britain even as they expanded some of the political ideals of England – notably religious toleration, representative government, and voluntary citizenship – into a distinctively American civic nationalism in which increasing numbers of white citizens fervently believed. Even class divisions seemed to diminish among white citizens. Property qualifications for male voters disappeared first in the revolutionary constitutions of Pennsylvania and Vermont; by 1828, the election of Andrew Jackson as a common and rough-hewn frontiersman of the west symbolized the decline of class and status distinctions among male citizens.

Nor were ideas of white racial supremacy unknown or unpopular in the USA. Europeans had been cataloguing human physical difference since the late Middle Ages. Racial theorists like François Bernier (1620–1688), Georges Louis Leclerc Buffon (1707–1788) and Johann Friedrich Blumenbach (1752–1840) rejected divine explanations for human differences, tracing them instead to adaptation to the environment and the biological reproduction of acquired, cultural characteristics. Over the course of the eighteenth century, the ideas of these racial theorists linked biological inheritance to a hierarchy of "savage," "barbarian," and "civilized" cultures, replacing earlier spiritual distinctions between heathens and Christians arranged hierarchically in a divine "Great Chain of Being."

Colonials in British North America, like John Harrower, had long focused on color as the most important marker of biological difference. After noting the small number of "purely white People" in the world, and the vast number of "blacks" and "tawnys," Benjamin Franklin had found it wrong "to darken [America's] people." "Why," he asked should Britain "increase the Sons of Africa, by Planting them in America, where we have so fair an opportunity, by excluding all Blacks and Tawnys, of increasing the lovely White . . . ?"[15] After studiously avoiding the use of color categories in the first US censuses, census takers in 1820 began enumerating the "colored" free population, distinguishing them from both free whites and from slaves.

Nevertheless, in some respects, the ill treatment and exclusion of slaves and Indians from the nation was also a source of division among white Americans. Historians tell us that the indirect and vaguely worded references to slavery in the American Constitution were themselves the result of compromises reached in sharp debates among opponents, supporters, and tolerators of slavery among the founding fathers. Slavery and the exclusion of Indians from desirable agricultural lands may have been the twin foundations of economic development and prosperity for white Americans. But they did not always unify whites. While northern white New Lights argued paternalistically for the conversion and gradual "civilization" of slaves and of Indians, abolitionists of both colors soon demanded the eradication of slavery not only as a moral blot but also as a violation of the principles of the country's civic religion.

Debates like these quickly revealed the continued, and evolving, importance of regional cultures in the new nation. The division of the west between slave and free territories and the reconfiguration of regional economies and cultures – an industrializing northeast, a southern plantation economy, and a west of small farmers on the frontier – had encouraged the development of political parties with clear regional foundations. Debates over slavery and racial diversity would become increasingly important dimensions of regional American cultures and dividers of white citizens in the years ahead, as newcomers again flocked to the USA. In seeking to become Americans, the emigrants of the nineteenth century could scarcely hope to avoid choosing sides in this great regional debate.

Further Reading

Joyce Oldham Appleby. *Inheriting the Revolution: The First Generation of Americans* (Cambridge, MA: The Belknap Press of Harvard University Press, 2000).

Ira Berlin and Ronald Hoffman, eds., *Slavery and Freedom in the Age of the American Revolution* (Charlottesville: University Press of Virginia, 1983).

David Hackett Fischer and James C. Kelly, *Bound Away: Virginia and the Westward Movement* (Charlottesville: University Press of Virginia, 2000).

Marcus Lee Hansen, *The Atlantic Migration, 1607–1860* (Cambridge, MA: Harvard University Press, 1940).

James H. Kettner, *The Development of American Citizenship, 1608–1870* (Chapel Hill: University of North Carolina Press, 1978).

Frank Lambert, *Inventing the "Great Awakening"* (Princeton: Princeton University Press, 1999).

Peter S. Onuf, *Jefferson's Empire: The Language of American Nationhood* (Charlottesville: University Press of Virginia, 2000).

Theda Purdue and Michael D. Green, eds., *The Cherokee Removal: A Brief History with Documents* (Boston: Bedford Books of St. Martin's Press, 1995).

3

Emigrants and Regional Strife, 1820–1860

Agoston Haraszthy ought to have found quick welcome in the USA for he seemed exactly the type of emigrant nineteenth-century Americans wanted to welcome to their country. When he came to the USA in 1840, he was a republican fleeing the aftermath of a failed revolution in his homeland, and he quickly became a citizen. Americans almost certainly would have attributed Haraszthy's hard work and energy to his escape from the constraints of the Old World to which they felt superior. Because they believed emigrants fled from a narrow, illiberal, and impoverished past, they would have been reluctant to attribute Haraszthy's energies to his origins. Yet Haraszthy had been born to considerable privilege, a member of an old and wealthy family of Hungarian landowners, and he had enjoyed an excellent European education before coming to the USA.

Indeed, much of Haraszthy's difficult life in the USA can be seen as the product of Old World privilege uncomfortably transplanted to the New World. Haraszthy's vast ambitions and considerable energy did not make him a well-respected man among Americans. Charges of fraud, deception, and dishonesty trailed him as he migrated first to Wisconsin, then to southern California, and finally to San Francisco. In Wisconsin, and then again in southern California, Haraszthy failed as a construction entrepreneur and town-builder, and he fled from both places in the middle of intense political controversies. In the early 1850s, a stint as assayer at the government mint in San Francisco ended in much the same way. Soon thereafter, however, Haraszthy and his growing family seemed to find a less controversial life, successfully raising grapes in Sonoma County at their newly acquired Buena Vista estate. There, they quickly prospered, built a large, commodious home and began entertaining visitors in grand style. Nevertheless, within ten years, Haraszthy was again bankrupt. With one of his youngest sons, he promptly ventured off to Central America, where he hoped to grow sugar for export to San Francisco's developing refineries. In 1869, Haraszthy drowned unexpectedly in Nicaragua. His sons in California subsequently struggled to rebuild their lives as independent wine- and champagne-makers.[1]

In many critical ways, Haraszthy failed because he did not adopt the opinions and lifestyles of his American businessmen peers and he could find no approval from them anywhere he settled. In the 1850s, some pro-slavery Democrats newly arrived in California from the south may have tolerated Haraszthy's aristocratic manners. But they also viewed even the elite of recently conquered native Spanish-speaking and Catholic californios as "mongrels." By contrast, Haraszthy was perfectly happy to see two of his Catholic sons married to the daughters of his californio and Catholic neighbor – the rancher, winemaker, and elite Mexican political leader, Mariano Guadelupe Vallejo. Becoming a winemaker himself, Haraszthy also quickly attracted the enmity of skilled emigrant workers from Europe in the Democratic Party by employing, and loudly declaring his preference for, the Chinese workers, whom they despised as "rat-eating celestials" (from "the celestial empire of the east") or simply as "orientals" (with their eastern, rather than western, civilization).

Nor did California Whigs or Republican businessmen newly arrived in California from the north or midwest necessarily welcome Haraszthy. Nativist and sometimes virulently anti-Catholic, both parties attracted the growing numbers of Americans who took temperance pledges, abstained from the consumption of alcohol, and feared the baneful moral influence of emigrant brewers and beer-drinking "German Sundays" on American virtue. Soon after Haraszthy sent his elder sons to Europe to learn new winemaking techniques and traveled there himself to purchase new vines in anticipation of reimbursement from the state legislature, the Civil War began. Republicans dominated California's government by the time he returned, and they refused to pay a penny for the vines he had purchased. In less than two years, he was bankrupt.

In the years between 1820 and 1860, a massive migration that would continue almost uninterrupted for 100 years began to transform life in the USA. Look again at Figure I.1 (p. 4). Concerned with creating a nation of voluntary white citizens, the founding fathers had called earlier new arrivals aliens – those without citizenship. After 1830 Americans more often call newcomers from abroad "emigrants," even after they acquired citizenship. While the term focused negatively on what foreign migrants left behind, it said little about the country that received them. Perhaps that reflected Americans' uncertainty about the future of their nation. For the 40 years after the country began collecting information on the newcomers, vast new international migrations facilitated the geographical expansion of the USA but it also intensified sectional conflicts developing between north and south. These sectional conflicts had been obvious already in 1789; after 1820, they sharpened. The new emigration thus provided small foundation for unifying a dividing nation; if anything, it exacerbated differences between north and south and helped to make the west a region of recurring, violent confrontation.

Emigrants in the Antebellum USA

Between 1815 and 1860, five million new emigrants entered the USA, and on the eve of the Civil War newcomers made up about 13 percent of the American population. Fulfillment of the country's "manifest destiny" to expand westward at the expense of its Indian, Mexican, and British Canadian neighbors would have been unthinkable without this influx. So was the 1823 Monroe Doctrine with its declaration of the country's intentions to prevent foreign domination of the American hemisphere. The onset of American industrialization, along with the national strength and influence it promised, drew on the resources, ideas, and brawn of the newcomers. Migration and nation-building thus remained closely linked, if still controversial, in the minds of many Americans in the antebellum USA.

Worldwide as many as 150 million migrants traversed national borders in the century that followed the end of the Napoleonic Wars, and easily twice that many moved about within their own countries. Whether they traveled internationally or within national territories, migrants felt themselves pushed by their perceptions of hardship at home and pulled by the relatively better opportunities they perceived elsewhere. For much of the century, Europe was at peace but rapid population growth in its rural regions pushed out poorer young people hoping to marry and raise families. Great Britain's empire also now reached into India and China, luring underemployed rural workers there into ever wider migratory labor circuits as the British abolished slavery. With independence, the USA, Mexico, Argentina, and Brazil opened huge territories to agriculture and settlement by pushing indigenous peoples to marginal lands. At the same time, the growth of industry created new jobs in the cities of Europe and America, undermining the lives of small-scale artisans, especially in rural Europe. Finally, with the advent of the steam engine, railroads and ships could also now move large numbers of people over long distances at diminishing costs.

Responding to the country's westward expansion and its industrial and commercial expansion, Americans themselves continued as the largest group of migrants in the nineteenth-century USA. And they moved from the country to the city and from east to west in record numbers. During no other period of American history did cities in the USA grow so rapidly. In 1820 only seven percent of Americans had urban residences; by 1850 25 percent lived there. Many Americans migrating toward cities were young men from the countryside who crowded boarding houses and sought jobs in commerce, business, and the skilled trades. Almost simultaneously, thousands of men and family groups left New England for western New York State and the northern parts of the midwest. Already in the 1820s, southerners and their slaves were also moving across the Mississippi into Texas, and scholars estimate that white Virginians alone sold 300,000 slaves to southern Gulf coast markets in the antebellum period. By 1850 over 85,000 persons born in Virginia lived in Ohio, 55,000 in Kentucky, 46,000 in Tennessee, 42,000 in Indiana, and 41,000 in Missouri. In addition, by 1860, undetermined numbers of runaway slaves had fled north into Canada, beyond their masters' reach. But the largest and best-organized emigration out of the USA was surely the flight of the Mormons, almost all of them Americans, into the deserts of northern Mexico in 1846. There, the USA quickly engulfed them again. Having annexed the independent republic of Texas (created in 1836 by southern slave-owners' rebellion again Mexico), it then fought a war with Mexico in 1846–7.

With the treaty of Guadalupe Hidalgo in 1848 and the Gadsen Purchase of 1853, the USA had acquired more than half of Mexico's original territory and almost 100,000 of its Spanish-speaking hispano (in New Mexico and Arizona), tejano (in Texas), and californio (in California) farmers, along with significant new Indian populations, especially in the first two territories. Eighty years after its revolution, the USA stretched "from sea to shining sea," as Crèvecoeur had predicted. Westward migration to the Pacific coast captured the imaginations of Americans in the east. The discovery of gold in California in 1848 so abruptly provoked a migration that contemporaries labeled it a "rush." Most of those clambering into ships or walking across Panama in 1850 were men but in the next decade, groups of white American families from the east and the more recently settled midwest gathered at launching places along the Mississippi river to begin the long journey to Oregon and California through territories still occupied and claimed by Indians.

Watching so many Americans head west in the 1830s, Alexis de Tocqueville, a visitor from France, surely exaggerated when he claimed that an emigrant arriving from abroad "always lands . . . in a country that is but half full."[2] Still, Tocqueville was correct that the USA was attractive to emigrants and that newcomers often settled apart from longtime Americans. Between 1830 and 1930, the USA was by far the most popular destination worldwide for the 55 million emigrants leaving Europe. (It drew only a tiny percent of the 30 million who left Asia, however.) The vast majority of Europeans liked what they found in the USA and remained as settlers; half or more of the smaller numbers of Chinese who ventured across the Pacific found a harsh reception and instead left again.

Like Agoston Haraszthy, most of the emigrants who arrived in the USA between 1820 and 1860 came from outside Great Britain. By far the largest groups were from Germany and from Ireland. Migrations from Great Britain remained sizeable, and the numbers of migrants from French- and English-speaking Canada also increased as American industry developed in the northeast and around the Great Lakes. The emigrants from the Netherlands and from China who settled in Michigan and California respectively attracted attention only because they seemed so different from Americans; the much larger Anglo-Canadian and English migrations remained largely invisible to American eyes, and they remain that in most immigration histories.

From 1820 to 1860, almost two million emigrants crowded first into boats in the German cities of Hamburg and Bremen and then onto emigrant trains in Baltimore, New Orleans, and New York. Religiously they were a diverse group of Catholics and Protestants, and many originated in the southwestern and western lands that had not then unified as a single nation, Germany. Perhaps as many as a third of the emigrants Americans classified as German were Jewish, and while many left behind Bavaria or Berlin, many others were from German-speaking areas in Poland, Bohemia, Hungary, and Austria.

Among these German Jewish emigrants was Ottilie Assing. Assing's father was Jewish and her mother a free-thinking Protestant German; as a child, she had experienced anti-Jewish riots in Hamburg – for while German-speaking Jews were newly eligible for citizenship there, social prejudice against them remained intense. Leaving Germany in the aftermath of the failed republican revolutions of 1848, Assing believed German-speaking liberals in Europe would be eager to have her reports about the republican experiment in the USA.[3] Assing was, of course, a highly unusual, articulate, and independently wealthy young woman who seemed especially excited by the prospect of life in the USA. More typically traveling as parts of family groups, Jewish men may have anticipated humbler futures. Most began their careers in the USA as peddlers before opening small businesses specializing in clothing and other dry goods throughout the country.

Joining emigrants from Germany in America's growing cities were Irish newcomers like John Hughes – almost all of them Catholic. Hughes had faced a beating by Protestants as a young boy; emigrants of this era were pushed by even harsher circumstances. In the 1840s and 1850s, over a million fled Ireland to the USA alone when the island's potato crop failed and famine and epidemic ensued; another million died at home. Few had much money or hope of returning. "It cannot excite the least surprise," a diarist who traveled on an emigrant "coffin ship" concluded, "that these wretched beings should carry with them seeds of that plague from which they were flying and it was but natural that these seeds should rapidly germinate in the hot-bed hold of ships crammed almost to suffocation with their distempered bodies," turning some emigrant ships into "floating lazar houses."[4]

Even after Ireland's potato crops recovered, Irish emigrants continued to see life in the USA as a voluntary exile from a beloved homeland colonized by the anti-Catholic British. While some Irish traveled in family groups, many more left home as young men or young women desperate to find work for wages. In the USA, the men found it in construction, on the docks, and in manual trades. Irish women became charwomen, laundresses, or domestic servants. For both men and women, the early textile and shoe factories of New England also proved attractive.

Crowded with German and Irish emigrants, cities became the most demographically and culturally foreign places in the antebellum USA. In 1855, 52 percent of New Yorkers and about the same proportion of San Franciscans in 1860 were emigrants; at the same time in once-homogeneous New England, the city of Boston was 35 percent emigrants, two-thirds of them Irish Catholics. Even in the American south, a few port cities housed sizeable emigrant populations. New Orleans was 44 percent foreign-born in 1860 and Savannah 33 percent; fully 61 percent of the residents of St. Louis, on the Mississippi, were emigrants, mainly German-born.

While many emigrants repopulated eastern cities, others like Agoston Haraszthy traveled west alongside longtime Americans. While most wanted land, few probably considered themselves conquerors. Texas proved particularly attractive to German, Irish, Scandinavian, and British emigrants, and in California, a very mixed crowd of South Americans, Germans, Irish, Italians, other Europeans and Mexicans joined the rush to the gold fields. The lure of the "gold mountain" reached even to Asia, and in 1854, 13,000 Chinese arrived in California; thereafter about 4,000 workers, traders, and some prostitutes and servants from China followed each year.

Typical of the westward-bound emigrants were William Seyffardt and Sophie Frank, who both arrived in the USA from Germany in 1850. Unlike the majority of mobile peasants, artisans, and female domestic servants among Germans, William came from the family of a successful businessman; Sophie's father was a Protestant minister. Both traveled to communities in Michigan where friends and family from Germany already resided. Their new homes near Frankenmuth lay somewhat outside the distinctive "German triangle" of rural settlement between the heavily German cities of Milwaukee, Cincinnati, and St. Louis, but otherwise resembled areas of concentrated German settlement in Iowa, Illinois, Missouri, Wisconsin, and Minnesota.

The transformation of the antebellum USA by internal and international migrations was impressive. Unlike their Spanish- and Portuguese-speaking neighbors in South America, the USA never claimed to recruit European settlers like the Seyffardts in order to whiten their racially diverse population. Yet that was the result. In the 50 years after 1810, descendants of Africans declined from 19 to only 14 percent of the American population; emigrant newcomers now equaled them in numbers. But while most descendants of Africans lived in the south, most emigrants settled in the northeast, midwest, and far west. As new cross-cultural encounters ensued and new groups formed in these regions, north and south became ever more different, and their quarrels increasingly focused on the future of the west.

Group Formation: Communities and Associations

Most emigrants from Europe, like white Americans from the east coast, chose their own destinations in the USA, and they typically settled among their own kind. For them, and often for Americans too, new identities emerged from life in new communities forming among mobile people. These communities were rarely homogeneous however; to form cultural, regional, and religious identities, emigrants typically had to ignore sizeable differences among themselves.

The midwestern districts settled in the nineteenth century by migrants from Germany, New England, and the south were visibly different in some respects. Migrants from New England carved out square landholdings; Virginians who prospered in Indiana built grand plantation-style manor houses. Germans' churches, houses, and barns modified designs from their homeland using American materials; able to grow their own food, emigrant farmers introduced new crops (like rutabagas or gooseberries) and ate them in ways unknown to Americans. Emigrants also managed their farmlands differently from Americans. German farms in Texas often boasted extensive orchards, and farmers foddered their cows year-round in order to have fresh milk; Americans more often turned the animals loose to pasture and moved on before a tree bore fruit. Germans brewed and made wine at home and drank it after church on Sunday; migrants from New England baked beans on Saturday night so as to avoid all work and devote Sundays instead to worship and Bible study.

By the 1850s, a typical German settlement in the midwest was a cluster of 50 or more farms around a village with a church, one or more general stores, and perhaps a creamery, mill, or granary. The German emigrants Sophie Frank and William Seyffardt married soon after their arrivals in Michigan, starting life together on a farm near a cluster of such villages. Their early years together were difficult: William lost his milling business in a disastrous fire, and Sophie mourned the death of at least one small child in the 1850s. At such times, friends and neighbors – most of them German-speakers – came to their aid and comfort. Like many Germans in rural America, the young couple seemed interested in recreating the comfortable, family-oriented, small-town life they had enjoyed in Germany, and their letters home were full of reports of social events with other Germans.[5] Almost all their friends were Protestants, however. It is unlikely that the Seyffardts would have considered Ottilie Assing or even the German Catholic farmers living in separate towns nearby as members of their community.

No casual visitor could have confused these German settlements with the Indian settlements created during the forced removal of Cherokee and Seminoles from the southeast to Oklahoma. There, too, however, new groups were in formation, in a veritable melting pot of eastern Indians that generated recurring plots for rebellion against the US army. The Seminoles – groups that had originally fled from Creek territory in the west to take over empty lands in Florida – had been forced to Oklahoma along with their African adoptees and slaves in the late 1830s. Although settled on their own lands, some chose to go to live among the Cherokee (whom they regarded as more culturally advanced); remnants of the Creek confederation also tried to reclaim the Seminoles as their descendants. Under the leadership of Micanopy, one group of Seminoles became successful, settled farmers, celebrating their autonomy with their traditional green corn festival. But faced with harsh environmental challenges, and under constant pressure from both government agents concerned about former slaves living among them and from enemy tribes of the Plains, rampant alcoholism also threatened community survival.

In a large city like Chicago, internally divided emigrant enclaves were the rule. As the largest single group in the city of Chicago – about 15 percent of the city's population by 1880 – emigrants from Germany were so numerous that they lived almost everywhere. Not only were they Jewish, Catholic, and Protestant but they also spoke half a dozen different German dialects. Germans in Chicago included a large group of workers, concentrated in the skilled trades – notably construction, butchering, and baking – and in the new meatpacking and brewing industries. These workers lived alongside wealthier emigrants who ran small businesses and shops, preserved traditional crafts in small workshops or worked in the professions, as did Ottilie Assing. Still, neighborhood clusters known as "Little Germanies" appeared on the near north side and their businesses, clustering along main streets, provided a spatial focus for a unifying group identity.

Whether in the western countryside or in Chicago, emigrants organized formal institutions to strengthen their informal communal bonds. Knowing that the American government supported no one religious faith, Alexis de Tocqueville in his travels reported nevertheless that "the religious aspect of the country was the first thing that struck my attention." He quickly realized why this was so: "In no country in the world," he wrote, "has the principle of association been more successfully used or applied to a greater of multitude objects than America."[6] The most important of those objects was religion. Although unnoticed by Tocqueville, a second object was ethnic solidarity. If churches or community institutions were to exist, Americans had to build and finance them themselves, with no help from government.

Emigrants quickly learned this lesson of American life. In rural communities, Catholic German churches sponsored German-speaking parish schools, and sometimes also choir groups for men and for women. Towns where German emigrants predominated even made German the language of instruction in their public schools. Because they hired Germans as teachers, schools in rural areas typically offered prayers familiar to children of the local Lutheran or Catholic church. In the 1840s, rural German Lutherans banded together regionally to form their own synod or alliance of churches to promote the use of the German language, to maintain uniform worship services and articles of faith, and to isolate believers from American Protestantism with its preference for individual religious choice. Their Missouri Synod provided training for teachers and ministers, distributed reading materials in German, and discouraged parents from sending their children to English-speaking public schools well into the twentieth century. The Missouri Synod had no counterpart in Germany – there, state governments funded churches.

German Chicago supported an even wider range of secular associations. Apart from the ubiquitous Lutheran and Catholic churches, there were social clubs and insurance societies for emigrants of a particular regional background. Over time, however, most fraternal and masonic lodges welcomed all German-speakers, whether they were Swabians, Berliners, or Prussians. Once again, Germans unified more easily in the USA than in Europe. German nationalists transplanted their gymnastic club the "Turnverein," and emigrants read their own newspaper, the *Illinois Staats-Zeitung*, enjoyed theater in their own cultural center, and belonged to dozens of choral groups. In the 1840s, German workers began to organize their own groups; 30 years later they too had their own newspaper, where the principles of trade unionism, anarchism, and socialism were hotly debated in German. While men formed and led most German organizations, German women also organized separately, at first to sing and later to provide welfare services – for example, a home for the German-speaking elderly – not provided by city or state governments.

Jewish emigrants from Bavaria and central Europe also experienced sharp changes in identity as they organized religiously in the USA. As Yiddish- and German-speakers, few felt comfortable with the synagogues founded by the Americanized refugee Sephardic Jews of the Spanish Empire who had arrived in North America in the eighteenth century. Since few rabbis accompanied the newest Jewish migration, the first institutions of Jewish communities were usually fraternal lodges, that later allied nationally as B'nai Brith. Brotherhoods of men and sisterhoods of women provided for recreation (Young Men's and Women's Hebrew Associations), burial, insurance, and charity. Sisterhoods helped raise the money to build synagogues, while brotherhoods sought rabbis to lead them. Most congregations of Jews opted for "Reformed" expressions of Judaism developing in Germany and requested rabbis willing to interpret Talmudic law liberally and to offer worship services for men and women together and partially in English or German rather than in Hebrew. As a result, Jewish forms of worship – like those of American Protestants – differed considerably from one local congregation to the next.

As emigrants poured into American cities, urban communities of free Africans also grew and became more diverse, challenging the early leadership of ministers like Richard Allen. Free men and women organized abolitionist societies beginning in the 1820s and a weekly newspaper, *Freedom's Journal*, began publication in 1827. National conventions of African community leaders began meeting in 1830 to discuss – and quickly to disagree about – what freedom could promise slaves in the south. Born to a slave father and a free mother in West Virginia in 1812, Martin Delany, who claimed descent from a Mandingo prince, argued for a future and autonomous Black nation apart from whites. Moving north, Delany became a journalist and organizer of Black anti-slavery organizations in the 1840s before applying to Harvard Medical School, which, in admitting him, required him to emigrate and practice medicine in Africa. Subject to constant harassment throughout his early life, Delany went to explore the Niger Valley in Africa, and he signed a treaty with Yoruba rulers in 1859, hoping to create an asylum for free Africans from America. "Africa for the African race," he pronounced, "and black men to rule them."

In sharp contrast to Delany, Frederick Douglass, the child of a white man and born to a slave mother in Maryland, escaped to freedom but always insisted "I thank God for making me a man simply."[7] Douglass worked closely with the white abolitionist William Lloyd Garrison and later with John Brown, and he consistently called on freed Africans to think of themselves as colored Americans or as hyphenated Afro-Americans with claims to citizenship and inclusion in the American nation, rather than to dream of return to Africa. Following Douglass's arguments, a newspaper *The Colored American* began publication and a National Colored Convention first met in 1843, followed by the National Council of Colored People in 1853. Douglass's frequent appeals to the republican ideology of the founding fathers also made him an early ally of the American women who met in Seneca Falls in 1848 to demand equal rights for themselves.

As voluntary associations, the institutions, churches, and rituals of Coloreds or Blacks and of Reform Jews, German "Turners", or Missouri Synod Lutherans were all as much products of American life as of Old World cultures. Tocqueville even argued that churches, like the other voluntary associations that proliferated in the USA, prepared Americans for participatory citizenship in a republican government. Along with churches, competing secular institutions – which individuals were free to join or to avoid as they pleased – held much the same promise for escaped slaves and emigrants from Europe. Among Indians, by contrast, association was not related so directly to republican citizenship. Even in defeat, they chose their own leaders, either democratically or through kinship and charisma; they also continued to assert their independence as nations and to negotiate with the "Indian Agents" of the federal government who, by contrast, increasingly viewed them as their dependents or wards.

New Contacts; New Conflicts

Because emigrants rarely went south, except to Texas and to a few southern cities, and because they preferred to farm among their own kind, the cities of the northeast and west were the most important sites of cross-cultural contact in the early nineteenth century. And because many of these encounters were conflict-laden, American cities quickly gained a reputation for violence as Catholics and Protestants, whites and blacks, and older and newer citizens clashed over turf, jobs, and local politics. In the rural midwest cultural isolation allowed for a more peaceful co-existence while farther west conquest instead pitted newcomers against Indians and Mexicans. Everywhere, differences in gender and family relations, in language and color, and in religious practice remained important markers of group boundaries in these interactions too.

Western encounters

Emigrants who ventured to Iowa and Minnesota to farm often found themselves living near Natives who – like their counterparts in the east – were quickly learning that frontiersman wanted their lands. In 1862, emigrant Gro Svendsen arrived from Norway with her husband Ole in St. Ansgar, Iowa. Among their first experiences in the USA was an uprising of the Santee Sioux who lived nearby. Provoked by the federal government's refusal to provide food and supplies as negotiated, the Sioux attacked the nearby German settlement of New Ulm, killing more than 500 emigrants. The newly arrived Svendsen reported her terror in letters home, wishing that "not a single one who took part in the revolt should be permitted to live. Unfortunately," she continued, "I cannot make the decision in the matter."[8] Emigrants like the Svendsens often commented on the lowly status of women among groups such as the Sioux, pointing to their hard physical labor and contrasting their subordination to the respect women enjoyed in Christian families, where men supposedly protected and supported their wives and children. While Svendsen did not consider herself a conqueror, she certainly shared many of the assumptions of white Americans about the "savages" she met in her new home.

From Texas to the Pacific coast, too, conquest resulted in violent conflicts over land and schooling with the former residents of Mexico and this was the case whether the newcomers were Americans or emigrants. In fact, to the many

Spanish-speaking hispanos, tejanos, californios, and to the Indians of this region Americans arriving from the east and emigrants from Europe were all "Anglos" with common goals – to possess their lands. In Texas, Americans from the south quickly succeeded in revoking tejanos' land titles. But in California, wealthy Catholic and Spanish-speaking rancheros like Mariano Guadelupe Vallejo more often held onto their possessions by strategically arranging marriages between their daughters and prosperous newcomers such as Agoston Haraszthy. In New Mexico and Arizona, too, the largest Indian groups – Pueblo, Navajo, and Apache – maintained some sovereignty over their lands as surrounding areas became part of American national territories. Smaller groups withdrew into their farming or herding communities on American soil, seeking to avoid conflicts with the newcomers. Still, Protestant and Catholic missionaries arrived even in relatively small and isolated communities in the southwest, offered schooling to such communities in order to teach English and American customs to Spanish-speaking and Indian children, hoping to "uplift" them to American standards of culture.

Urban encounters

In American cities in the northeast, the arrival of emigrants instead encouraged longtime and wealthier white Americans to move away, and seek to segregate themselves in outlying "street car" suburbs. The result was cities populated largely by laborers and small businessmen of diverse emigrant backgrounds. Thus it was unsurprising that much urban conflict in the nineteenth century resulted from competition over jobs in the country's new urban industries, pitting workers of varied backgrounds against each other in local job markets.

In the textile mills of Lowell, Massachusetts, the daughters of New England's farms had been the first American factory workers; after the depression of the mid-1830s, emigrants from Ireland, England, Scotland, and French-speaking Canada replaced them. The American mill girls protested sinking wages and working conditions but then withdrew from the industry. Similar transitions in male workplaces more often sparked violence. In New York in 1835, gangs of American workers attacked Irish gangs in the "Five Points" district as unskilled, ignorant "wage-breakers." Fifteen years later in California, Americans and emigrants from Europe united to drive Orientals from the gold fields. Efforts to unite workers into trade unions typically foundered over conflicts like these between 1830 and 1880, and many early labor organizations, especially in the west, were organized explicitly to oppose the continuation of free migration from China.

Economic competition between unskilled Irish men and free African-Americans was equally intense in northeastern cities. The occupations open to African men shrank noticeably as ever more emigrants crowded into cities after 1830. German tradesmen replaced them as barbers and waiters, while Irish emigrants increasingly dominated in unskilled work on the docks and in construction. The competition of African and Irish women for work in middle-class kitchens was more complex, however, as many Americans hesitated to employ Irish women who were not only Catholic but who also had a reputation for rebelliousness.

Religious encounters

In the early republic, few Americans outside Maryland or Louisiana had met many Catholics. Less than one percent of the American population in 1790, Catholics became the largest single religious denomination in the USA by 1860. Almost all the Irish emigrants arriving in the USA during these years were Catholics, as were all the conquered Mexicans and about a third of emigrants from Germany. Thus the Catholic Church itself became a place where emigrants of many backgrounds met – and often competed – with each other, especially in American cities.

As a young priest in 1826, the Irish emigrant John Hughes entered a Catholic Church still dominated by American

Bishops of English and French descent. He and other English-speaking Irish emigrants soon displaced them – he became bishop of New York in 1840 – only to face incessant demands for still greater cultural diversity in the priesthood and Church hierarchy. German Catholics in particular repeatedly argued for the creation of national parishes staffed by priests who shared emigrants' language and background. Irish-American bishops, including John Hughes, preferred a diverse but American (that is, English-speaking and Irish-dominated) church. Still, they also made many concessions and often appointed priests of the same background as the residents of an urban or rural parish. The controversy over national parishes nevertheless raged until the latter years of the century, refreshed by each wave of Catholic newcomers.

In their first encounters with it, many American Protestants found the Catholic Church to be an alien and dangerous import. Unlike America's many Protestant sects, the Catholic Church was a vast, international, and centralized institution with clearly articulated and relatively homogeneous principles of faith. Its parishes were no voluntary associations or congregations governed by their members but rather territories mapped out and manned by priests appointed and paid not by their parishioners but by a church hierarchy culminating in the Pope in Rome – who was also ruler of his own country, the Papal States.

Exacerbating perceptions like these, the Americans who watched Catholic Churches springing up in American cities were themselves Protestants in the throes of yet another religious revival, the Second Great Awakening of the 1830s. Once again, recent converts enthusiastically pledged themselves to making American society a morally better place through their good works and evangelism, reaching out to the unconverted. Many reformers of this era, including large numbers of women converts, committed themselves to working with the urban poor, many of them Catholics. Protestant fervor among long-time Americans fueled every reform movement of the antebellum USA, from abolition and temperance to women's rights and nativism.

The confrontation of awakened, Protestant American citizens and Catholic emigrants sometimes became a violent one. Bringing with them a long history of opposition and hostility toward their British Protestant rulers, Irish emigrants rightly feared that moral reformers wanted to make them both culturally English and Protestant. To isolate the poorest Catholics from the influence of reformers and proselytizers, Catholic priests such as John Hughes sought to create Catholic institutions – notably schools, charities, and hospitals – to serve the needs of the urban poor. To do it, Hughes and others turned to the religious orders or sisterhoods of Catholic nuns who in Europe devoted themselves mainly to prayer and contemplation in their isolated cloisters. Responding to appeals from the USA, Catholic nuns migrated enthusiastically from their "mother houses" in French Canada and Europe knowing they would instead lead lives of activism in the USA. Catholic sisters soon specialized in teaching, nursing, and working with the poor in American cities.

Unmarried women in distinctive garb or "habits" working under the leadership of celibate and distinctively clad Catholic priests provoked intensely hostile responses from Protestant Americans who had inherited the anti-Catholicism of British and German reformations and of New England's Puritans. Already in 1833, as a young priest, John Hughes had begun publishing a newspaper, *The Catholic Herald*, to counter mounting anti-Catholic polemics in Philadelphia newspapers. Verbal conflicts soon escalated into physical violence. In 1834 Protestant rioters attacked a convent of Ursuline nuns outside Boston (see the Student Exercise at the end of the chapter). In 1836, the purported confession of a young woman named Maria Monk about moral depravity and infanticide in convents made a nation-wide best-seller of a falsified and prurient story. Cultural differences between Catholics and Protestants in turn heightened passions in apparently unrelated political controversies at the local, state, and national level.

Political encounters: the local level

Because emigrants from Europe could attain American citizenship quickly, urban politics generated intense conflicts between longtime Americans and recent emigrants in the years before the Civil War. German and Irish emigrants began arriving in the USA in large numbers just as the second "system" of two competing American parties – Whigs and Democrats – consolidated after the election of Andrew Jackson. Although enjoying the support of southern planters, too, Jackson's Democrats boasted of having created a party for common men – notably western frontiersmen and urban workers – while the Whigs represented the commercial and new industrial interests of the cities and of the northeast generally. This system would collapse rather quickly in the 1850s as a result of rising sectional tensions but it shaped many male newcomers' introduction to American political life and governance and made politics itself a place where cultural differences found expression among white citizens.

In American cities of the 1820s and 1830s, and especially in the northeast where emigrants first clustered, the formation of new Democratic Party political "machines" offered workers "a kind of primitive welfare state" – patronage jobs when they were available, charity when they were not – in exchange for electoral support.[9] American reformers, often in the Whig Party, were horrified that self-interest rather than the virtue of individual candidates should sway voters but they blamed the change – equally apparent in western frontiers settled by Americans – on emigrants. Reformers especially noted the swiftness with which Irish emigrants moved into political activism and even leadership of urban machines. Not only were most Irish emigrants English-speakers, they also possessed a long-term, if negative, familiarity with the political traditions of their British colonizers. Building political machines also worked to the advantage of their communities, providing networks of personal influence that linked Irish office-holding to patronage of city jobs open to Irish workers, notably as policemen and firemen, as holders of city contracts and as workers in garbage collection, street cleaning, and the construction of urban public works.

Political battles over urban public schools also frequently pitted Catholic, and Irish, Democrats against Whig reformers. Copying New England models, reformers saw urban public schools as the best place to teach the literacy and the republican values required of American citizens. Newly appointed as Bishop of New York, and unable to fund separate schooling for most Catholic children, John Hughes saw things differently: to him Protestant reformers used school funds to hire anti-Catholic teachers who then forced students to read the Protestant (King James) translation of the Bible. In a petition, Hughes reminded Americans that "in Ireland [the Catholic] was compelled to support a church hostile to his religion, and here he is compelled to support schools in which his religion fares little better, and to support his own schools besides."[10] Supporting a controversial proposal of Governor William H. Seward to provide public funds for secularized schools sponsored by the Catholic Church, he sought support for this program from Catholic voters. Outside Philadelphia, a somewhat similar local political debate provoked the Kensington riots of 1844, when armed Protestants attacked Catholic homes and institutions for three days. In New York, Hughes's residence was bombarded and broken into, and his furniture demolished.

While Irish hostility to English culture and American moral reform often led them directly into the Democratic Party, non-English-speaking emigrants moved more slowly into local political activism. By the 1850s Germans living in culturally diverse towns where large numbers of Irish had entered the Democratic Party often responded by taking up membership and pursuing leadership within the new Republican Party. Even Protestant Germans, however, looked askance at the moral reform movements fueled by the Second Great Awakening. Germans saw no moral taint in drinking beer and wine, and they resented efforts by awakened Americans to limit their enjoyment of drink with prohibitionist "blue laws." They disparaged the masculinity of American men taking water pledges and the femininity of female moral reformers, abolitionists and feminists, dismissing them as "bloomers" (the reformed dress some feminists had adopted). Conflicts between natives and newcomers over morality, religion, and reform in turn deeply affected emigrants' views on slavery, the burning national political issue of the day.

Political encounters: the national level

No bigger political issue confronted emigrants as voters and as new residents of the USA than that of slavery. Slavery had already divided the founding fathers. In 1820, the Missouri Compromise drew a line through the Louisiana Purchase separating territories opened and closed to slavery. Thereafter, white and black abolitionists, many of them inspired by the moral fervor of the Second Great Awakening, devoted themselves to eliminating slavery as a moral blot and a violation of American civic values.

As millions of Irish and German emigrants poured into the country, the Mexican War again focused the nation's attention on the future of slavery in the west. In 1846, Congressman David Wilmot unsuccessfully tried to exclude it from the new territories gained from Mexico. The ensuing conflicts between pro- and anti-slavery whites split the Whig Party, and new parties – Free-Soilers, the American Party, the Republicans – formed to represent the reformers. A new compromise in 1850 declared some western territories free of slavery in exchange for a stricter fugitive slave law but in 1854 the Kansas–Nebraska Act forced western migrants to resolve the issue themselves. The result was organized migration of northerners and southerners followed by open warfare between pro- and anti-slavery supporters in "bloody Kansas." In 1857 the Supreme Court's rejection of the slave Dred Scott's appeal for freedom rendered all these compromises moot: devastating abolitionists' gains, it permitted slave-owners to take their human property wherever they chose.

In the nation-wide debate over slavery, emigrants seemed natural allies for abolitionists. Emigrants rarely chose to settle in the rural south where slavery and the cotton plantation economy prevailed. Few newcomers met either slaves or slave-owners in their urban homes or midwestern farming communities. And many – perhaps even most – found slavery repugnant. Republican exiles from Germany such as Ottilie Assing were outspoken abolitionists. Even politically uninformed emigrants easily recognized slavery as a "peculiar" institution – unknown in their homelands – that was difficult to reconcile with Americans' boasts about their land of liberty. Unfortunately, as Agoston Haraszthy learned, the abolitionists whose ideas might have been attractive to emigrants were often Protestant anti-Catholics eager to limit emigrants' access to citizenship and its full rights.

By the 1850s, as emigrants poured into the USA, many American reformers had become outspoken nativists, opposed to increasing alien influence on American life. Nativist organizations like the Order of the Star Spangled Banner and the American or "Know-Nothing" Party emerged after the collapse of the Whig Party in 1848; their influence peaked in states such as Massachusetts just before the Civil War. Like the founding fathers, American nativists believed republics were fragile creations, endangered by diversity. With its view of emigrants as a threat to American stability, nativism appealed to both opponents and supporters of slavery, and some nativists hoped to reverse the rising tide of sectionalism. They sensibly observed that emigrants could claim American citizenship long before they had learned the language or customs of the USA, and they demanded that emigrants wait 21 years before acquiring full citizenship and the franchise – just as American-born babies did. At the local and state level, the American Party opposed office-holding and even appointment to patronage positions for citizens born abroad. Significantly, however, nativists did not try to restrict migration itself.

The largest and most vocal group of nativists of the 1850s were northerners who opposed Catholic Irish influence on American politics. Know-Nothing activists first succeeded in imposing legal limits on the amount of property owned by the Catholic Church; their American Party actively opposed Catholic candidates for political office. In their hostility to Irish voters and machine politicians, Know-Nothings portrayed Catholic values as inimical to voluntary citizenship. Nativists contrasted Protestantism as a republican and voluntary religion to the obedience to papal authority required of Catholics. Pointing to Irish Catholics' move into the Democratic Party (the party also of southern planters) and to their battles over urban turf and jobs with free colored Americans, abolitionist nativists went still farther. Massachusetts Congressman and Know-Nothing Anson Burlingame concluded that "Slavery and priestcraft . . . have a common purpose: they seek [to annex] Cuba and Hayti and the Mexican States together, because they will be Catholic and Slave. I say they are in alliance by the necessity of their nature, – for one denies the right of a man to his body, and the other the right to act for himself."[11] Indeed some nativist abolitionists saw free Africans – as longtime and usually Protestant Americans – as potentially better citizens than Catholic emigrants. Such arguments did little to draw emigrants, or at least the Irish Catholics among them, into the abolitionist campaign.

Emigrants and Regional Cultures

Nor could nativist sentiments like these bridge the growing chasm slavery was creating between Americans. By 1860, the American Party had itself split into competing factions of northern and southern Know-Nothings, as had many other American voluntary associations, including the Baptist Church, home to many Protestants awakened in the latest religious revivals. The USA was about to collapse into warring regions that imagined themselves as separate nations, and vast new migrations from abroad had helped to produce that outcome.

In the north, migration from Europe made industrialization possible and created cities that were cosmopolitan and creative but also dirty and sometimes dangerous places. Watching the rise of industry, northern intellectuals began to create the myth of an earlier "Yankee" culture, rooted in New England, that had blended the best of British culture with Puritan moral idealism and the common sense of industrious mechanics and traders. Yankees promoted a national government that would unify the nation by promoting its general welfare through industrial and commercial expansion and the abolition of slavery.

Boston's elite intellectual "Brahmins," New York's Whig reformers and Cincinnati's abolitionists could not easily welcome newcomers as fellow Yankees. Separated from Yankees by class, religion, and nativity, the culture of the emigrants was urban, plebeian and culturally complex. In northern cities, Catholics sometimes intermarried across ethnic boundaries, as did Protestants, but longtime and more prosperous Americans contributed little to this linguistic and marital blending. An emigrant living in rural Sheboygan county, Wisconsin, observed what was even more true of northern cities when he proclaimed "there are not ENGLISH Americans here to intermarry with."[12]

There were Afro-Americans in cities, of course, but emigrants rarely intermarried with them. A color line shaped northern culture even when it did not unify all whites. The Irish came to the USA burdened with British stereotypes of them as wild, uncivilized blacks, and northern reformers' contempt for Catholics evoked many of the same images of simian, drunken, and violent Irish. Emigrants from Ireland, along with other poor laborers, claimed whiteness for themselves without - gaining acceptance from white Yankees. For their part, elite abolitionists accepted Africans' souls as equal but rarely chose to live anywhere near them, as the Irish more frequently did.

Emigrants, free Colored Americans, and working-class Americans created a new culture in northern cities that violated Yankee norms of propriety and blended their separate traditions. Young urban male dandies – stereotyped as "Zip Coon" (if black) and "bowery b'hoys" (if white) – enjoyed new commercial entertainments – notably saloons and beer gardens – operated by Irish and German emigrants.

Identifiable by their distinctive, urban clothes, such young men dominated downtown streets at night with their quest for lager beer and prostitutes. Emigrant thespians entertained them, as did foreigners and white Americans who corked themselves to perform in "black face" and to compete with the banjo music, songs, and dances free Africans had introduced to the city. (One of their stock subjects was a jumping, dancing, simple-minded slave named "Jim Crow.") Foreigners also directed the first American museums and introduced Yankees to music and opera, while outside of northern cities, few "high" or "low" cultural institutions like these could be found.

Except in a few western border regions of the expanding south (Texas, Missouri) and a few cities (notably New Orleans), the antebellum south remained a rural region of longtime and overwhelmingly Protestant Americans, divided by a color line between black and white. From their home regions, southern whites viewed the industrializing north as more like Gomorrah than Zion or a "city on the hill;" they claimed its urban emigrants were more impoverished and exploited than slaves. The planter elite of the south increasingly portrayed themselves as the opposites of Yankees and as descendants of the English gentry or "cavaliers" – men of substance who continued to treat their poorer white neighbors as human subordinates, rather than as factors in capitalist production. To southern thinkers, the absence of class conflict in the south explained the common participation of humble frontiersman, yeoman farmers, and planters alike in the Democratic Party. Little touched by migration from abroad, the south was spared the conflicts of urban Protestants and Catholics or the violence, strikes, and crises of periodic unemployment associated with industrial wage-earning. Where emigrants did settle in the south, furthermore, even Catholic Irish emigrants and Jewish peddlers found ready acceptance as white citizens and viewed themselves as such.

Thus the elite of the south could claim that slavery provided a superior foundation for a peaceful and homogeneous white republic. Southerners elaborated republican traditions of opposition to central government and glorified local and states rights that protected individual liberty and religious freedom for humble white farmers while simultaneously defending the institution of slavery with all its violence. They reminded northerners that slavery had existed also in the ancient republics of Greece and of Rome. And during the revivals of the Second Great Awakening, they also developed new religious justifications for slavery, insisting it uplifted Africans from a state of savage depravity into Christian morality. Planters understood themselves as paternalists or patriarchs obligated morally to care for their child-like slaves as they did for their own wives and children.

Northern and southern elites thus developed regional cultures that provided radically differing models for the nation's future, while both assuming that the future of the nation increasing lay in the west. In 1860 the American west was both culturally diverse – like the north – and still overwhelmingly rural – like the south. Northern and southern cultures clashed most directly in the west, and emigrants' choices sometimes mattered in determining which vision prevailed there. From colonial times, newcomers from Europe had avoided settling areas dominated by plantation agriculture but whether because they hated slavery, feared the competition of enslaved labor, or disdained contact with Africans is not yet known. In Texas and parts of the southwest, emigrant Germans and Jews often resisted southerners' lead in rejecting all contacts with Spanish-speaking natives or Indians. But in California – where emigrants from Europe and Asia more often competed directly for gold stakes and jobs – southern, northern, and foreign-born settlers quickly united along color lines, demanding that California become a "white man's country," by excluding the hated Orientals, who lived in fear of constant harassment and attack.

Mainly concerned with building their own communities and cultural organizations, emigrants in antebellum America commonly adopted national, American identities rather than espousing regional ones as southerners or northerners. Thus, for example, organizations founded by German-Americans and Irish-Americans, unlike those of other Americans in this era, rarely fractured along sectional lines. Still, emigrants did increasingly take sides in the sectional controversies of the 1850s and ultimately most – even the Irish and Catholic activists of the northern, urban Democratic Party – sided with national union over southern secession.

In viewing the west as a place where free men should have access to free soil, northern Republicans especially confirmed the special place of emigrants in building the future of the American nation in the west. Speaking out on the Kansas–Nebraska Act in in Peoria in 1854, Abraham Lincoln summed up the north's appeal to emigrants when he expressed his desires for the western territories. "We want them for homes of free white people," he insisted. "This they cannot be, to any considerable extent, if slavery shall be planted within them. Slave States are places for poor white people to remove FROM; not to remove TO." The western territories, he emphasized later in his 1858 debates with Stephen A. Douglas, must be "an outlet for free white people everywhere, the world over – in which Hans and Baptiste and Patrick and all other men from all the world, may find new homes and better their conditions in life." [13] In the west, unlike the east, Lincoln seemed to imply, emigrants and Americans could unite as founding fathers of the new region.

The international migrations of the antebellum thus exacerbated sectional tensions while ultimately helping the north to prevail in its quarrels with the south. At the same time, they strengthened Americans in their longstanding battles with Indians for control of North American lands. In appealing to emigrants as free men but also as whites, Abraham Lincoln's words foreshadowed future conflicts. Even Civil War between north and south would not easily resolve the central tension between civic and ethnic nationalism that had festered at the heart of the American nation since its foundation.

Further Reading

Kathleen Neils Conzen, *Immigrant Milwaukee, 1836–1860: Accommodation and Community in a Frontier City* (Cambridge, MA: Harvard University Press, 1976).

Hasia R. Diner, *A Time for Gathering: The Second Migration, 1820–1880* (Baltimore: Johns Hopkins University Press, 1992), vol 2. *The Jewish People in America.*

Jay P. Dolan, *The Immigrant Church: New York's Irish and German Catholics* (Baltimore: Johns Hopkins University Press, 1975).

Charlotte Erickson, *Invisible Immigrants: The Adaptation of English and Scottish Immigrants in Nineteenth-Century America* (London: Weidenfeld and Nicholson, 1972).

David Gerber, *The Making of an American Pluralism: Buffalo, New York, 1825–1860* (Urbana: University of Illinois Press, 1989).

James Oliver Horton and Lois E. Horton, *In Hope of Liberty: Culture, Community, and Protest among Northern Free Blacks, 1700–1860* (New York: Oxford University Press, 1997).

Noel Ignatiev, *How the Irish Became White* (New York: Routledge, 1995).

Dale T. Knobel, *America for the Americans: The Nativist Movement in the United States* (New York: Twayne Publishers, 1996).

Eric Lott, *Love and Theft: Blackface Minstrelsy and the American Working Class* (New York: Oxford University Press, 1993).

Kerby A. Miller, *Emigrants and Exiles: Ireland and the Irish Exodus to North America* (New York: Oxford University Press, 1985).

Student Exercise

Catholic Nuns Testify in Court after the Burning of the Charlestown Convent

"The first witness called was Mary Anne Ursula Moffatt, otherwise called Mary Edmond Saint George, the Lady Superior of the Ursuline Community. This lady appeared in Court in the costume of her order, and closely veiled. One of the Counsel for the prisoner (Mr. Farley) expressed a desire that she should unveil. With this requisition the witness hesitated to comply; but on being informed by the Court that it was absolutely necessary for her to do so, in order that her voice might be distinctly heard, she reluctantly removed the veil from her features, and gave her testimony as follows:

> I am the Superior of the Ursuline Community in this State. I had the entire jurisdiction of the institution at Charlestown. Have held my present rank ten years. There was a school in our establishment, of which I was the director. On the Thursday preceding the day on which the outrage was committed, I was told that the Convent would be pulled down, and on the Saturday following, several papers were sent to the institution concerning the "Mysterious Lady." On Sunday one of the Selectmen of Charlestown called upon me and told me the Convent would be destroyed if the "mysterious lady" could not be seen. By the "mysterious lady," I understood him to mean Miss Harrison.
>
> . . .
>
> A little after 9, on the 11th of August, when I had retired into my room, I heard a great noise on the Medford road – I heard, "Down with the Convent," "Down with the Convent" from the mob. I could not judge of their numbers; but when they came up, there seemed to be about 30 or 40 . . . I went into an adjoining apartment and gave directions to two of the sisters to inform the community I thought there was some danger. There were 56 pupils, from 6 to 18 years of age – 47 were there that night – all females – there were ten members of the community – three female domestics – two of the ten, were novices – the novices are not called Ursulines or nuns. The nuns are named as in the list, I sent to the Attorney General. When they assume the white veil, they take any name they please, instead of the name by which they are known in the world, and are always known by that in the religious community.
>
> . . .

The community sometimes call me "ma mere" (mother). The words *divine mother* are never applied to me. Confessions are never made to me, but to the Rt. Rev. Bishop, or, in his absence, to some other clergyman. I confess to the Bishop. The confessions are made once a week. We apply the word *divine* only to the Divinity. I do not represent the Virgin Mary, but am considered in the light of the mother of a family.

. . .

I was the last of my family that left the house. I did not remain in the summer house more than half an hour . . . It was when I came down again, that I saw the men in my room. I called Miss Harrison "the mysterious lady" in allusion to the piece in the paper they showed me – the piece alluded to Miss Harrison's going from the convent. She went to Mr. Cutter's without my knowledge. She left at 4 P.M. on Monday the 28th of July. She is a professed nun, and has belonged to the community twelve years. She was senior teacher of music. She returned in 24 hours, with Bishop Fenwick and her brother, Thomas Harrison. It was at my repeated solicitation that the bishop went for her. The occasion of her leaving, was weakness of mind, debility, and fever of the brain, brought on by excessive application. She had been composing music – she had given 14 lessons a day – each lesson of 25 minutes or more. When she returned, she appeared very much excited – and she said she did not know what it meant.

. . .

I have never recovered the property, except some small articles. The building had the necessary furniture for the establishment – beds and bedding – there was about $50,000 property of the pupils – there were three Spanish children, who had great quantities of jewelry. The children were required to have a silver tumbler, teaspoon, desert-spoon and table-spoon. There were harps and pianos – a harp is worth from 300 to 400 dollars – about 4 in the institution – 9 or 10 piano fortes – 3 of them perfectly new, and worth about 350 to 370 dollars each – an harmonicum . . . The windows were broken by stones &c, before I left the house – the pupils and sisters heard the windows broken. I can't say they were broken by clubs held in their hands.

Mary Ann Barber, sworn

The mob made use of a great deal of abusive language to the Superior – they called the Superior "the Figure Head" – I should think about 40 and 60 persons were assembled – this was before the bonfire was kindled – I saw them making the bonfire and collecting in larger numbers.

The Trial of John R. Buzzell, Before the Supreme Judicial Court of Massachusetts for Arson and Burglary in the Ursuline Convent at Charlestown (Boston: Russell, Odiorne and Metcalf, 1834) and *The Trial of the Persons Charged with Burning the Convent in the Town of Charlestown, (Mass.) Before the Supreme Judicial Court, Holden at East Cambridge, On Tuesday, Dec. 2, 1834* (Boston: Allen & Co., 1834).

Questions for Discussion

1. What clues do you find in the nuns' account to the motivations of the mob that attacked their convent in August, 1834? What seems to be the problem of the "mysterious lady" mentioned in the testimony?
2. What evidence would you point to in this testimony that the jury hearing this case were unfamiliar with

the practices of Catholicism? Can you find evidence of hostility to Catholicism in these testimonies?

3. What evidence would American Protestants have found in this testimony to link Catholicism to foreigners? The men charged with the burning of the convent were working-class men of British descent. What would have seemed particularly upsetting to Protestant working men of the 1830s about the lives of these nuns?

Further Reading

Nancy Lusignan Schultz, *Fire & Roses: The Burning of the Charlestown Convent, 1834* (New York: The Free Press, 2000).

4

Redefining the Nation, 1850–1900

In 1856, Ottilie Assing traveled to Rochester, New York, in order to meet Frederick Douglass for the first time. Before becoming a prominent abolitionist and spokesman for colored Americans, Douglass had escaped from slavery with the help of his free wife, Anna Murray Douglass. Assing went to their home in Rochester hoping to translate Douglass's memoir for her German readers. The meeting was a happy one, and Assing continued to work closely with Douglass for two decades, living part of each year with his family, traveling with him, and coming to know and love him and his children.

Assing never understood or liked Douglass's wife Anna, however. Anna Douglass was an illiterate but self-reliant and intensely religious woman who devoted herself exclusively to her children and household responsibilities while showing little outward interest in her husband's public activism. In her letters to Douglass, Assing referred to Anna Douglass enigmatically as "Border State." Herself a sophisticated, well-educated, and independent emigrant, Assing openly flaunted American gender conventions even after she became an American citizen. By contrast, Anna Douglass seemed determined to prove herself truly American. And for her that meant fulfiling Americans' cult of domesticity as woman's sole destiny.

Assing may have been Douglass's lover. She certainly hoped they might marry someday, and Douglass was himself quite happy to have the emotional and intellectual support of a woman whose republican devotion to liberty matched his own.

Still recovering from a scandal over an earlier love affair with a British abolitionist, Douglass had recently quarreled with white abolitionist William Lloyd Garrison. He also faced the new challenges to his leadership of Black nationalist leaders such as Martin Delany. In the aftermath of John Brown's raid, Douglass temporarily fled his home and then watched as the USA collapsed into warring sections.

During the war years, Douglass faced an equally difficult path. He objected to Lincoln's insistence that the north fought to save the Union, not to end slavery. He protested the Union army's discrimination against colored Americans while also encouraging slaves to escape and serve in it. In 1865, Douglass advocated full citizenship for emancipated slaves but angered many female supporters – former abolitionist allies – by supporting an amendment granting the right to vote only to emancipated men. Throughout these controversies, Assing remained a faithful supporter.

Nevertheless, by the mid-1870s, the two were drifting apart. Douglass had become a political appointee in Washington, and he remained a loyal Republican even after his party abandoned its commitment to racial equality in 1877. Assing's republican principles proved more unbending; she did not hide her contempt for white Republicans who had betrayed the freedmen's aspirations. When Anna Douglass died, Assing hoped she could convince Douglass to join her on a trip to Europe. But while she was there on family business, Douglass instead married Helen Pitts – his young, white, and well-educated secretary. Depressed or in ill health – we cannot know which – Assing later committed suicide.

White Americans had long scorned love across the color line. Rejecting the ethnic nationalism of Europe, the founding fathers had ignored Crèvecoeur's observations about intermarriage and biological reproduction creating a new American race, and had insisted instead that a man's political beliefs held the only key to citizenship and membership in the American nation. At the same time, they had made it almost impossible for those of Native and African descent to become citizens or to exercise the rights of citizens. In the antebellum USA, white Americans not only prohibited marriages between blacks and whites but they also had long classified children born to inter-racial couples such as Assing and Douglass as black, thus preventing the recognition of racially mixed identities such as those found throughout the nations of Latin America. Until the nation split over slavery, few white Americans had considered how such racial fears and prejudices contradicted and undermined the high ideals of civic nationalism. Even most abolitionists had focused on the moral blot of slavery, not that of racial prejudice.

Foreigners noticed, however, and found the contradictions disturbing. The more pessimistic among them, including some of Ottilie Assing's fellow German-speaking journalists, often expressed fears that the exclusion of Africans from citizenship could easily become the foundation for excluding others, including emigrants like themselves. But Ottilie Assing was more optimistic; she assumed that the Civil War would open to former slaves the rights of citizenship available through naturalization to emigrants. Assing's optimism proved wrong. By the time she died, the USA had opened citizenship to Africans, but white northerners and southerners had also quickly reunited by narrowing access to its full rights, not only for the freedmen and other natives but also for emigrants.

Re-assessing Citizenship

Voluntary citizenship had created the foundation for an American nation, and neither Assing nor Douglass had ever accepted that only free white men were capable of choosing it freely. By the 1850s, movements for equal rights as citizens had emerged among both free colored Americans and among American women, black and white. Along with demands for the abolition of slavery and equal rights for women, the rise of industry and waged work, and the conquest by the USA of Mexican and Indian populations that were neither white, English-speaking, nor Protestant posed for many white Americans substantial questions about the future of voluntary citizenship.

Along with emigrant Catholics, Mormons – most of them longtime white Americans, natives, and citizens – were among the first to discover that the principles of civic nationalism had their limits. Americans, they soon learned, would not extend toleration to some forms of religious diversity. Acting on the vision of an angel he claimed came to him in 1820 in western New York State, the founder of the Church of Latter Day Saints, Joseph Smith, wrote of finding golden tablets telling how Christianity had actually originated in the New World. Much like others awakened to religious enthusiasm in the 1830s, Smith's followers, called Mormons, or Latter Day Saints, sought to purify a world they saw as threatened by moral decline. Much like emigrants from abroad, Mormons withdrew into frontier communities among their own kind, first in Ohio, and then in Missouri, to practice a religion they – but few of their neighbors – imagined to be uniquely suited for Americans. Mormons' belief in plural marriage made them the object of constant attack even on the frontier. Many American Protestants refused even to accept Mormons as fellow Christians. In 1839 Missouri's governor Lillburn Boggs actually urged citizens of the state to drive out the Mormons. Withdrawing to Nauvoo, Illinois, Mormons briefly found peace but a mob lynching of their founder in 1846 shattered their hopes to remain there.

After Smith's murder, about 15,000 Latter Day Saints followed Brigham Young as emigrants out of the USA to build their own city, "Deseret" – not on a hill but on the shores of the Great Salt Lake of Utah, then part of Mexico. Among them was a young woman, Louise Barnes, who had been born in Canada in 1802, had become a Mormon in New England in 1838 and had then migrated to Nauvoo with her husband and four daughters in 1841. When the Church sent her husband on a mission to the Society Islands, in the Pacific, Barnes supported her children in Nauvoo, working as a seamstress. After migrating to Utah in 1848, she reunited with her husband and accompanied him to the Society Islands before returning, first to a Mormon community in California and then to Salt Lake City.[1] The USA had by then taken Utah from

Mexico. Federal officials battled verbally and militarily for almost 45 years over the plural marriages and citizenship of these American emigrants. Only a formal rejection of polygamy allowed Utah to become a state in 1896.

In the years before the Civil War, the continued territorial expansion of the USA and rising levels of international migration raised additional questions about voluntary citizenship and membership in the American nation. In 1848, Mexicans of Spanish descent automatically became citizens of the USA if they failed to move south into their now much-reduced homeland of Mexico. Although federal census takers were officially told to record these new citizens as white if they (unlike most of the Indians) spoke Spanish, few newly settled Anglos in the southwest – many of them southerners who were highly aware of the dark skins of many tejano and hispano natives – regarded them that way. A few years later, an 1855 act of Congress granted citizenship automatically to the minor children and wives of naturalizing emigrant men, while American women lost their citizenship if they married aliens. And while Supreme Court judges denied citizenship to the American-born fugitive slave Dred Scott, Congress granted it to babies born abroad to American citizen fathers. All these decisions made American citizenship less a matter of individual choice and more a product of blood or reproduction, and of ethnic rather than civic principles of defining the nation.

Sectional conflicts also became, in part, a conflict over voluntary citizenship. White southerners argued with particular vigor that Americans were citizens of the individual states and that the states, not the national government, therefore defined the rights of citizens. The assumption was popular enough to allow the Know-Nothings of the north to pursue some successful campaigns to exclude foreign-born citizens from state and local political office. Still, the Constitution was quite clear that national government alone specified conditions for the naturalization of aliens. In 1849, a court decision further declared migration to be a type of "foreign commerce," to be regulated and taxed by the federal Department of Treasury. In New York, Castle Garden became a kind of customs house for emigrants but states still processed their applications for citizenship.

With the beginning of Civil War, the obligations of citizenship became a life and death matter for many men. Volunteering to fight for one's nation had been an important foundation for consensual citizenship since the Revolution, and service in state militias remained an important obligation of citizenship in both the southern Confederacy and the northern Union. Whether naturalized or not, emigrants along with free Afro-Americans and even slaves sought acceptance into the nation by volunteering to fight. As many as 200,000 German-born and 150,000 Irish emigrants served among the two million soldiers of the northern army, some of them in militias limited to Irish or German emigrants and their sons and commanded by officers of their own origins. The slaves who followed Frederick Douglass's advice and joined the Union forces (where they served under white officers) earned their freedom even while their status as citizens remained unclear.

Requiring military service of all men, rather than calling for volunteers, was more controversial, however, and the Union's decision to draft soldiers revealed how sharply class divided the north. When drafted in Michigan, the German emigrant William Seyffardt was struggling to escape from the debt caused by a fire that destroyed his mill; his wife Sophie wrote home hopefully that his brother had volunteered to substitute for William. In Iowa, Gro Svendsen complained in letters home because her husband was drafted as soon he announced his intention to become a citizen in order to claim a farm homestead. Gro was left to farm alone with only the help of her young children; ultimately she was forced to work as a schoolteacher in order to earn money to support them.

Emigrants even poorer than Ole Svendsen sold themselves as draft substitutes for wealthier men. For urban Catholics and Democrats, the draft thus seemed particularly odious. In New York's 1863 draft riot, mobs of poor men and women, many of them Irish, attacked pro-draft newspapers, Union officers, and the local armory. But they also attacked freedmen they encountered on the street and even burned down an orphanage for colored children. Ottilie Assing, living in nearby New Jersey, was too horrified even to report the riot to her German readers.

At war's end, the Republican-controlled Congress knew it could break the political power of Democrats only if freedmen joined Republican ranks. After the wartime emancipation of slaves in rebel territories in 1863, they added a thirteenth amendment to the constitution to prohibit slavery and involuntary servitude anywhere in the USA except as punishment for crime. A fourteenth amendment made citizenship a product of either birth on American soil or naturalization, and it prohibited states from abridging citizens' rights or failing to provide them equal protection. A fifteenth amendment specifically prohibited abridgment of men's voting rights "on account of race, color, or previous condition of servitude." Responding to the fifteenth amendment in 1870, Congress permitted naturalization for "aliens of African nativity and to persons of African descent" as well as for whites. And a federal 1875 civil rights law provided for equal access to public accommodations and jury duty. Citizenship had opened to all born in the USA, but the full rights of citizenship remained limited to adult men. Citizenship was now also explicitly national.

The American nation – and American citizenship – had nevertheless been "reconstructed" during years when northern soldiers occupied the south and when most former rebels – including most white southern men who refused to swear allegiance to the amended constitution – were prohibited from voting or holding office. At the same time, the federally supported Freedman's Bureau and the Republican Party made sure that emancipated men could vote, and they served in state legislatures and in Congress for the first time. Under Republican control, biracial reconstruction governments created public schools in the south; they encouraged railroad building and industrial development. But they also found themselves charged with corruption by angry white Democrats.

While slaves had become freedmen, the 1870 federal census still counted the first Americans as "Indians, not taxed" and thus as alien nations – and they would continue to do so for another 20 years. The 1862 passage of the Morrill Act (which provided new-citizen farmers like Ole Svendsen with homesteads on "unoccupied lands" on the Great Plains) assured that conflict with the Indian natives of the west would continue. In California, volunteer militias of white settlers had already waged war on the Shoshone (killing 4,000 of them) as the Civil War raged. With the postwar completion of the transcontinental railroad and the arrival of settlers from the east, warfare moved steadily westward. In the 12 years between the US Army's 1864 defeat of the Cheyenne and Arapaho in the Sand Creek Massacre and the confrontation of Sitting Bull and former Civil War soldiers under General Custer at Little Big Horn in 1876, battles raged for sovereignty in the west. White settlers still regarded western Indians as the largest single impediment to their own liberty to move about as they chose.

The Liberty to Move

Freedom of movement had been central to Americans' notions of liberty since the Declaration of Independence, with its complaints about British prohibition of westward migration. As late as 1868 the former Know-Nothing Anson Burlingame negotiated a treaty with China that again confirmed "the inherent and inalienable right of man to change his home and allegiance." The Civil War itself had scarcely interrupted the robust migrations of the antebellum era. Over 800,000 newcomers arrived during the War itself; over 7 million more followed before 1893. Most came from the same places (Germany, Ireland, the British Isles, Scandinavia, Canada, and China) as before the Civil War. The defeat of the western Indians and the Morrill Act also encouraged renewed migrations of Americans including new migrations out of the defeated south.

West or south?

With the south's plantation economy in ruins, the west remained the most popular rural destination for white Americans and for emigrants from Europe and China. Defeated white southerners complained vehemently about "Yankee Carpetbaggers" arriving in their communities but in reality only 200,000 persons born in the north lived in the south in 1870, and many of these had emigrated there prior to the war. Some were businessmen or investors in local industries; others were simple farmers. The carpetbaggers southerners most despised – soldiers, Republican activists, and teachers in freedmen's schools – usually returned to their northern homes.

Homesteading in the Dakotas and other parts of what had been called "the Great American Desert" (the Great Plains) was far more attractive to restless northern farmers and newcomers than the south. During the economic depression of the 1870s, poor white southerners farming marginal lands east of the Mississippi moved into the equally harsh lands of Indian Territory (Oklahoma), Arkansas, and west Texas. Even where soldiers had removed hostile Indians, settling the west was no easy undertaking. The poorest Americans and emigrants could not sustain themselves there, even when they received land at no cost. The vast expanses of the west filled rather quickly, if also rather thinly. Already in 1890, American census takers proclaimed the closing of the western frontier. By then, railway ties linked the Great Plains to the mills and slaughterhouses of Minneapolis and Chicago, providing a ready market for the wheat and cattle raised by newcomers in the west for the newcomers of the east.

Gro Svendsen and her husband were two of almost a million Scandinavian emigrants arriving in the USA between 1860 and 1893 and settling in the west. Like many other Norwegians, Danes, and Swedes, they claimed a homestead; they also subscribed to a Norwegian newspaper and worshiped in a Protestant church with other Norwegians. When Gro died, at age 37, Ole and their nine children set out again for a new homestead in the Dakota territory. Reflecting the effective missionary work of Mormons in Europe, thousands of Scandinavian emigrants (along with significant numbers of British converts, many of them women) also traveled to Utah to join the growing community of Mormons there. Foreigners were more than a third of Utah's population by 1900.

Because the Union army experimented only briefly with dividing the plantations of southern rebels among their former slaves, few freedmen received the "forty acres and a mule" that would have provided them with the southern equivalent of the Svendsens' homestead. But freedmen did acquire the liberty to move once emancipated. Those who had been sold west before the war began long, difficult searches for wives, husbands, siblings, and parents left behind, and one of the major tasks of the Freedmen's Bureau for many years was to assist wanderers in finding not only their relatives but also jobs to sustain them. Both searches often proved difficult.

The expense of settling the Great Plains was far too great for most emancipated slaves. Demographers tell us that freedmen moved mainly from the lower south to the border states of the upper south or they headed toward southern cities, where opportunities to earn wages were better, especially for women working as domestic servants. Still, in the 1870s, Benjamin "Pap" Singleton – a native of Tennessee sold south during slavery – began encouraging freedmen to migrate to Kansas. In the states bordering the Mississippi, "Kansas fever" had developed by 1879 and freedmen began organizing themselves into groups to leave the south. In the language of the Old Testament, they described their "Exodus" from a south portrayed as Egypt and called themselves "Exodusters."

Panicky white southerners responded to even this relatively small migration by threatening to recruit Chinese "coolies" (whom they labeled "Oriental Yankees") to replace the freedmen as agricultural workers. But a man such as Huie Kin, along with most of the approximately 300,000 Chinese emigrants of the nineteenth and early twentieth centuries, continued to prefer the west to the south. Born in 1854 in Toi Shan in a tiny coastal village near Canton, Kin grew up in a region wracked by the Taiping Rebellion – led by a Christian convert against governmental inefficiency – in which 20 to 30 million had recently died. Age 14 in 1868 and able to pay his own passage, he traveled with three older cousins to San Francisco. There he received assistance from their Chinese district association before going to Oakland to join a relative.[2]

While thousands of his compatriots labored on the transcontinental railroad, and in California's rapidly developing agricultural enterprises, Huie Kin found work as a house servant. In 1874 he converted to Christianity, joined the Presbyterian church and then entered a midwestern seminary to become a minister. The small numbers of Chinese who went instead to Louisiana and Mississippi opened small businesses rather than taking up the agricultural work of the departed Exodusters. (On Louisiana's sugar plantations, newcomers from Sicily accepted the work in the 1880s.) Overall, however, the south was – once again – relatively untouched by the international migrations transforming other parts of the country.

Freedmen or Emigrants? The urban north

Industry had facilitated the north's triumph in the Civil War, and after war's end industrialization of the region intensified. In theory, with the south's agricultural economy in collapse, the freedmen of the south could have provided the labor postwar northern industry demanded. However, even those northern employers who supported abolition, citizenship, and legal equality for freedmen were as little inclined to hire them after the war as they had been to live among them before the war. The Afro-Americans who had long lived in the north thus continued to face fierce opposition from emigrants and both freedmen in skilled trades and free women in domestic service continued to lose the competition for urban jobs. The place of colored Americans in northern cities remained marginal and tenuous, creating no powerful magnet to the newly mobile freedmen of the south.

The urban north instead continued to attract a diverse mix of newcomers from Europe. Among the more prosperous emigrants was Jacob August Riis. The son of middle-class parents, Riis had been a young rebel in his homeland of Denmark; he had worked as a carpenter and in 1870, at age 21, escaped an unhappy love affair by emigrating to the USA, where he survived for a time as a tramp. Later, as a journalist and police reporter for the *New York Tribune*, Riis became one of the most important interpreters of life among poor newcomers in the neighborhoods of New York City. He was surprised how little natives seemed to know about this dismal urban world. "For more than a year," he reported, "I had knocked at the doors of the various magazine editors with my pictures, proposing to tell them how the other half lived, but no one wanted to know."[3]

In New England, newcomers from French-speaking Canada could have provided poignant subjects for a photographer such as Riis. Typical of these emigrants was Antonia Bergeron who grew up on an impoverished farm, one of 13 children, in French-speaking Quebec; her father worked winters in a logging camp. At 15, she went to Manchester, New Hampshire, where one of her former schoolteachers helped her to find a job in the Amoskeag mills, weaving bags. Her mother and younger siblings soon followed. After living in a boardinghouse and in an Irish neighborhood, and complaining about the favoritism German supervisors showed toward their own countrymen, Bergeron married in Manchester in 1900.[4] Much like Germans earlier in the century, newcomers from Canada contested Irish control of the Catholic Church, read French and Canadian newspapers, and formed their own mutual aid societies. Unlike emigrants from Europe, however, they often returned home many times before settling more permanently in Canada or the USA.

Northerners like Abraham Lincoln had promised free soil to free white men emigrating to the USA from abroad. And northern employers clearly preferred emigrants over freedmen as laborers in their factories. With international migration so central to the economic development of both the west and the north, it therefore seems doubly puzzling that Americans nevertheless began guarding their borders more jealously once the north had defeated the south and the question of slavery seemed resolved. Why would the redefinition of the American nation require limitations on free peoples' liberty to move to the USA or to choose American citizenship? One answer emerges from the new ideas of "scientific racism," also sometimes called Social Darwinism. These ideas provided a handy bandage for whites seeking to bind up the wounds of sectional division by casting new doubts on the capacity of emigrants, along with Indians and freedmen, to fulfill the duties citizenship opened to them. Over the next 50 years, Social Darwinists would effectively argue that in differing ways all three groups threatened the well-being, and even the survival, of the American nation.

Narrowing the White Nation

With the abolition of slavery and the establishment of biracial citizenship between 1865 and 1870, Americans seemed momentarily open to the possibility of defining their nation in ways that Latin Americans had opted for 50 years earlier. With the end of Civil War in the USA, only Brazil and the Spanish colony of Cuba still allowed slavery in the New World; everywhere in Latin America, slavery's abolition had also ended officially sanctioned racial discrimination. But love across the color line, and the mixing of races, continued to trouble American nationalists in the USA. Not unlike the colonial Spanish, US census takers in 1850 began to record racial amalgamation by listing free but racially mixed "mulattos" such as Frederick Douglass, and until 1890, they distinguished among white, black, mulatto, quadroon (one black grandparent), and octoroon (one black great-grandparent). But they counted the mixing of blacks and whites because they feared the racial amalgamation Brazilians would later glorify as racial democracy.

As white southerners and northern Democrats in the 1870s

increasingly objected to reconstruction and to the consequences of extending citizenship and voting rights to freedmen, they also frequently claimed it promoted racial amalgamation and love across the color line. Democrats circulated a pamphlet (supposedly written by a Republican) that argued Americans could "become the finest race on earth" if they would blend "all that is passionate and emotional in the darker races, all that is imaginative and spiritual in the Asiatic races, and all that is intellectual and perceptive in the white race." Knowing that most northern and southern whites, unlike Ottilie Assing, would regard such thoughts with terror, Democrats imagined the daughters of the nation pleading with them, "Fathers, save us from nigger husbands."[5]

Dramatically claiming to protect white womanhood, southern whites organized secret societies – the Ku Klux Klan (KKK) being only the best known – to intimidate freedmen and prevent them from exercising the rights of citizenship even during reconstruction. More quietly but to the same effect, northerners began to withdraw their support from federal activism in the south and especially from the military occupation that had been required to guarantee voting rights for freedmen. As life in antebellum northern cities had proved, few whites in the north desired equality for, let alone social relations with, freedmen. The civic nationalism of radical republicans and abolitionists such as Ottilie Assing and Frederick Douglass had foundered on the racial prejudices that southern and northern whites apparently shared.

Beginning in the 1860s, Charles Darwin's theories of evolution provided northerners, southerners, and westerners alike with a new, powerful and purportedly scientific basis for narrowing their white nation by denying the full privileges of citizenship to freedmen and emigrants alike. Well before Darwin published his treatise on the origin of species and his thoughts on natural selection (or "survival of the fittest" as it was popularly called), American ethnologists had been accumulating evidence of human variations that reached well beyond skin color. The study of cranial forms and the popular cult of phrenology had linked physical differences to the cultural and personality traits theologians had once explained through stories of separate creations or divinely inspired "great chains of being." In the antebellum north, racialized portraits of short, ape-like, and drunken "wild" Irish emigrants appeared alongside images of simple-minded enslaved "Jim Crows" and more urbanized "Zip Coon" dandies with huge lips and noses, as well as pictures of hawk-nosed, blood-thirsty, tomahawk-wielding Indians.

Darwin's research suggested a new explanation for how biological reproduction of physical differences such as these generated cultural and social hierarchy. "Survival of the fittest" provided Social Darwinists like Herbert Spencer with explanations for white domination and the cultural superiority of an American civilization rooted in northern Europe. North, south, and west, whites could agree that blacks and Indians were savages who had lost the competition with white, civilized Europeans. Scientific racists predicted that as the "less fit" became citizens, they would contaminate the American nation and destroy its republican government.

For Social Darwinists, even Ottilie Assing, a European and a naturalized citizen, posed a danger for the republic. Scientific racists argued that Europeans, too, represented many races, and some of them were still barbarians, or close to it. The Germanic, Teutonic, Anglo-Saxon, and other Protestant "Aryan" or Nordic races of northern Europe were the fittest, thus explaining their spread throughout the world as white conquerors and bearers of the "white man's burden" to civilize the people they conquered and colonized. From them, white Americans had inherited their capacity for voluntary citizenship, leadership, and economic progress, in the form of rapidly expanding corporate capitalism. Jews and Irish instead represented inferior "Semitic" and "Celtic" races, while Latin Americans were degenerate products of amalgamations between Spanish, Portuguese, Africans, and indigenous peoples. Large numbers of all these races had become American citizens in the past decades, also endangering the nation.

Social Darwinism thus creatively linked northern nativists' earlier fears of Catholic and Jewish emigrants to southerners' fears of emancipated slaves, and in the process reunited warring whites around a new, racially charged and purportedly more scientific version of ethnic nationalism that had long simmered beneath white Americans' paeans to voluntary citizenship. It also allowed northerners and southerners to abandon finally their decades-long quarrels over the west's future. Throughout the nation, white Americans united in a new nativist movement to exclude the "yellow peril" on the west coast while worrying in ever-growing numbers over the impact on the east of Jewish emigrants like Ottilie Assing and the still newer emigrants from southern and eastern Europe they dubbed "the Chinese of Europe."

Restricting the Liberty to Move

Defending a nation of racially superior Nordics or Anglo-Saxons from contamination by new citizens justified new restrictions on two liberties the founding fathers had regarded as essential – the right to move and the right to choose one's own citizenship. Americans had consistently denied these liberties to Indians and slaves before the Civil War. After the Civil War, Indians were again force-marched onto western reservations by American soldiers, and they again suffered and died in the process. Precisely because so many took to the road after their emancipation, mobile freedmen also soon found their liberty to move about freely circumscribed by the reassertion of white power. In many parts of the south, sharecropping contracts left freedmen permanently in debt (and thus legally bound as debtors) to the white planters who still controlled access to land, the only important resource of the still-agricultural south.

Dramatic restrictions on the liberty to move were now also imposed at the borders through which emigrants had continued to pour. Only by regulating entry could nativists hope to prevent racially unfit emigrants from first claiming and then exercising the rights of American citizenship and thereby threatening the republicanism white Americans believed symbolized the superiority of their race's civilization. Unsurprisingly, the 63,000 Chinese living in California were the most vulnerable to scientific racist campaigns. The 1870 naturalization act had granted only Africans, along with whites, the right to naturalize, and court cases quickly confirmed that Chinese emigrants were not whites eligible for citizenship (a provision that remained in effect until 1943). Because the thirteenth amendment guaranteed citizenship to all children born on American soil even to Chinese parents, however, citizenship still remained accessible to those with roots in the hated and racially disparaged Orient.

Already in the 1850s, Chinese miners and laborers in California had encountered the type of violent opposition from emigrant workers that freedmen faced on the east coast. Immediately, political coalitions of white emigrants (most of them poorer and less enthusiastic about the employment of Chinese laborers than Agoston Haraszthy) and southern Democratic settlers had sought new ways to exclude emigrants such as Huie Kin. These coalitions gained momentum during the postwar economic depression of the 1870s. Americans and European emigrants alike joined Irish emigrant Dennis Kearny's Workingmen's Party in arguing that "the Chinese must Go" from California. Western workers claimed to fear competition from unfree coolie or indentured labor, but in fact few Chinese emigrants were coolies; at most they had borrowed money to pay their passages.

Unable to restrict migration (a federal prerogative), California ordinances of the 1870s prohibited Chinese emigrants from exercising particular trades, testifying against whites in court, or owning land; Chinese workers faced special taxes and constant harassment especially when they continued to wear Chinese-style clothing and long hair, as Huie Kin did during his first 15 years in the USA. "We were simply terrified," he recalled. "We kept indoors after dark for fear of being shot in the back. Children spit upon us as we passed by and called us rats."[6] State laws had rendered federal promises of equal protection under the law meaningless to Chinese aliens or their children in the west even before reconstruction ended in the east.

Since only the federal government could regulate emigration and foreign trade, white Californians in the 1870s sought an alliance linking their concerns to northern workers' fears of job competition and Social Darwinists' fears of racially inferior citizens. Republicans in Washington remained committed to free labor, and proved happy enough to ban the "coolie trade" as unfree. But California's Dennis Kearney did not receive a universally warm reception when he traveled east, even among emigrant laborers. The National Labor Union opposed the recruitment of any foreign laborers as strikebreakers but seemed unconcerned about Chinese laborers in particular. Besides, most Chinese emigrants were neither coolies nor strikebreakers.

In 1875 Congress nodded toward white westerners' concerns when it passed the Page Act, which barred entry into the USA to prostitutes. Consuls abroad and emigration officials in San Francisco interpreted the Page Act strictly and excluded almost all female emigrants from China, arguing that Chinese women most often found work as prostitutes among the overwhelmingly male Chinese population. Ultimately, however, it was a congressional coalition of westerners, southern whites, and Republicans hoping to regain the presidency with western support that finally passed an act to restrict Chinese immigration in 1882. That restriction applied only to Chinese laborers and it was limited to 10 years (although subsequently renewed twice more). Even in 1904, when the exclusion of Chinese workers became permanent, small numbers of students, businessmen, and clergy continued to enter the USA from China. Strictly racial exclusion of all Chinese awaited the further spread of scientific racism.

Demands for restriction of emigration from Europe built, albeit slowly, on the precedents of the anti-Chinese campaign. In 1885, responding to complaints from the newly formed and east-coast based American Federation of Labor (AF of L) and the older Knights of Labor, Congress passed the Foran Act to prohibit the entry of any laborers contracted abroad. In fact, few American employers directly recruited laborers outside the USA. The importance of the Foran Act was thus largely symbolic; it had no impact on the numbers entering the USA from Europe or Canada in the 1880s or 1890s. Nor could its passage be attributed only to the power of American labor – the Knights of Labor, for example, was about to collapse. Instead, its passage reflected mainly the re-emergence of nativism among white Americans in 1880s.

In many respects the new nativism of the 1880s would have seemed familiar to the Know-Nothings of the 1850s. The most important new nativist organization, the American Protective Association (APA), founded in Iowa in 1887, repeated and elaborated Know-Nothing objections to emigrants as citizens. Its members wanted to extend the time newcomers waited before naturalizing. Nativists wanted to assess the English-speaking skills of all voters and to deny automatic naturalization to emigrants' American-born children. Like the Know-Nothings, the APA most feared Catholics becoming citizens. By the 1890s, however, anti-semitism was also rising, especially among wealthier Americans who began to exclude upwardly mobile Jewish businessmen from their private schools, clubs, and private resorts.

The ideas of Social Darwinism broadened nativists' concerns and gave impetus to new demands for restrictions on migration itself. In the last two decades of the century, Congress focused special attention on emigrants who might not be fit for citizenship. Thus it barred entry to prostitutes and certain classes of criminals in 1875, contract laborers in 1885, and in 1891 added to the list of those excluded, "all idiots, insane persons, paupers or persons likely to become a public charge, persons suffering from a loathsome or dangerous contagious disease, persons who have been convicted of a felony or other infamous crime or misdemeanor involving moral turpitude, [and] polygamists [a provision specifically aimed at emigrant Mormons]." In 1903, anarchists and persons advocating the overthrow of the American government joined the list of the unfit.

To supervise the growing numbers of new arrivals more carefully, Congress created a Superintendent of Immigration in the Department of Treasury in 1892 and opened a large, new processing center at Ellis Island. There, federal agents oversaw a growing bureaucracy to "guard the gates" against those unfit for citizenship. Somewhat later, in 1906, the Commissioner of Immigration would be transferred to the Department of Labor and the requirements of naturalization changed to require of all applicants the ability to speak and read English.

Demands for still greater restrictions on European emigrants' liberty of movement originated within the Immigration Restriction League, founded by east-coast educators at Ivy League institutions in 1896. The Immigration Restriction League demanded that no illiterate should enter the USA, since illiteracy alone marked a person as unfit for citizenship. Congress first passed a restrictive literacy act in 1895, and would do the same four more times, in the next 20 years, only to have American presidents veto the bills as inappropriate limits on the right of free persons to choose where they lived and worked.

No group did more to popularize scientific racism among Americans in the east than the Immigration Restriction League with its emphasis on the racial inferiority of southern and eastern Europeans. Yankee intellectuals such as Prescott F. Hall and Henry Cabot Lodge pointed to the eastern (Oriental) and "Semitic" origins of "Hebrews" (Jews), who along with Arabs shared a racial homeland in Asia, as well as to the possibility of African blood in the dark peoples living on the Mediterranean shores of Europe. They predicted the decline or – in the words of Theodore Roosevelt – the suicide of the American race of Anglo-Saxons as it was overrun by emigrant mongrels. How much impact Social Darwinists' ideas had on black Americans in the east is less well known. (For one prominent American Negro's view of newcomers, and their place in the south, see the Student Exercise at the end of the chapter.)

Beginning in 1899, American immigrant agents began categorizing every emigrant at the border by race. Since a long-standing tradition forbade them from asking the religion of newcomers, they transformed even free-thinking German Jews like Ottilie Assing into members of the Hebrew race. And they distinguished between two Italian races – one "Alpine," northern and round-headed, the other "Mediterranean," southern and narrow-headed. Beginning in 1900, the federal government also asked census takers to give the "race or color" of every person listed in their decennial count. Although scientific racists had not succeeded in excluding all the emigrants they deemed unfit for citizenship, they had begun to collect evidence to strengthen their own case for further restrictions.

While slave-owning founding fathers had discussed the American nation abstractly as political philosophers, Social Darwinists sounded more like animal breeders concerned with the nation's racial pedigree. By the 1890s, discussions of American diversity focused on a complex and dangerous hierarchy of racial groups deemed more and less fit for citizenship and membership in a nation founded by Anglo-Saxons from northern Europe. The first result was a series of legal Dutch doors – part open, part closed – to citizenship rights and to membership in the nation. The second was the formation of new group and individual identities among those whose fitness scientific racists had put under surveillance.

Dutch Door Citizenship; New Identities

The same American nationalists of the 1890s who boasted of their Anglo-Saxon superiority and questioned the fitness of freedmen and emigrants for citizenship paradoxically also demanded that the "unfit" prove their fitness by adopting the culture of Anglo-Saxons. Americans lower on the Social Darwinists' racial hierarchy generally denied their unfitness for citizenship while also finding ways to resist demands for cultural conformity. Still, their experiences with prejudice and discrimination at the hands of scientific racists, and with the limitations placed on their access to citizenship and its rights, also shaped their identities in significant ways.

At the bottom of Social Darwinists' racial hierarchy were the freedmen who had gained citizenship only to lose access to most of its rights. Freedmen's acquisition of American citizenship had briefly diminished the appeal of Black nationalists such as Martin Delany. Immediately after the war, a Colonization Council gathered information about emigration to Liberia, and the newly freed slave Henry Adams claimed to speak for 98,000 freedmen prepared to leave the USA. But few freedmen actually left the USA. Instead, new citizens reacted to scientific racism with efforts to prove their fitness.

They did so under extraordinarily difficult circumstances. With the end of reconstruction in 1877, white majorities throughout the south (and in many northern states, too) began passing "Jim Crow" laws to segregate black from white citizens in almost every arena of life. These laws made it almost impossible for freedmen citizens to own land or to vote. Freedmen could not marry whites, or ride with them in railroad cars; they could not serve on juries, or get an education alongside whites. In 1883 the Supreme Court declared the Civil Rights Act of 1875 unconstitutional, allowing individuals everywhere to discriminate openly against black citizens. An 1896 Supreme Court case even approved the Jim Crow principle of separate "but equal" schools and public accommodations. Unlike women and children, who also lacked full rights of citizenship, freedmen in the south were subject to violent physical assault whenever whites perceived them as disrespectful, particularly to white women – lynchings, murders, mob assaults on their homes, and riots were common events in the south. Equal protection for American citizens had been eliminated with surprising speed.

In 1900, 95 percent of Afro-Americans faced these obstacles while living in extreme poverty in the rural south. Rather than demand rights as citizens, many freedmen in what whites called the "New" south attempted mainly to prove the Social Darwinists wrong. Their goal was to "uplift" their own race, thus proving their fitness for citizenship. Booker T. Washington believed segregation could actually promote racial harmony among black and white southerners if it gave freedmen an opportunity to prove their worthiness. Through his Tuskegee Institute (founded in 1881), Washington urged freedmen to work hard at humble tasks while building strong and moral, if segregated, communities. Mutual aid societies, schools, churches, and businesses organized and run by freedmen were more important to Washington than mixing socially or economically with whites. Signaling their efforts to build autonomous communities, Washington and many activists by 1900 had begun to call themselves Negroes. But many poorer Negroes scoffed at a leadership advocating hard work and moral uplift as the privileged or "talented tenth" of their segregated communities.

In contrast to Negroes, American Indians would not gain automatic citizenship by birth on American soil until 1924. Having lost most of their battles for sovereignty, they also found that the federal government no longer signed treaties with them as foreign nations. Almost 250,000 Indians lived on reservations where the federal government posed as their guardian while declaring them capable of becoming civilized Americans. In 1871, 1875, and again in the 1887 Dawes Act, federal law encouraged the division of Indians' communally held reservation lands into privately held homesteads. Monogamous family groups willing to adopt sedentary farming in turn became eligible for citizenship. In the words of Commissioner of Indian Affairs T. J. Morgan in 1890, "The American Indian was to become the Indian American" by demonstrating his fitness to belong to the American nation.[7] Indian men soon served in the military as members of the "Indian police" on reservations. In 1907, the former Indian territory of Oklahoma even became a state.

The pressure to prove themselves fit for citizenship by adopting American culture carried a high price, however, and few embraced it wholeheartedly. The Dawes Act probably did less to facilitate Indian citizenship than to cause a precipitous drop in Indian-owned lands, from 138 to 78 million acres. And as guardians, government-sponsored or missionary boarding schools for Indian children sometimes proved to be unnecessarily harsh parents. One young girl, Gertrude Bonnin (Zitkala Sa), a Dakota Sioux, remembered her first boarding school experience with horror. "I cried aloud, shaking my head all the while until I felt the cold blades of the scissors against my neck, and heard them gnaw off one of my thick braids. Then I lost my spirit . . . my long hair was shingled like a coward's! In my anguish I moaned for my mother .. now I was only one of many little animals driven by a herder."[8] While desiring an education and citizenship, Bonnin felt little desire to become an Anglo-Saxon American.

Limits on citizenship in the era of scientific racism were particularly complex in the western territories that had once been Mexico. Emigrants from Asia had long been explicitly excluded from American citizenship nationwide. In the west, their citizen children typically attended segregated schools and faced prohibitions against marriage with whites. By contrast, under federal law, and in federal censuses, Catholic Spanish-speaking hispanics were still deemed white citizens. Locally, however, they rarely could claim the full rights of citizenship, especially in Texas and in California where large numbers of southern whites had settled. In both places, schools were often segregated and voting booths closed. Although New Mexico had long possessed a population of Indian natives and newcomers large enough to qualify it for statehood, it did not succeed in becoming a state until 1912.

For European newcomers, the Dutch doors that separated them from full citizenship were still decidedly more open than closed, allowing immigration to peak after 1890. But only English-speaking emigrants from Canada and Great Britain found easy acceptance as fit citizens among old-stock Americans. Facing no particular social barriers, these emigrants rarely formed groups or identities that separated them from old-stock Americans. Unlike Huie Kin's compatriots, furthermore, emigrants from Europe could choose to become citizens and since more remained in the USA, rather than returning home, most did so. Somewhat less than two-thirds had naturalized by 1890 although the proportions declined rapidly thereafter. Nevertheless, aliens remained a distinctive legal category in the USA. Since 1820, federal census takers had distinguished citizens from aliens in their lists. Until emigrants naturalized, furthermore, they did not enjoy the rights of citizens (for example, free speech); they could be summarily deported without judicial review.

By the 1890s, newcomers from Europe also knew from personal experience that their liberty to enter the USA was under attack. When entering, they had to convince immigration officials that they were not paupers likely to become a public charge (a particular problem for women travelling alone) without thereby suggesting that a job already awaited them – a violation of the Foran Act. They were assigned a race, inspected for diseases, given tests meant to identify illness or mental competence, and sometimes even rejected at the border.

Scientific racism also soon convinced American census takers to collect evidence of foreign origins even among the native-born children of naturalized citizens. Beginning in 1870, the census invented a new category of citizens (scholars would eventually call them the "second generation") by recording the birthplace of the parents of all residents of the USA. As a result, American-born citizens of foreign parentage seemed tainted by foreign origins in ways older stock "native-born whites of native parentage" were not. In 1890, census takers also began to record whether citizens and aliens alike could speak English, and it would later record whether English-speaking citizens had a mother-tongue, home, or childhood language other than English. Many recent arrivals wondered, with some cause, why the American government wanted all this information, and census takers often reported resistance, mistrust, and silence in urban neighborhoods crowded with newcomers from abroad.

For most emigrants, Spanish-speakers, Negroes, and Indians, the preservation of distinctive religious practices proved one of the most effective forms of resistance to Social Darwinists' demands for cultural conformity. Protected by law, religious diversity also provided a positive counter-balance to experiences of prejudice, discrimination, and exclusion as elements in group and individual identities. In a short-lived era of religious revival and church-building among freedmen following the Civil War, most Protestant churches had split into segregated branches. New, and "enthusiastic" forms of worship, which included dancing, singing, and "speaking in tongues," spread as a new holiness movement through the segregated churches of poorer Negro southerners. Black ministers in these churches, along with a small black middle class of teachers, doctors, and small businessmen who were sometimes less enthusiastic and belonged to older Baptist and Methodist churches, also focused on moral uplift among their congregations.

Beginning in the 1880s, a new wave of spiritual revivals also helped give Indians adjusting to reservation life the strength to resist government demands for cultural conformity. Known as the Ghost Dance, this religious revival promised that the buffalo, along with Indians' slaughtered relatives, would return to help them resist. American soldiers so feared the influence of Ghost Dance preachers that they precipitated a massacre of Sioux worshipers at Wounded Knee in 1890. Somewhat later, Gertrude Bonnin's contemporary, Sam Blowsnake, a Winnebago, converted to the Peyote religion – an amalgam of Native and Christian beliefs that later gave birth to the Native American Church.

Most emigrant newcomers also refused to adopt the beliefs and practices of American Methodists, Baptists, Episcopalians, or Presbyterians in order to gain acceptance from older stock Americans. Children of Missouri Synod Germans spoke English in public but prayed in German. Their church especially sought to isolate them from the religious individualism of evangelical Protestantism. At home, German-speaking farmers emphasized the importance of family solidarity under the authority of a strong father, and criticized Americans for their independent women and disrespectful children. Missouri Synod ministers claimed authority both in doctrinal matters and in issues related to community morality. (In a somewhat parallel fashion, German Socialists in Chicago bemoaned the individualism that made American workers suspicious of collective action and blind to class struggle.)

For Catholic and Jewish emigrants, an even broader panoply of community institutions insulated emigrants and their children from painful experiences of exclusion as well as from the missionary zeal of Protestants. Jewish children attended public schools and sought professional integration but responded to anti-semitism by withdrawing into their own institutions. Poorer Jews could depend on assistance from Jewish charities. Jewish recreational organizations – from Jewish clubs to summer resorts – encouraged emigrants' children to marry within their own class and religion.

By the end of the century, an ambitious German Catholic child could remain within Catholic institutions from grade school through university; if he prospered he donated to Catholic charities and if he fell ill he was nursed in Catholic hospitals. Significantly, Catholic voluntary associations, such as the Knights of Columbus founded in 1881, claimed to prepare believers for what they called Catholic-American citizenship. Inherent in Catholic citizenship was a critique of the same Anglo-Saxon American individualism that the Missouri Synod Germans descried. Anton Wallburg, a German-speaking Catholic priest in Cincinnati, summed up his followers' resistance to cultural transformation with a trenchant critique of Anglo-Saxon America, thundering that "the American nationality .. is often the hotbed of fanaticism, intolerance, and radical, ultra views on matters of politics and religion. All the vagaries of spiritualism, Mormonism, free-loveism, prohibition, infidelity, and materialism generally breed in the American nationality."[9] Clearly, Wallburg had few doubts that Catholics were fit for citizenship.

Enjoying the full rights of citizenship, the second-generation children of Europeans often chose identities different from their parents. Many expressed their desire to join Anglo-Saxon America by adopting their forms of Protestantism. Although unusual for Chinese of his generation, Huie Kin decided to become a Presbyterian. Even the nativist, and anti-Catholic, APA attracted membership among Protestant emigrants and their children. And the leaders of the American Federation Labor – a group that regularly argued for immigration restriction after 1895 – included Irish, British, and German activists of the emigrant and second-generation. The president of the AF of L was himself a Jewish emigrant cigar-maker, Samuel Gompers. But while many children of emigrants sought acceptance as citizens, most also tried to combine cultural loyalties to both their parents and to the American nation.

Social Darwinism and the ideals of scientific racism clearly left their marks on the identities of Americans by 1900. At the bottom of the racial hierarchy, Americans with roots in Africa nurtured identities characterized, according to Negro sociologist and Harvard graduate W. E. B. DuBois, by double-consciousness: "One ever feels his twoness," DuBois wrote, "An American, a Negro, two souls, two thoughts, two unreconciled strivings; two warring ideals in one dark body."[10] When Theodore Roosevelt a few years later complained of "hyphenated Americans," however, he was not referring to American Negroes such as DuBois but commenting critically instead on German-American, Catholic-American, and Irish-American citizens. Plural, dual, and hyphenated identities had become an important form of American diversity, but they still allowed Anglo-Saxons such as Roosevelt to claim they alone were real Americans. To some considerable degree, the proliferation of hyphenated identities by 1900 reflected the scientific racism that had dismissed ever-greater numbers of Americans as unworthy for the full rights of citizenship and thus for full membership in the American nation.

Further Reading

William Cohen, *At Freedom's Edge: Black Mobility and the Southern White Quest for Racial Control, 1861–1915* (Baton Rouge: Louisiana State University Press, 1991).

Jon Gjerde, *The Minds of the West: Patterns of Ethnocultural Evolution in the Rural Middle West, 1830–1917* (Chapel Hill: University of North Carolina Press, 1997).

Tamara K. Hareven, *Family Time and Industrial Time: The Relationship between the Family and Work in a New England Industrial Community* (New York: Cambridge University Press, 1982).

John Higham, *Strangers in the Land: Patterns of American Nativism, 1860–1925*, 2nd. edn. (New Brunswick: Rutgers University Press, 1992).

Matthew Frye Jacobson, *Barbarian Virtues: The United States Encounters Foreign Peoples at Home and Abroad, 1876–1917* (New

York: Hill and Wang, 2000).

Michael C. LeMay, *From Open Door to Dutch Door: An Analysis of U.S. Immigration Policy since 1820* (New York: Praeger, 1987).

Odd Sverre Lovoll, *The Promise of America: A History of the Norwegian-American People*, Rev. Ed. (Minneapolis: University of Minnesota Press, 1999).

Nell Irvin Painter, *Exodusters: Black Migration to Kansas after Reconstruction* (New York: Knopf, 1977).

George Anthony Peffer, *If They Don't Bring Their Women Here: Chinese Female Immigration before Exclusion* (Urbana: University of Illinois Press, 1999).

Lucy E. Salyer, *Laws Harsh as Tigers: Chinese Immigrants and the Shaping of Modern Immigration Law* (Chapel Hill: University of North Carolina Press, 1995).

Barbara Miller Solomon, *Ancestors and Immigrants: A Changing New England Tradition* (Cambridge, MA: Harvard University Press, 1956).

William E. Van Vugt, *Britain to America: Mid-nineteenth-century Immigrants to the United States* (Urbana: University of Illinois Press, 1999).

Student Exercise
Can a Negro be a Nativist?

To those of the white race who look to the incoming of those of foreign birth and strange tongue and habits for the prosperity of the South, were I permitted I would repeat what I say to my own race, "Cast down your bucket where you are." Cast it down among the eight millions of Negroes whose habits you know, whose fidelity and love you have tested in days when to have proved treacherous meant the ruin of your firesides. Cast down your bucket among these people who have, without strikes and labor wars, tilled your fields, cleared your forests, builded your railroads and cities, and brought forth treasures from the bowels of the earth, and helped make possible this magnificent representation of the progress of the South. Casting down your bucket among my people, helping and encouraging them as you are doing on these grounds, and to education of head, hand, and heart, you will find that they will buy your surplus land, make blossom the waste places in your fields, and run your factories. While doing this, you can be sure in the future, as in the past, that you and your families will be surrounded by the most patient, faithful, law-abiding, and unresentful people that the world has seen. As we have proved our loyalty to you in the past, in nursing your children, watching by the sick-bed of your mothers and fathers, and often following them with tear-dimmed eyes to their graves, so in the future, in our humble way, we shall stand by you with a devotion that no foreigner can approach, reach to lay down our lives, if need be, in defense of yours, interlacing our industrial, commercial, civil and religious life with yours in a way that shall make the interests of both races one.

Source: Booker T. Washington, *Up From Slavery, An Autobiography* (New York: Dodd, Mead and Co., 1965), pp. 140–1.

Questions for Discussion

1. What objections does Booker T. Washington offer to immigration from Europe? How does he describe the newcomers?
2. Would you consider the author a scientific racist? Why or why not? How are his objections to immigration different from those of the scientific racists?
3. To whom does Washington appear to be directing his appeal?
4. What exactly does he mean when he asks his readers to "Cast down your bucket where you are"?

5

Immigrants in a Nativist America, 1890–1920

In 1919 Nicola Sacco, a skilled worker in a shoe factory, lived with his wife Rosina and their school-age son Dante in Stoughton, Massachusetts. "Those day," he would remember later, "they was a some happy day." Sacco was well liked in the small community of workers employed at the Three-K Shoe Company. His employer, George Kelley, the son of Irish emigrants, had trained Sacco years before in another shoe factory in Milford, Massachusetts. Kelley described Sacco as a steady and dependable worker who was up early every morning to tend his vegetable garden before beginning a long day at work. There was just one small problem with Sacco – the meetings. A quiet family man and good worker, Nicola Sacco was also an anarchist.

In the years before and after 1900, Americans typically viewed the rapidly growing industrial power of the USA, along with its attractions to humble workers such as Nicola Sacco, as additional signs of American superiority. Many also saw the country's free markets and large-scale corporate, capitalist businesses as expressions of the economic liberty that political democracy had facilitated. And they were convinced that immigrants such as Andrew Carnegie, the wealthy steel magnate, had demonstrated the benefits of American liberty for rich and poor alike by rising from rags to riches. Unlike their counterparts 50 years earlier who saw newcomers as "emigrants" fleeing restraints in the Old World, Americans who now labeled men such as Carnegie and Sacco "immigrants," emphasized the obvious benefits of New World life.

Nicola Sacco saw things differently. Born in 1891 into a family of peasants in Torremaggiore, near the city of Foggia, in southern Italy, he became an anarchist only after he came to the USA, during the short but sharp depression of 1907–8. As a follower of the exiled anarchist theorist Luigi Galleani, Sacco disdained union membership but nevertheless participated in a shoe workers' strike and raised money for the striking textile workers of the Industrial Workers of the World (IWW) in nearby Lawrence, Massachusetts in 1912. Unlike most Americans, when Sacco looked at the economy of the USA, he thought mainly of people such as his friend, Bartolomeo Vanzetti, who worked at temporary, dangerous, low-wage jobs with little hope of finding material comfort or even respect in American society.

Sacco was no intellectual. To him anarchism meant simple moral truths – "capitalism is evil, government is slavery, war is crime against humanity, freedom is essential for human development," and churches existed only to lull people into submitting to tyranny.[1] Unlike anarchists who rejected individual acts of violence, this otherwise gentle, modest man saw nothing wrong with the assassination of corrupt political leaders or the bombing of the property of governments and capitalists. As rank-and-file anarchists, Sacco and his friend Vanzetti sometimes acted on their principles. Refusing to register for the draft in 1917, Sacco left his family behind and fled to Mexico. When he was arrested in 1920, and charged with the robbery murder of a shoe company guard, he was carrying a gun. "Give up the radical stuff! Be an American!" Sacco's employer had recommended. But to no effect. While most Americans saw class struggle as a threat to economic liberty, Sacco remained true to political beliefs that Americans devoted to liberty as they understood it refused to protect. In an increasingly nativist country, he and his friend Vanzetti would later be executed for a crime they probably did not commit.

America, Migration, and the Wider World

In many ways, Nicola Sacco's migration, work, and resistance to Americanization reflected the rapidly changing place of an industrializing USA in the wider world. If the USA in the late nineteenth century had focused on mending sectional divisions, Americans' attentions after 1890 increasing turned outward. Prosperous American businessmen heading abroad in search of markets, natural resources, and investment opportunities crossed paths with humble immigrants such as Sacco who were looking to earn wages in the country's burgeoning industries. By 1910, almost 15 percent of the American population was of foreign birth. Most of the newcomers were poor, industrial wage-earners.

Mobile businessmen and immigrants represented two faces of a new, and truly global, world economy. By 1910, corporate investors had helped Europe's expanding empires to build transportation – steam ships and railroads – and communication – telegraphs and telephones – that spanned the globe, facilitating the transfer of natural resources, manufactured products, laborers, and even anarchist ideals around the world. Americans agonized over ignoring George Washington's warnings against entangling foreign alliances but seemed firmly committed at least to the Monroe Doctrine of 1823 – that the USA should lead its hemisphere toward independence from European influence. In 1898 the USA fought against Spain and gained control over its former colonies in Cuba, Puerto Rico, Hawaii, and the Philippines. While American soldiers went to Mexico and Nicaragua to protect American investments there, and to the Philippines to suppress a nationalist revolution against American rule, they also offered protection to corporations against immigrant revolutionaries such as Sacco at home.

In the past, global migrations had flowed toward the plantations of Asia and the Americas and toward the prairie frontiers of North and South America. After 1900, industry and the commercial agriculture that fed its urban workers motivated most new migrations. In Europe, Britain, Germany, Switzerland, and France employed large numbers of Italians and Poles; in the British Empire, Indians migrated to South Africa and Europeans and Chinese to Australia and Canada. Nicola Sacco could easily have joined other Italians working in France, Argentina, or Brazil. But like the largest number of Europe's migrants in these years, he instead chose to search for work in the USA.

There, by 1890, Social Darwinists were already commenting critically on the changing races of the newcomers without having resolved how to restrict their entry. See Table 5.1, which uses the racial categories of the era of scientific racism to show the changes that so concerned nativists of the day. Italians now outnumbered the Irish; Polish Catholics and Jews outnumbered the Germans; Japanese, Koreans, and Filipinos had replaced the excluded Chinese. First railroad building, then revolution, lured and then pushed Mexicans across the Rio Grande, and the building of the Panama Canal, along with Florida's growing cigar industrysparked migrations from Cuba and Jamaica. Few of these new immigrants were Protestants. While the numbers of immigrants entering the USA fell off slightly during the depression of the 1890s, they peaked at a million yearly in the decade after 1900. Nativists felt they had all the evidence they needed that a "new" – and less desirable migration from southern and eastern Europe, and from lands populated by peoples with dark or swarthy skin, was about to inundate Nordic America. (See student exercise at the end of the chapter.)

The economic expansion of the USA was a strong magnet to immigrants, yet many European and other immigrants – like the Chinese of the previous century – came to take jobs only to leave again. Well over half of Russians and Rumanians returned home, as did about half of the immigrants from Italy, Greece, and Hungary, about a third of those from Poland, and southeast Europe, and about a quarter from Great Britain, Mexico, Japan, and the Caribbean islands.[2] So many jobs in the USA were seasonal, and open only to men, that families often separated for years while male "birds of

Table 5.1 Race of immigrant aliens admitted to the USA, 1899–1924

Race	*Numbers of immigrants*
North and south Italian	3,820,986
Hebrew	1,837,855
Polish	1,483,374
German	1,316,614
English and Welsh	1,110,749
Scandinavian	956,308
Irish	808,762
Slovak	536,911
Greek	500,463
Magyar	492,031
Croatian and Slovenian	485,379
Mexican	447,065
Scottish	441,172
French	415,244
Ruthenian	265,478
Lithuanian	263,277
Japanese	260,492
Russian	258,985
Finnish	226,922
Dutch and Flemish	205,874
Spanish	190,521
Portuguese	186,244
Bulgarian, Serbian, and Montenegrin	165,091
Bohemian and Moravian	159,319
Rumanian	148,251
African	135,029
Syrian	97, 716
Armenian	76,129
Chinese	57,058

Source: Calculated from data in Imre Ferenczi, compiler, and Walter F. Willcox, ed., *International Migrations*, vol. 1: Statistics (New York: National Bureau of Economic Research, 1929), tables 10 and 13.

passage" – along with their cash savings – commuted back and forth across the Pacific and Atlantic Oceans. Perhaps this explains why immigrants often referred to Ellis Island as "the isle of tears" through which they entered a country that did little to hide its nativist hostility toward them.

Italians were the largest group of immigrants at the turn of the century but they were also among the most likely to return home again. Among the women in this heavily male stream of immigrants was Rosa Cassetteri. A foundling from the mountains of northern Italy, Rosa had grown up very poor, which meant that she started work as a young child, in her case producing silk thread and working as a domestic servant. Her foster mother arranged Rosa's marriage to a returned immigrant and Rosa left her baby behind when she followed him back across the Atlantic. In the USA, Rosa's husband worked as a miner while Rosa cooked and cleaned for boarders. Like many immigrants, they sent money to Italy to help support relatives.[3] In much of Italy, remittances allowed struggling peasants to survive long years of severe agricultural crisis while still hoping for a future in a country where they could feel more at home than in the USA.

Rosa, too, eventually returned to Italy to reclaim her son. Unusual for immigrant women, she then left her first husband and chose a new partner after emigrating again. Much like other Italian men, Rosa's new husband found work in construction and as a fruit peddler in Chicago. There Rosa also found work, cleaning at Chicago Commons, one of many new Settlement Houses emerging in the city. But while Rosa scrubbed floors, many more women immigrants from Italy worked in the Chicago's and New York's garment industries.

Not long after Rosa Cassetteri arrived in Chicago, Israel Antin left his family in Polotzk, Russia, and migrated to Boston. Like the Antins, most Jewish immigrants after 1880 left Russia and Russian or Austrian Poland, where they had faced harsh lives. Land ownership was forbidden to them, and many schools closed to them. Jewish men feared conscription into the Russian army and whole families fled in terror as physical attacks on Jewish property and lives escalated into a veritable epidemic of violent anti-Jewish pogroms (massacres) in the 1880s.

As refugees, Jewish immigrants traveled in family groups and very few subsequently returned. The Antins were fortunate to be reunited in the USA in 1894. Less Orthodox in their religious practices than many of their neighbors, their daughter Mary dreamed of a bright future in a new "promised land." Israel Antin, a former rabbi, struggled to support his family; many of his small businesses failed. Although originally a Yiddish-speaker, daughter Mary relished learning English and was proud of her American education. She eventually wrote an autobiography that described her admiration for America but also defended immigrants from hostile nativists, calling the newcomers the Pilgrims of their era.[4] Unlike many Jewish immigrant girls, Mary Antin was fortunate and did not have to leave school at an early age to work as an "operative" at a sewing machine in a garment factory or as a "cash girl" clerk in a department store.

Slavic-speaking peoples in central and eastern Europe – from Poland, Russia, Austria–Hungary, and the Ottoman Empire – formed one of the largest and newest groups of immigrants at the turn of the century. Antonina Rzeszutko, born in 1889 into a peasant family in a small town in Poland, feared that as a young girl travelling alone she might be excluded as a potential "public charge." She entered in 1906 posing as the daughter of a man from her home village. She first joined her half-sister in Utica, New York and then moved to Webster, Massachusetts, where friends had found her a job in the spinning room of a cotton mill. In 1909 she married John Ruda. At first both worked in the mills; giving birth to seven children, Antonina Ruda then raised her family in mill town housing.[5]

Smaller in number than the Jewish, Italian, and Polish migrations, but equally new, were the Mexicans venturing northward, at first mainly into the southwest. For the American businessmen who invested simultaneously in the southwestern USA and in northern Mexican railroads and mines between 1880 and 1910 and for the workers they sought among the Indians and Spanish-speakers of the adjoining regions, the border between the two countries was no great impediment. But had seasonal jobs in California agriculture, Texas cotton fields, or New Mexican mines and railroads been their only motivation, more migrants from Mexico might have returned to Mexico, as so many of their contemporaries in the east – notably Italians, Greeks, and Balkan Slavs – chose to do. After 1910, however, the political instability and violence that accompanied revolution in Mexico created economic chaos, discouraging many emigrated Mexicans from returning. By 1920, Mexicans had found their way to midwestern meatpacking cities like Kansas and Chicago, with their more stable industrial jobs, facilitating the relocation of whole Mexican family groups.

With the near-exclusion of Chinese labor after 1882, Japanese and Koreans found their way from Asia and from Hawaii to replace them on the west coast. California's "agribusinesses" – appropriately called "factories in the fields" – now raised crops on a massive scale for export eastward. Their demand for seasonal harvesters was almost insatiable, and Mexicans, Filipinos, Portuguese, Koreans, and Japanese all found work as farm laborers. After studying law in Tokyo, the father of Kazuko Itoi arrived in Seattle in 1904 hoping to earn money to continue his studies. He first worked on a railroad gang and in the potato fields of Yakima, and then as a cook on Alaska-bound freighters. Returning to Seattle, he then purchased a cleaning shop.

Shortly after Itoi arrived in the USA, the segregation of Japanese children in San Francisco schools and Japanese government protests resulted in the 1908 "Gentlemen's Agreement" between the USA and Japan. While it ended the migration of laborers from Japan, it permitted Japanese laborers in the USA (unlike their Chinese counterparts) to send for "picture brides," who married them by proxy before departing Japan. Itoi, however, arranged to marry the daughter of a newly arrived Japanese missionary; he then raised four children, including Kazuko, while managing a hotel for transient men.[6] Like many immigrants from Japan, the Itoi family faced persistent discrimination; the newer arrivals did not escape the hostility experienced earlier by the Chinese.

New immigrations like these made American cities from Seattle to New York seem even more foreign in 1900 than they had in 1850. In cities, unskilled factory jobs characteristic of the country's second industrial revolution could be found in the greatest number and variety. Half or more of the residents of America's large cities – including New York, Chicago, and San Francisco – were foreigners and their children. In his book, *How the Other Half Lives*, Jacob Riis exaggerated only slightly when he concluded, "The one thing you shall vainly ask for in the chief city of America is a distinctively American community. There is none . . ."[7] He instead called the urban-dwellers of New York "the mixed crowd." The city's garment industry, like those of Chicago and Philadelphia, attracted disproportionate numbers of Italian and eastern European Jewish immigrants, and disproportionate numbers of women. Farther west, centers of heavy industry such as Buffalo, Cleveland, Pittsburgh, and Chicago, seemed equally foreign but attracted more men from Poland, Russia, the Baltic, and Balkans. In the southwest, San Antonio housed new arrivals from Mexico, while San Francisco mixed immigrants from Asia and Europe.

Not all immigrants found urban and industrial jobs. Seasonal construction of railroads, dams, highways, streets, sewers, and water systems scattered male laborers from Asia, Mexico, and Europe throughout the country. Huge agricultural businesses producing wine, wheat, cotton, sugar beets, and dozens of other crops, along with their packing sheds and canneries, drew seasonal migrants to California, Texas, and Colorado. As wage-earners in seasonal agriculture and industries, few of these immigrants could settle immediately. And by the early twentieth century, immigrant yeoman farmers such as the Svendsens and the Seyffardts had almost disappeared from the American scene, and the rural midwest had lost much of its earlier importance as a receiver of immigrants. Over time, however, intensive cultivation of strawberries, asparagus, and potatoes in California became a specialty of Chinese, Japanese, and Italian "truck farmers," allowing for a more settled life even in areas of large-scale agriculture.

Points of Contact

Thus, once again, immigrants' most significant cross-cultural encounters occurred in cities and in the rural southwest. Newcomers exchanged ideas and material aid with other immigrants and with the working-class children of earlier emigrants from Germany and Ireland. These urban encounters were less violent than their antebellum antecedents. But violence erupted instead when immigrant workers tried to unite against their employers, the corporate "robber barons" old-stock Americans glorified as symbols of economic liberty and the superiority of Anglo-Saxon civilization. Class temporarily eclipsed region and race as the most controversial source of diversity in American life.

Immigrant men most often met old-stock Americans in positions of considerable authority over them. As the Mexican Ernesto Galarza observed in California, "the bartenders, the rent collectors, the insurance salesmen, the mates on the river boats, the landladies, and most importantly, the police – these were all gringos."[8] So were most of the managers and executives of the mines, enormous factories, and agribusinesses where immigrants worked long hours in poorly paid, dangerous, and seasonal jobs. It was a volatile encounter. Drawing on the ideas of Social Darwinism and scientific management, American employers often assigned different tasks to workers of different races, hoping to prevent solidarity and to maintain control over immigrant employees they scarcely knew. In Pittsburgh's steel mills, Hungarians, Poles, Italians, and Negroes all received jobs deemed appropriate for their distinctive racial fitness for work.

To communicate with workers, American employers hired bilingual supervisors who had arrived earlier or were second-generation children of immigrants. In California, Italian, Mexican, Filipino, and Japanese labor bosses recruited, supervised, and even fed and paid gangs of harvesters assigned by race to separate bunks and dining facilities. In the garment factories of New York City, a complex skill hierarchy based on gender, background, and length of time in the USA also emerged. Men – first of German, then of Jewish, and eventually of Italian origin – held the most highly skilled jobs as cutters, pressers, and supervisors. Some subsequently became jobbers, subcontractors, and employers in small, sweatshop businesses. Old-stock American women, along with the daughters of German and Irish women supervised first Jewish and then Italian female operatives at their sewing machines.

Especially in the south, physical violence occasionally replaced managerial manipulation to intimidate and divide workers. In New Orleans in 1891, Americans lynched nine Sicilian dockworkers accused of the murder of Irish-American police chief David Hennessy. Twenty years later, the Jewish Leo Frank was lynched in Atlanta after having been convicted of raping a young white mill operative on the testimony of a colored witness.

Ultimately, however, no employers' strategies could be counted on to prevent immigrant workers from occasionally unifying to challenge their power. Already in 1892, the heterogeneous workforce of the Carnegie Steel Plant in Homestead, Pennsylvania united to strike when Andrew Carnegie announced he intended to hire non-union laborers. Carnegie had arrived from Scotland in 1848 as a young boy. By the 1880s, his steel trust symbolized the power of huge corporations to monopolize national and even international markets. Carnegie had prided himself on good relations with "his men" but he, like most American employers, increasingly left their management to subordinates as business grew. Carnegie's subordinate was the American Henry Clay Frick. Knowing his decision would provoke conflict, and fearing criticism, Carnegie departed for Scotland after advising Frick, "My idea . . . is always to shut down and suffer. Let them decide by vote when they decide to go to work."[9]

Frick disagreed; he was determined to lock out workers and replace them with non-union labor. When Carnegie left town, he built a stockade with watchtowers and barbed wire around the Homestead mill. The arrival of 300 Pinkerton detectives to protect the mill began a violent day-long battle with strikers. While Pennsylvania's governor sent 8,000 troops to secure the plant, Russian-born anarchist Alexander Berkman traveled from New York with a gun. But he failed in his attempt to assassinate Frick, who promptly re-opened the Homestead mill with non-union, "scab" labor. Still in Europe, Carnegie lamented, "I was expecting too much of poor men to stand idly by and see their work taken by others."[10]

Of course immigrant workers shared many grievances – from dangerous working conditions and long hours to job insecurity and reductions in pay. But what most often united them, as it did in Homestead, was the threat of being replaced by new workers they labeled "wage depressors." In West Virginia mines, the wage depressors were often southern Negroes or Italians; in western mines they were more often Mexicans; in eastern factories they were Italians, Serbians, or Syrians. In San Francisco, immigrants from Europe objected to the employment of Chinese men and women in garment shops, while white miners continued to attack Chinese workers throughout the Rocky Mountains.

The result was a division between a mainstream labor movement that rejected class conflict, revolution, and radical political ideals while advocating immigration restriction, and a radical, labor movement organized by the wage depressors, often across racial lines. Both were culturally diverse labor movements, where "Americanization from the bottom up" facilitated different forms of class solidarity. America's first national labor organizations – the National Labor Union of the 1860s, the Knights of Labor of the 1870s and 1880s and the American Federation of Labor of the 1880s – united old-stock American skilled workers and earlier emigrants from Ireland, Great Britain, and Germany in a movement to maintain autonomy and wages. By 1900, only the American Federation of Labor, with its president, the Jewish immigrant cigar worker, Samuel Gompers, survived, and its solidarity was founded, in part, on advocacy of immigration restriction. AF of L unions of skilled German, Irish, British, and American workers routinely barred female, Negro, or immigrant workers from membership, calling them wage depressors.

But even within the AF of L, several industrial unions promoted cooperation between older and newer immigrants. In the mining towns of Pennsylvania, West Virginia, the midwest, and Colorado, the United Mine Workers (UMW) welcomed membership from foreign and African-American miners; their Irish-born organizer "Mother Jones" worked with both. In the west, Filipinos, Japanese, Mexican, Italian, Portuguese, and Chinese workers struggled to organize as cannery and agricultural workers. In the east, the International Ladies Garments' Workers' Union (ILGWU) solved conflicts among German- Yiddish- and Italian-speaking members by organizing workers into separate language locals. In the aftermath of a 1909 strike of women workers, and the tragic Triangle Shirtwaist Company fire in which more than 200 female operatives died, the ILGWU organized the largest group of women workers in the country. Jewish and Irish women predominated at first; after 1910, Italian women became more active. The goal of the ILGWU, like that of the AF of L generally, was to reform capitalism and restrict corporate power through collective bargaining or political pressure on legislators, not to overthrow legislatures or capitalists.

Unlike AF of L leaders, some old-stock Americans and earlier emigrants saw capitalism, not wage depressors, as the enemy. Americans such as "Big Bill" Hayward led the IWW in western mines, and leaders of the Socialist Party of America were also mainly natives; the best-known American socialist of the era was Eugene V. Debs, the son of immigrants from Alsace. Nicola Sacco was more typical of new immigrants with his passionate devotion to anarchism. And, the radical union alternative to the AF of L, the syndicalist IWW, was often more successful than the AF of L in leading strikes among culturally diverse immigrant workers, for example in the textile towns of Lawrence and of Paterson, New Jersey. IWW leaders included foreign-born radicals such as the Italian Carlo Tresca and the second-generation Elizabeth Gurley Flynn, both of whom hoped workers organized in one big union could control their industries, creating democratic workplaces where workers enjoyed the profits of their work. In the Lawrence strike, a dozen language groups sent representatives to the strike committee; appeals for funds appeared in German, Italian, French, Serbian, Russian, Finnish, Polish, Greek, Armenian, and Spanish newspapers. The IWW even welcomed women and Negroes as members.

Anarchism was an equally diverse movement of Germans, Russian Jews such as Alexander Berkman and his sometime lover Emma Goldman, Italians such as Galleani and Sacco, and Indians from Asia such as Dhan Ghopal Mukerji.[11] Goldman prided herself on her anarchist advocacy of sexual liberation but expressed nothing but contempt for American women reformers' interests in moral reform and the right to vote. The American Socialist Party, too, was culturally diverse; it organized its membership into language sections and published newspapers in many languages advocating the democratic conquest of the American government by a coalition of naturalized and old-stock socialist voters.

The fact that immigrants lived in far greater intimacy with each other than with their American employers reinforced workplace solidarity across cultural lines. Although the children of immigrants later recalled growing up in homogeneous communities, most actually lived in mixed neighborhoods. In southern Manhattan, alone, Jacob Riis found "an Italian, a German, a French, African, Spanish, Bohemian, Russian, Scandinavian, Jewish and Chinese colony."[12] In Sacramento, the Mexican boy Ernesto Galarza discovered Japanese, Chinese, Filipinos, Hindus, Portuguese, Italians, Poles, Yugoslavs, Koreans, and Negro neighbors all within walking distance. East and west, simple material assistance – the sharing of cash, clothes, and food – established relations among even the poorest neighbors. More than one historian has pointed out that entire communities, including housewives and children, went on strike in places like Homestead or Lawrence.

Religion and local politics further strengthened cross-cultural neighborliness. In New York, an important center of Jewish life by 1900, the so-called uptown Jews who had arrived earlier from Germany and central Europe feared that the poverty and orthodox religious practices of Yiddish-speaking Russian and Polish Jewish newcomers on the Lower East Side were provoking anti-semitism among scientific racists and Americans generally. Nor were they happy with the free-thinking atheism that inspired Mary Antin to announce one day to her schoolgirl classmates that since no God, but rather "nature made me'" she would not even observe Passover. Invoking a long history of Jewish communal traditions, uptown Jews provided educational programs and charity for newcomers, much as the Catholic bishop John Hughes and immigrant sisters had for newcomer Irish and German Catholics a half century before.

Augmenting programs that linked older and newer immigrants through Catholic and Jewish welfare services, urban political machines also continued to incorporate new voters. In fact, the first step toward political participation for many new immigrant men was assistance in obtaining citizenship from a naturalized immigrant ward heeler who expected nothing except a vote for his help. Some cities even required citizenship of workers hoping for jobs collecting municipal garbage or building municipal services such as streets or subways. By 1890, however, the machine politicians' traditional opponents, American reformers, also had something new to offer newcomers. Upset by the class conflict that corporate power and radical ideologies encouraged, old-stock Americans now demanded that efficient and nonpartisan governments provide welfare services to help the poor adjust to American life without empowering ward heelers and corrupting electoral politics. Reform of municipal government became a centerpiece of reformers who called themselves "Progressives" after the turn of the century.

Many of the Progressive reformers seeking to bridge the class divide were old-stock American women – the first generation of well-educated, professional (and usually unmarried) women escaping from the cult of domesticity that had shaped Anna Murray Douglass's life. In public schools and social settlement houses, women enjoyed relatively peaceful encounters with clients who, as women and children, were already well accustomed to subordination to authority. In her book *The Promised Land*, Mary Antin, who attended a private Catholic girls' school, eulogized her teacher Miss Dillingham – who shared the name, but not the prejudices, of an influential, anti-semitic, and nativist Congressman, William P. Dillingham. Miss Dillingham invited Antin to tea; Antin remembered Dillingham as an inspiring woman who taught her important lessons about America's civic religion and about religious toleration. Farther west, in Sacramento, Ernesto Galarza remembered the racial insults of his schoolyard but also recalled "We were sure to be marched up to the principal's office for calling someone a wop, a chink, a dago, or a greaser. The school was not so much a melting pot as a griddle where Miss Hopley and her helpers warmed knowledge into us and roasted racial hatreds out of us."[13]

Still, when Miss Dillingham invited Mary Antin to tea, she served the young Jewish girl ham – a reminder that public school teachers were as devoted to Anglo-Saxon civilization and to ensuring the cultural conformity of immigrants as were Gertrude Bonnin's Indian school instructors. Teaching English generally came first. Concerned that new immigrants lacked the facility or willingness to learn a new language, worried census takers from 1890 until 1930 categorized every person they listed as "able" or "unable" to speak English. Meanwhile their teachers experimented with teaching small groups of immigrant children in their native languages – today we would call it bilingual education – largely to discourage older children, otherwise assigned to the first grade, from leaving school completely, thus ending their exposure to English-speakers.

For Antin as for Bonnin, cultural transformation meant more than learning English or America's civic religion or respect for representative government. Public schools sought to transform immigrant boys into workers immune to radicalism and immigrant girls into American mothers who were also good consumers. State laws increasingly required children to remain in school until age 14 and school days now started with pledges of allegiance followed by vocational training for factory, domestic service, and housework. Lessons in personal hygiene –

some public schools even installed bathtubs for instruction – entered the curriculum, as did textbooks introducing American cooking and home decoration.

Educational experiments such as these had originated as experiments in settlement houses much like the one employing Maria Cassetteri. Jane Addam's Hull House in Chicago was the best known of dozens of settlement houses established in immigrant neighborhoods between 1880 and 1920. Addams and her largely female co-workers opened Hull House with nursery programs for the children of working mothers and a wide variety of educational and athletic clubs for boys and girls. Settlement houses taught girls American housewifery and lured immigrant mothers with clubs and parties. Hull House organized campaigns to improve garbage service, public schools, and factory conditions in Chicago. Groups like the Women's Trade Union League, an initiative of middle-class reformers and immigrant labor activists in New York and Chicago, often met in settlement houses.

Maria Hall Ets, the woman who recorded Maria Cassetteri's life story at Chicago Commons, shared with Addams a conviction that immigrants had gifts to give their new homeland. Hull House thus built a labor museum that displayed and demonstrated immigrant arts and crafts. New York's settlement houses sponsored programs where immigrants performed their dances and songs for appreciative audiences. While never abandoning their distaste for class struggle or their desire to see immigrants culturally transformed, women professionals' relatively harmonious relations with their neighbors did counterbalance workplace conflict and nativist rhetoric. Immigrant children such as the Italian Leonard Covello fondly recalled that "Miss Ruddy [Protestant director of the East Harlem Home Garden Settlement] filled a need we could find nowhere else."[14] But the adult Rosa Cassetteri summed up her contacts with the American women somewhat less enthusiastically, noting "They used to tell us that it's not nice to drink the beer, and must not let the baby do this, and this . . . I went to sleep when they started the writing. I couldn't learn it."[15]

New Groups and Identities

Without question, the early twentieth century was one of the most important periods of ethnic group formation in American history. Group identity still originated at home, in immigrants' families and in their neighborhood communities. Immigrant businesses reinforced that domestic culture by making it a part of an emerging consumer marketplace. And immigrant voluntary associations extended that domestic culture by giving it institutional expression.

Foreigners and old-stock Americans alike agreed that differing expectations of family solidarity, different patterns of childrearing, and different relations between men and women divided them. For the child Leonard Covello, family solidarity meant starting work at age 12 and turning his $1.75 earnings over to his mother. For Kazuko Itoi it meant obeying her mother and going to Japanese language instruction after school every day. For Rose Gollup, a Russian Jewish immigrant girl several years older than Mary Antin, it meant respecting her father's request when he showed her a red paper book and announced "This is my union book. You too must join the union."[16] Not all immigrant children subordinated their individual desires for education or for the purchase of American clothes, food, or books willingly of course. But even their conflicts with children drove home to parents the stark contrast between their family ties and the individualism of Americans.

Gender ideologies particularly clashed in schools and settlement houses. Most immigrants agreed that daughters, and even mothers, should help support their families, and the daughters of immigrants dominated the female workforces of most northeastern and western cities. Yet female wage-earning, especially by mothers, violated Americans' expectations of female domesticity. For women reformers, the wage-earning mother symbolized male tyranny, while it revealed immigrant men as failures as breadwinners. For immigrants, unmarried women reformers often symbolized female autonomy, especially as the American suffrage movement grew to its peak, and American women gained the right to vote in 1919. With no other way to understand the American women, Catholic immigrants sometimes called the women reformers "nuns without God." While some admired the unmarried female reformers and suffragists as American role models, many more pitied and resented them.

Immigrant parents supervised the work and family behavior of their daughters with special anxiety, believing that they, as mothers, would determine the survival of the entire group. Leonard Covello not only married an Italian Catholic girl, he married one from his parents' native town of Avigliano. When she died, he chose her younger sister as a second wife. Nevertheless, rates of intermarriage did rise in the second generation. But children who found spouses of different cultural background generally continued to respect religious boundaries, creating separate Catholic, Jewish, and Orthodox Christian marital "melting pots." Newly arrived Catholic immigrants married the children of earlier German or Irish immigrants, but all three religious melting pots isolated newcomers from contact with Protestant families of old-stock Americans. The free-thinking Mary Antin was quite unusual in eventually marrying outside her faith.

In west coast Chinatowns and Koreatowns, it was the absence of women and the prominence of immigrant bachelors that instead marked group boundaries. The mother of Korean immigrant Mary Paik cooked for four years for 30 Korean men without families who worked in the citrus groves of Riverside, California.[17] In New York, Jacob Riis observed that only a very few Chinese merchants (whose wives, along with those of students and ministers, were the only Chinese women able to enter the USA) lived in families. He frightened American readers with lurid descriptions of Chinese bachelors seeking white "wives" among the female opium addicts they had lured into their "dens." But he also urged Americans to consider a more humane immigration policy that would allow Chinese men to bring Chinese wives into the country.[18]

Whether called "Little Italy," the "Jewish Ghetto," "Polonia," "Koreatown," or "el Barrio," neighborhood communities extended solidarity beyond the family. For Ernesto Galarza, the ability to speak Spanish and to recognize regional differences among recent refugees from the Mexican revolution created a sense of living in a culturally homogeneous neighborhood even with other immigrant groups nearby. "All our immediate neighbors were old friends from Korea," Mary Paik also remembered; one had even been the boyhood friend of her father.[19] No Jim Crow laws forced European immigrants into these neighborhood communities. Even Mary Paik's family had traveled by choice to Los Angeles with Korean friends from Hawaii and were glad to have the assistance of other Koreans in Riverside when finding a job and a place to live. Thus, even the adoption of American clothing and the pronunciation of an immigrant's first words of English typically occurred in the company of a friend or neighbor of the same cultural origins.

Although otherwise quite different, Jews, Italians, Poles, and Koreans contrasted their communal ties and their intense sociability to the individualism and privacy Americans more highly valued. Jewish immigrants praised the "mensch" among them, as a person honored by his friends and neighbors for helpfulness and concern for others. Italians sought "respect" from a face-to-face community, with the result, according to Riis, that "those who are not in the street are hanging half way out of the windows, shouting at some one below. All 'the Bend' must be, if not altogether, at least half out of doors when the sun shines."[20] Foreigners shared their cramped homes with relatives and boarders; their doors were open to neighbors; the family kitchen doubled as adjunct to the factory when neighborhood groups of women and children took in industrial homework. Relegated to the worst jobs in the industrial economy, new immigrants understood economic liberty less as individual mobility – as Americans viewed it – and more often as the collective achievement of economic comfort by a family, a community, or the entire working class.

Immigrant neighborhoods nevertheless provided an insecure foundation for group stability. A typical "Little Italy," for example, had emerged in the 1880s as a cluster of saloons, restaurants, banks, and boarding houses serving transient male laborers. Newcomers subsequently arrived as young married couples or reuniting families; as children began earning wages their families could often afford better housing and so moved away in search of it. A dismayed social worker living in New York's Little Italy reported "One never becomes accustomed to the kaleidoscopic changes of one's neighbors."[21] In addition, few American cities had only one Little Italy or Jewish Ghetto, and even most Chinese immigrants lived outside New York's Chinatown, not within it. In New York, the Jewish Lower East Side became a launching pad into smaller Jewish neighborhoods in Harlem, Brooklyn, and the Bronx.

In constantly changing cities, immigrant businesses made cultural diversity a more enduring feature of urban markets. Immigrants often preferred to do business and to work among their own kind. A Polish immigrant wanting to buy and eat kielbasa would expect a Polish immigrant grocer or butcher to know his consumer preferences. Grocery stores like the one Israel Antin opened, along with saloons and cafes, provided centers for sociability, where neighbors quickly met and gossiped. By trusting their clients with credit, grocers assured that both the Antin and Paik families ate during periods of temporary unemployment. Immigrant businessmen also offered services immigrants needed – sending money to the homeland, selling insurance, translating documents, arranging travel. Ernesto Galarzo, Kazuko Itoi, Maria Cassetteri, Antonina Rzeszutko, and Leonard Covello all described the importance of immigrant businesses in their memoirs of community life.

For Italian and Jewish immigrants living in huge urban communities and in cities such as New York, the production of culture also became an important business. Actors and actresses in the Yiddish- and Italian-language theatres specialized in stories with immigrant themes. The Italian actor Farfariello created a new genre of comedy by joking about immigrant mixing of dialects with American English and standard Italian. Sicilians even supported their own puppet theatre for a time. Yiddish literature enjoyed a renaissance in the USA because of the large population of Yiddish readers living on New York's Lower East Side. Books, novels, political pamphlets, and newspapers in Yiddish poured from Jewish presses between 1890 and 1920.

Immigrant businessmen also often preferred to hire and do business with immigrants of their own background. A Tuscan immigrant gave Maria Cassetteri's husband the money and advice he needed to start his own business as a banana peddler. On the west coast, Chinese merchants first loaned Mary Paik's mother the money she needed to begin cooking for citrus grove workers. Out of practices such as these, distinctive "ethnic niches" developed in urban economies. Italians worked in disproportionate numbers in construction, produce marketing, and restaurants. Chinese clustered in groceries, restaurants, and laundries. Some scholars even describe New York's garment industry as an ethnic enclave economy dominated from top to bottom in the last two decades of the nineteenth century by Jewish immigrants.

Market relations so shaped group formation, that competition, diversity, and individual consumer choices could easily threaten group solidarity. A shopper in San Francisco's Chinatown could buy from dozens of competing Chinese groceries or restaurants. Yiddish-speaking Jews in New York could select from a wide variety of newspapers, each reflecting its editor's political and religious ideals. Immigrant churches and synagogues survived only if they could successfully raise funds to build meeting places like the one where Mary Paik's father occasionally preached on Sundays. Even anti-capitalist clubs of socialists and anarchists produced plays and sponsored May Day celebrations in order to raise money.

Little wonder, then, that immigrant businessmen filled many of the leadership positions of immigrant community associations. Members of a particular family, kinship group, or hometown organized the smallest societies – Italians' paese clubs, Jewish Landsmannschaften, and Chinese district associations. Smaller societies often confederated. Chinese immigrants had their Six Companies. More characteristically, the Sons of Italy generated a competitor – the Columbian Federation – while, for Poles, the Polish National Alliance (which placed no religious limits on its members) competed with its counterpart the Polish Roman Catholic Union, which limited membership to Catholics.

Immigrants could choose among associations with differing agendas, too. Most offered to do "what had to be done" in order to take care of "our own kind." The smallest societies offered sociability, usually for the adult men who gathered in their club rooms. Their picnics, banquets, and dances generated cash while creating important, if temporary, moments of family recreation. Among the Japanese, Chinese, and Finns, voluntary associations also sometimes functioned as cooperative businesses, operating small grocery stores. Japanese mutual aid societies supported farming and marketing cooperatives, while Chinese societies organized trade and commerce between Chinatown and China, or guaranteed that the bodies of the dead returned to their homes. Many societies offered members some of the same services – insurance, charity, healthcare, burial – as urban machines, private businesses, and the municipal welfare programs old-stock American reformers increasingly preferred. Others united around ideology: Italian socialist, anarchist, syndicalist, and nationalist clubs published their own papers in Italian and either supported or opposed union organization, strikes, Mussolini, American ward heelers, or candidates in municipal elections. Some societies sponsored English classes, others supported cultural programs in the immigrants' native tongues or taught the language to immigrants' children.

Irish, Polish, as well as Jewish Zionist organizations united newcomers to lend support for independence or the creation of a national homeland outside the USA. The first Yugoslav newspaper, addressing all South Slavs, appeared in the USA before Yugoslavia became a country. Women's associations also became more common in the late nineteenth century. Jewish women's clubs federated as the National Council of Jewish Women, and the Zionist movement had its own female organization, Hadassah. Even relatively small fraternal societies eventually generated women's auxiliaries and – often somewhat belatedly – children's organizations, often in an effort to attract second-generation members.

Because membership in communal societies was completely voluntary, many – perhaps even most – immigrants joined not a single one. While she remembered no society important to Antonina and John Ruda, for example, their great-granddaughter in the 1990s did recall that "the Polish Catholic Church was the center of their lives . . . Many men donated a lot of money to the church and would work free for the church's needs. The church was a great unifying factor."[22] Far more than secular voluntary associations, religious institutions ensured group survival into the second generation. In Homestead, Pennsylvania, for example, Orthodox Christians speaking half-a dozen Slavic languages formed separate congregations, some of which survived for over half a century.

Among Catholics, Polish and Italians replaced Germans and French-Canadians as challengers of Irish hegemony. Italians were not content to worship in the basements of churches dominated by Irish worshipers and by their English-speaking priests but attracted missions funded and staffed by Italian-speaking Catholic brothers, notably from Italy's Scalabrinian Order. These brothers were independent; not subject to Irish-American bishops, they learned to tolerate immigrants' cults of particular patron saints, which generated loud, yearly, and very public celebrations in which the patron's statue was paraded through the streets. Although the Catholic Church organized dozens of "nationality parishes", and tried to guarantee that priests and nuns could speak the languages of the parishes to which they were assigned even nationality parishes were territorial and the property of their founding religious order or of the bishops of the Church. Still, the proliferation of clubs and organizations for Catholic parishioners, along with parish schools and social services and public processions, reinforced the association between neighborhood and parish in the minds of many immigrants. It may even have encouraged higher rates of homeownership among Catholic than Jewish immigrants of the era.

Among new Jewish immigrants, the aid and assistance of

"uptown Jews" could not impose religious homogeneity, and it often reinforced a sense of cultural difference between immigrants of German and eastern European origin. Most Jewish immigrants from Russia and Poland continued to prefer their own, small Orthodox congregations, with their own synagogues, to the reform temples of the uptown Jews. Over the next half-century, new Jewish immigrants generated a wide variety of American Jewish congregations from Reformed, to Conservative and Orthodox. Each congregation in turn developed somewhat distinctive adaptations of kosher culinary restrictions, Sabbath domestic rituals, and forms of synagogue worship. Each represented a different adaptation to American life and a somewhat different strategy for cultural survival. Even in matters of faith, then, immigrants had cultural options. As this suggests, Nicola Sacco, and other anarchists, were also particularly unusual among immigrants in rejecting religious practice altogether.

Immigration and American Culture

The almost continuous immigrations of the nineteenth century created a growing cultural chasm between rural and urban dwellers, significantly transforming the regional cultures and identities of the USA. By 1920, a slight majority of all Americans lived in cities. As mixed crowds, cities were most characteristic, and most foreign, in the industrialized northeast. In the west and southwest – New Mexico, Arizona, Texas, and California – where commercial agriculture also produced a diverse society, older emigrants were numerous among the natives welcoming or rejecting newcomers, many of them from Mexico or Asia. New immigrants had again bypassed the rural south but in the twentieth century they also avoided the rural midwest and Great Plains. Shaped by distinctive histories and distinctive cross-cultural encounters, new and diverse urban, western, and rural American cultures would not result in a second Civil War in the USA. But they did promote a new political coalition to support the nativists with their rising demands for racially based immigration restriction.

East, west, or southwest, American cities again generated a larger-scale, impersonal, and polyglot urban culture. This culture was increasingly commercial and inevitably secular; it blended elements from the foodways, dialects, and leisure-time preferences of religiously diverse new immigrants. The vast beer gardens and saloons opened by earlier German and Irish immigrants gave way in the early twentieth century to music halls, nickelodeons, street snacks, candy stores, dance halls, and amusement parks such as Coney Island. Here, mixed crowds of young people met and experienced the pleasures of a consumer culture that pleased neither their parents nor their school teachers or social settlement neighbors.

The blending of popular theatrical, culinary, and musical traditions of Europe, Asia, and – with the slow but increasing migration from the south – of Africa gave the country vaudeville, dance crazes, Hollywood, hot dog "red hots," "dago red" wine, singing waiters, and chow mein restaurants. In California, Mary Paik vividly recalled seeing her first movie – a cowboy story – in 1914; in the east, Leonard Covello, as a teacher, tried to help newer Italian immigrants understand why their sons seemed more interested in baseball and basketball than in wage-earning.

In rural areas, old-stock American farmers viewed this new urban commercial culture as more than disturbingly foreign – to them it was also morally dangerous. And in the years before World War I, nothing seemed more dangerous to rural Americans than urban-dwellers' toleration of alcohol production and consumption – an issue that had separated old-stock Americans from newcomers at least since the days of Agoston Haraszthy. Like Haraszthy, the vast majority of new immigrants saw nothing morally wrong with drinking beer, wine, or spirits. On the contrary, they believed drinking became a problem only for old-stock Americans. In California, Andrea Sbarboro, an immigrant Italian winemaker and banker, lectured a delegation from the Women's Christian Temperance Union (WCTU) that women's most effective contribution to temperance would be to serve their sons wine as part of a good meal. Even a child like Ernesto Galarza believed that "on skid row we rarely saw a drunk wino who was not a gringo."[23]

Even as Sbarboro lectured the women temperance activists, a Chicago minister in 1903 predicted that "deliverance [from alcohol] will come . . . from the sober and august Anglo-Saxon south, unspoiled and unpoisoned by the wine-tinted, beer-sodden, whiskey-crazed, sabbath-desecrating, God-defying and anarchy-breeding and practicing minions from over the sea."[24] The rural and southern America this minister praised in such fulsome language had remained Anglo-Saxon, unspoiled and unpoisoned by migration in large part because it was undergoing a profound economic crisis that would continue for almost a century. The rural south, along with the rural midwest and Great Plains, attracted few new immigrants after 1890 because large-scale commercial agriculture there left few opportunities for yeoman family farmers and generated few jobs for wage-earners. The depression of the 1890s drove large numbers of old-stock Americans, earlier emigrants, and hundreds of thousands of freedmen, off their marginal family farms in both regions.

Southern and western farmers responded to economic crisis both politically and culturally. They organized a populist political movement that glorified family farmers as the foundation for American democracy and they narrowly missed electing their candidate to the presidency in 1896. And some of these latter-day midwestern Jeffersonians who excoriated corporate capitalist modernity, urban consumer hedonism (including alcohol consumption), Jewish-dominated eastern banks, and the godless and un-American foreigners of the urban east now bore German, Czech, or Norwegian names.

Religious revivals among the rural poor formed a second response to painful economic change. Between 1880 and 1920 religious revivals again raged through the troubled fields and small towns of Protestant rural America. As in the past, too, urban dwellers at first seemed relatively immune to them. In cities, immigrants came into contact with wealthier, "mainline" Protestant reformers such as Jane Addams who were less interested in immigrants' souls or conversion than in a social gospel of neighborly good works that would inoculate immigrants from the temptations of radicals' calls for class struggle. In the countryside, Protestant revival instead encouraged the development of a rural religious culture broadly shared by poorer second-generation emigrants, freedmen and their children, and old-stock Americans alike.

The revival had started in the holiness movement spreading among freedmen in the 1870s. By the 1890s, Charles Price Jones, a Negro preacher from Selma, Alabama, and other Negro members of the Pentecostalist Church of God in Christ, were converting and ordaining hundreds of white southern worshipers. By the twentieth century the enthusiastic worship, praying, and preaching styles of poor southern Negroes and whites had spread to Charleston and Nashville, and from Kansas City to Los Angeles, often travelling with displaced farmers. On the Great Plains, Methodists, Baptists, and holiness preachers found new converts among children growing up in rural communities originally settled by emigrants such as Gro Svendsen or William and Sophie Seyffardt.

By letting the Holy Spirit into their hearts and by singing, dancing, and speaking in tongues, rural communities believed they could heal sickness and divine God's word. They spoke of being "baptized with fire." More importantly, they sought to restore America to moral purity in the new millennium. And in doing so they excoriated cities as foreign and un-American places, sought to ban the sale of liquor in state- and nationwide and supported "dry" candidates for office to achieve that end.

In the antebellum USA, nativism had failed to unite white southerners and northerners as they quarreled over slavery and abolition and the future of the west. After the Civil War, scientific racism helped to bind up their wounds, and to create a foundation for a new nativist movement focused on restricting foreigners' access to life in the USA and to American citizenship. By the twentieth century, nativist policies proposed by Yankee scientific racists sounded appealing even to rural and southern Protestant believers – both black and white – who otherwise rejected Darwin and his ideas about evolution as contrary to the word of God. In the two decades surrounding World War I, this odd political coalition delivered the more stringent restriction of immigration scientific racists had long demanded.

In fact, nativists in these years were probably correct in seeing immigrants as cultural, if not racial, threats. Linguistically, occupationally, economically, religiously, and – in Nicola Sacco's case – morally and politically, immigrants shared little enough with English-speaking Americans, many of them Protestants and influenced, at the very least, by the moral fervor of recurring Protestant revivalism. Although newcomers, like natives, appreciated liberty and material prosperity, they generally defined and evaluated them differently. Before they could find acceptance as Americans, many immigrants would have to learn – as Nicola Sacco could or would not – to worship a God, to respect private property, to admire representative government, and to solve their economic problems as individuals.

Further Reading

Sucheng Chan, ed., *Entry Denied: Exclusion and the Chinese Community in America, 1882–1943* (Philadelphia: Temple University Press, 1991).

Roger Daniels, *Not Like Us: Immigrants and Minorities in America, 1890–1924* (Chicago: Ivan R. Dee, 1997).

Matthew Frye Jacobson, *Special Sorrows: The Diasporic Imagination of Irish, Polish, and Jewish Immigrants in the United States* (Cambridge, MA: Harvard University Press, 1995).

Alan Kraut, *The Huddled Masses: The Immigrant in American Society, 1880–1921* (Arlington Heights: Harlan Davidson, 1982).

Ewa T. Morawska, *For Bread with Butter: The Life-worlds of East Central Europeans in Johnstown, Pennsylvania, 1890–1940* (New York: Cambridge University Press, 1985).

Gary Ross Mormino and George E. Pozzetta, *The Immigrant World of Ybor City: Italians and their Latin Neighbors in Tampa, 1885–1985* (Urbana: University of Illinois Press, 1987).

Orm Overland, *Immigrant Minds, American Identities: Making the*

United States Home, 1870–1930 (Urbana: University of Illinois Press, 2000).

Bruno Ramirez, *Crossing the 49th Parallel: Migration from Canada to the United States, 1900-1930* (Ithaca: Cornell University Press, 2001).

Mark Wyman, *Round-trip to America: The Immigrants Return to Europe, 1880–1930* (Ithaca: Cornell University Press, 1993.

STUDENT EXERCISE

DETERMINING THE GEOGRAPHIC ORIGINS OF IMMIGRANTS AT CENTURY'S TURN

When studying immigration and ethnicity, historians often have little choice but to use the categories employed by governmental officials in times past. Yet census takers and record keepers at the borders of the USA continuously revise the categories they use to describe the character of newcomers. This complicates historians' ability to make sensible comparisons between successive waves of immigrants.

You know from chapter 4 that Social Darwinist nativists argued that the immigrants of the turn of the century represented racial groups unfit for citizenship because they were not the "Nordic" northern and western Europeans who had dominated among earlier international migrations. But just how seriously did newcomers from the regions of southern and eastern Europe, Mexico, and Asia outnumber immigrants from northern and western Europe? To answer that question, first use the figures in Table 5.1 to complete the Table 5.2.

You may need to consult an atlas or a dictionary to complete this task. Where, for example, is Armenia? And where are the boundaries of eastern and southern Europe? Who are the Magyars? The Hebrews? The

Table 5.2 Immigrant origins, 1899–1924

Immigrants from	*Numbers*	*Percentage of total*
Northern and western Europe		
Southern and eastern Europe		
The Americas		
Asia		
Africa		
Other		
Total		

Ruthenians? This exercise should remind you that countries appear and disappear over time; their boundaries change; so do American understandings of what constitutes a racial or cultural group. All these changes complicate the work of historians who try to trace changes in immigrants over time.

You also need to remember that Table 5.1 is based on the racial categories used by record-keepers in the early years of the century, rather than on the country of birth of immigrants or the country from which they emigrated to the USA. This means, for example, that there are no Canadians or West Indians at all listed in Table 5.1. Instead, 567,941 English-speaking Canadians appear in the category "English and Welsh," while French-speaking immigrants from Canada outnumber those from France in the "French" category. Almost all the "African" immigrants in Table 5.1 actually arrived from the Caribbean, and were of African descent; most of the "Spanish" immigrants were Spanish-speakers who came from the Caribbean, not former residents of Spain, in Europe. To what geographic location will you assign these groups? To what geographic origin will you assign the Hebrews, who entered the USA in significant numbers from more than half a dozen countries and from three continents?

Once you have completed your calculations, compare

your findings to those of some of your classmates. Even if you have done additional research together, your findings may be quite different. In discussion, try to locate the origins of your differences in the choices you made when linking racial categories to geographical origins. Can you reach agreement about which of you made the best choices?

Finally, compare your findings to those in Table 6.1 (p. 180), which gives the distributions of immigrant origins before and after immigration restriction in the early twentieth century. Do your estimates of the geographic origins of immigrants before 1924 significantly differ from the ones you find there? To what could you attribute those differences?

6

Migrants, Immigrants, and Scientific Racism, 1900–1945

When Ignacio Reveles, a poor rancher from San Luis de Cordero in Durango, left the woman he had recently married to travel north in the early 1920s, he may not have exchanged even two words with government officials on either side of the long, land border between the USA and his homeland of Mexico. California's economy was booming after World War I, while Durango had become notorious for its rebelliousness during the Mexican revolution. With his home state still in turmoil, Reveles was one of many to leave the region. Once in the USA, he joined men from his hometown in Colusa, California, where they were laying railroad track. When the job in Colusa ended, Reveles again traveled north, to Mt. Shasta, where he found work in a lumber camp. Then, with his earnings, Ignacio Reveles returned to Durango and settled down to the hard job of supporting his family there.

The experience of fathering eight children over the next 15 years quickly convinced Reveles that his small ranch would never support so many, and during the 1930s, his son José was forced to leave school after only three years to help support the family. Still, during the Great Depression, as the senior Reveles watched the return from the USA of many neighbors, some with no savings at all, he may have felt a quiet satisfaction with his decision to return earlier. Unable to find jobs in a depressed economy in the USA and forced to seek charity and public assistance, as many as 300,000 Mexican immigrants had been rounded up by city officials in southwestern cities and, along with their citizen children, deported south of the border.

World War II again changed the options of the poor ranchers of San Luis de Cordero. Beginning in 1942, the Mexican and American governments signed a treaty to recruit temporary laborers ("braceros") for agricultural and construction jobs in the USA, where war production had sparked economic recovery. After the war ended, Reveles's son José Reveles would himself become a bracero, and work off several contracts in the USA. He would eventually settle and raise a family, first in El Paso and then in Colusa.[1]

Among the 200,000 Mexican men recruited as "braceros" during World War II was Arnulfo Caballero, who was born the son of a Spanish-speaking blacksmith and an Indian mother in Puebla, an ancient town 100 miles from Mexico City. Unlike Ignacio Reveles, Caballero interacted with government officials repeatedly as he became a temporary migrant to the USA. Caballero first answered a newspaper advertisement placed by the Mexican government; applying for a visa and work contract, he was selected and interviewed by Mexican officials who prepared his papers while promising fair wages during his employment abroad. His travel to the USA was then paid by the American government, and at the border his papers were again carefully inspected by American immigration agents. Unlike the vast majority of braceros (who worked in southwest agriculture and railroad maintenance), Caballero was sent in 1944 to work in New York, where he lived with five or six friends. All had jobs in the freight house of the New York Central Railroad. Like José Reveles, he too would later move to El Paso with his family.

Before 1924, immigrants such as Israel Antin, Mary Cassetteri, Nicola Sacco, and Ignacio Reveles had left home with few if any identifying papers. The liberty to move and to choose where one worked or lived, while under attack in the USA, had not been totally rejected. At the borders of the USA, migrants from Europe or the Americas (unlike those from Asia) faced at most an inspection to insure that they were healthy, mentally fit, and unlikely to become a public charge. After

1924, by contrast, immigrants entered the USA through carefully watched borders. Like Arnulfo Caballero, they often carried with them an impressive portfolio of papers acquired during the lengthy bureaucratic procedures required to obtain a visa to live and work in the USA. Potential immigrants now applied to American consuls for visas permitting them to enter the USA well before they arrived at the border. The visa that eventually became known as the "green card" – today it is not actually green – became the most sought-after and difficult to obtain because consuls faced limits, defined by the Congress of the USA, on the numbers they could issue each year.

Between 1917 and 1924, the USA imposed draconian new restrictions on immigration, permanently changing the immigration experience for all newcomers. While vehemently contested, the decision to restrict immigration represented the final triumph of the scientific racism of the nineteenth century. Not only did immigrants now face carefully watched borders, they continued until 1965 to enter a nation that tolerated blatant racial discrimination in its laws, employment practices, and everyday life. The triumph of scientific racism had unintended consequences for the USA. With a strong economy in the 1920s and again during World War II, American employers still needed workers. By restricting immigration from Asia and Europe in the 1920s, the USA provoked new mass northward migrations of southerners – from Mexico and the Caribbean, and from the bi-racial American south. Contacts among peoples of differing cultures and colors scarcely diminished as a result. As international migrations diminished and domestic migrations increased, Americans' toleration of scientific racism also waned, however. By 1950, many had begun to rethink the significance of American diversity and to imagine an American nation purged of its Social Darwinist prejudices.

Immigration Restriction and the Triumph of Scientific Racism

Nativists had been demanding additional restrictions on immigration since the 1890s. At first they made little headway against traditional notions about the liberty to move, especially in the face of a globalizing economy driven in no small part by American corporations and their seemingly insatiable demand for laborers. As ever more immigrants from southern and eastern Europe arrived in the USA after 1900, however, the appeal of nativist arguments grew. Congress appointed a commission to investigate immigration, headed by the anti-semitic Congressman William P. Dillingham. Dillingham's report, published in 1911, described the scientific basis for the country's racial categorization of immigrants. It claimed to document vast differences in attitude, behavior, and capacity between earlier emigrants and newer immigrants. New immigrants, it argued, were not becoming citizens at the same rate as earlier ones, even when they chose – as many did not – to remain in the USA.

Scientific racists also continued to insist that immigrants, along with native populations of blacks and Indians, would "mongrelize" an American nation of Nordics and Anglo-Saxons. The 1908 Gentlemen's Agreement restricting the migration of laborers from Japan and the passage of new anti-Asian legislation, limiting the right of Asians such as Kazuko Itoi or Mary Paik to purchase land or to marry whites, reflected the strong appeal of scientific racism throughout the country. Support for Jim Crow laws, as well as undiminished numbers of lynchings of black southerners, drew on the same font of ideas.

The rising tide of scientific racism in the USA did not go uncontested. But the very diversity of its opponents may have muted their influence. Among newcomers, Jewish scholars were among the most fervent opponents of scientific racism. The German Jewish immigrant Franz Boas, a Columbia University anthropologist who studied race, environment, and culture among American Indians, repeatedly exposed American racism as anything but scientific. Boas had studied the physical growth of American children since the 1890s, and he even reported to Congressman William Dillingham's Immigration Commission that the same immigrant children public schools and settlement houses transformed culturally were also – contrary to racists' predictions – changing physically.

Many Negroes, especially in the north, reminded scientific racists instead that they violated the earliest nationalist ideals of a civic America, repeating a question first posed by David Walker to white Americans in 1828, "Do you understand your own language . . . 'We hold these truths to be self-evident, that ALL *men are created* EQUAL.' "[2] Much like Frederick Douglass, those who called themselves the "New Negroes" of the north, including the Massachusetts-born and Harvard-educated sociologist W. E. B. DuBois, wanted to become Afro-American citizens in a color-blind civic nation.

Founded by DuBois in 1905, the Niagara Movement was an early expression of this traditional critique of racial prejudice. Its vision also appealed to many old-stock Americans from the northeast who considered themselves heirs to the abolitionists and the founding fathers. Certainly it appealed to the elite immigrants who in 1906 had formed the American Jewish Committee to "safeguard the civil and religious rights of Jews, to combat discrimination and to allay prejudice."[3]

For many new immigrants, the discovery of racial inequality in the USA proved as shocking as slavery had been to Ottilie Assing in the 1850s. Writing for the Yiddish press in 1919 a journalist anticipated moral outrage from his readers when he reported, "Yes, equal rights! Unfortunately that is what they lack in our democratic republic. Our black fellow citizens are still being held down, in spite of all the provisions of the United States constitution." Franz Boas became a life-long supporter of the National Association for the Advancement of Colored People (NAACP), which published some of his writings. Catholic clerics, too, insisted that anything short of a color-blind civic nation was morally unacceptable in the eyes of God.

Seeking coalition initially with like-minded white elite natives, DuBois soon became the most prominent spokesman for the integrated NAACP. Founded in 1909 the NAACP focused on ending segregation by removing racial barriers to the full rights of citizenship. DuBois and other Negro activists also joined the Urban League, founded in 1911, and read newspapers, such as *The New York Amsterdam News* or Chicago's *Defender*, that argued for full rights of citizenship for Negro citizens. They began a half-century campaign to pressure American governments to guarantee Negroes equal protection (from lynching and race riots) under the law, to broaden Negro citizens' rights – whether to vote or to serve equally in the Army and to end discriminatory practices in workplaces, neighborhoods, restaurants, and public transport.

Indian Americans' acquisition of US citizenship followed a somewhat similar strategy. In 1901 Gertrude Bonnin had met Dr. Carlos Montezuma, a Yavapai graduate of the Carlise Indian School, who – calling himself a "red progressive" – had dedicated himself to expanding citizenship rights for Indians. Bonnin herself helped to organize a pan-tribal Society of American Indians that resembled the NAACP in many of its goals.

Rural Protestants developed their own criticisms of scientific racism. Already aghast at Darwin's notion that humans were descendants of apes, rather than a creation of God, the white "holy rollers" who shouted and sang God's praises also violated the color line. True, the religious enthusiasms they shared with black Americans rarely provided common grounds for intermarriage, and most new churches emerging from the revivals of the turn of the century, much like the Assemblies of God, quickly developed into segregated institutions in the south. But the Pentecostalists who gathered in tent meetings and in urban revivals such as the ones held in San Francisco's Azusa Street mission were also often racially mixed crowds. And in the south, most early experiments in interracial cooperation occurred under religious auspices, bringing together elite Negro and white Protestants socially, even if only to organize segregated black southern YMCAS and YWCAs in the interest of racial uplift.

Rather than focus on color-blind equality in the civic world, recent immigrants proposed an alternative to scientific racism and a Nordic America that more resembled the ethnic nationalism of Hector Crèvecoeur. Israel Zangwill's 1908 play *The Melting Pot* again popularized biological metaphors of a more inclusive, although often presumably white, America. Oddly, Zangwill was a Zionist who believed Jews needed a homeland of their own. But his tales of life in and out of the Jewish ghetto of New York City instead typically treated interracial love, and his play described a marriage between Christian and Jewish immigrant children creating a new American race. Readers drew diverse conclusions from Zangwill's play: some imagined a homogeneous nation of flag-waving, English-speaking white citizens emerging from the melting pot, others an amalgamated but white American race much like the one Crèvecoeur had discussed. At times, however, Zangwill suggested that amalgamation through marriage included all races. "Ah, what a stirring and seething," he wrote passionately, "Celt and Latin, Slav and Teuton, Greek and Syrian – black and yellow . . . what is the glory of Rome and Jerusalem where all nations and races come to worship and look back compared with the glory of America, where all races and nations come to labor and look forward!"[4]

With the outbreak of World War I in Europe in 1914, Social Darwinists in the USA argued that racial diversity now threatened national unity. Chartered in Atlanta in 1916, a revived Ku Klux Klan (KKK) spoke for much of rural America in opposing immigration, demanding "America for Americans," and asking "WHICH SIDE ARE YOU ON? GET OFF THE FENCE!" The KKK saw a moral threat in "every pagan papal priest, every [Jewish] shyster, every K of C [Knight of Columbus], every white slaver, every brothel madam, every Roman controlled newspaper." In somewhat milder language, Vice President Calvin Coolidge's article "Whose Country is This?" repeated theories about racial decline accompanying intermarriage between Nordics and newer immigrants.[5]

When the USA declared war against Germany in 1917, nativists also raised the inevitable question. Would immigrants prove loyal? Nicola Sacco, the anarchist, remembering his creed of "No God, No Country" provided one answer by fleeing to Mexico. But many more foreign-born men and their sons volunteered in the American army, proving their commitment to the nation. Negro men also demanded and gained the right to serve. But scientific racists challenged even this evidence of loyalty with Army intelligence tests claiming to find immigrants and Negroes inferior to old-stock American recruits.

Newcomers also had their wartime defenders. Americanizers who called for "One Hundred Percent Americanism" generally did so with the expectation immigrants could transcend their unfitness. Americanizers such as the former settlement house worker Frances Kellor wrote not of immigrants' racial deficiencies but of an overstuffed melting pot. While she acknowledged that immigration restriction would hasten "melting," Kellor also wanted old-stock Americans to abandon their disdain for newcomers; the nation needed a domestic policy to incorporate immigrants – to teach them English and civic principles – as much as laws to exclude them.

And with Woodrow Wilson's wartime call for international self-determination, still other voices defending cultural diversity appeared. For the wartime writer and journalist Randolph Bourne, immigrants possessed a cosmopolitan familiarity with the wider world that all Americans would need as the USA rose to world leadership. Bourne argued that a culturally diverse, tolerant, and "transnational" nation could demonstrate at home that Wilson's internationalism could also guarantee peace worldwide.

Newcomers and natives under attack from scientific racists also mounted a vigorous defense of themselves during the war years. In 1913, Jewish Americans had formed the Anti-defamation League of B'nai B'rith. In 1915, NAACP supporters picketed the D. W. Griffith film *Birth of a Nation* for its vicious stereotypes of emancipated slaves as primitive rapists. Franz Boas critiqued the US Army's intelligence testing for measuring access to education, not intelligence. And, later, in the 1920s, immigrants in the Sons of Italy reminded Americans that the Roman Empire and the artists and scholars of the Italian Renaissance, not Anglo-Saxons, had created western civilization.

Nevertheless, in 1917, Congress finally passed a literacy requirement for immigrants over President Wilson's veto. The bill enjoyed widespread support. The literacy requirement was not a particularly strict one. It allowed immigrants to take a literacy test in their native language rather than requiring any knowledge of English. It even exempted illiterate wives if their husbands were literate. Groups not known for their support of scientific racism – both organizations of Negroes and of earlier immigrants – supported the bill – perhaps because they were tired of a century of job competition from newcomers.

A Bolshevik revolution in Russia in 1917 in turn raised new concerns about national security. Could immigrants' loyalty be trusted so long as vocal small groups of radical foreigners advocated the overthrow of capitalism or of representative democracy? By the time he returned to the USA, Nicola Sacco found the country gripped by a "red scare." The newspaper he read, Galleani's *Cronaca Souversiva*, had been banned as "the most dangerous newspaper published in the country" and Galleani himself had been deported, along with other radicals such as the Russian-born anarchist and naturalized citizen Emma Goldman. Federal agents had smashed the offices of the IWW and imprisoned leaders of the Socialist Party, including Eugene V. Debs.

Predictably, anarchists responded to such repression with violence. Unknown persons mailed a bomb to the home of Attorney General A. Mitchell Palmer (the man responsible for Galleani's deportation); others tossed a bomb into the Wall Street offices of the New York Stock Exchange. Back in Massachusetts, Sacco's closest comrades were in jail, suspected of manufacturing bombs. Sacco himself had applied for a passport to return to Italy before his arrest in 1920. With little evidence that either he or Bartolomeo Vanzetti had actually committed the murder they were charged with, their trial focused instead on their foreign origins and radical ideas. In 1927, the men whom their judge had dismissed as "anarchist bastards" were both executed.

Once the rapid postwar recovery of the US economy began, it quickly became apparent to nativists that the 1917 literacy requirement would not reduce immigration significantly. (See Figure I.1.) In response, Congress in 1921 finally gave scientific racists what they sought, in the form of an "emergency" quota act that imposed an overall restriction on immigrants from the eastern hemisphere (to somewhat more that 350,000 yearly), largely through racially discriminatory "quotas" on southern and eastern Europeans. In 1924 Congress made discriminatory immigration quotas permanent while leaving open their final definition. It also excluded almost all immigrants from Asia.

For another five years, researchers, including the first academic historian of American immigration, Marcus Lee Hansen, attempted a scientific analysis of the composition of the early white population of the USA to help Congressmen decide how to allot quotas. (Table 1.1 was based in part on their calculations.) Restrictive quotas came into full force in 1929 and then remained operative until 1965. Almost no Asians, and little more than 10,000 Poles and Italians combined, could enter the USA under the new provisions. Senator Albert Johnson, sponsor of the 1924 legislation, accurately summed up the significance of such restrictions. "The day of unalloyed welcome to all peoples, the day of indiscriminate acceptance of all races," he concluded, "has definitely ended."[6]

Yet oddly, visions of a culturally diverse America persisted even as scientific racism triumphed. During the 1920s, International Institutes replaced many settlement houses in northern and western cities and offered cultural programming to bring white newcomers and old-stock Americans together. Rejecting the language of scientific racism, they hosted "festivals of nations" and "nationality dinners" which presented newcomers' cuisine, dance, and music as sources of pleasure for their American neighbors. In 1927, university professor Horace Kallen, the son of a German rabbi and – like Zangwill – an active Zionist, expanded his wartime analysis of what he called cultural pluralism into a widely read book, *Culture and Democracy in the United States*. Kallen argued that a "federation" of immigrant nationalities made the USA a cultural as well as a political democracy; each immigrant nationality had a part in the American symphony, while fair laws and representative government kept the orchestra's many instruments in harmony. Much like Bourne, Kallen saw domestic cultural pluralism as an illustration of the harmony internationalists sought in the League of Nations, of which he was a strong supporter.

Despite these counter-currents, however, scientific racism had ultimately pushed the USA toward a form of ethnic nationalism in its public policy that differed significantly from its Latin American neighbors'. By the 1920s, Mexican nationalist José Vasconcelos celebrated the amalgamated "cosmic" race of his country, insisting it was "made up of the genius and the blood of all peoples and, for that reason, more capable of free brotherhood." Meanwhile, north of the Rio Grande, white Americans either insisted that democracy originated with Anglo-Saxons, imagined the amalgamation of many European nations into a "melting pot," white nation, or celebrated the persistence of cultural diversity among whites. And of these the most powerful voices influencing the country's policy toward immigrants remained those of men such as the Social Darwinist, nativist, and eugenicist Madison Grant who believed "The cross between white and Indian is an Indian. The cross between a white man and a Negro is a Negro; the cross between a white man and a Hindu is a Hindu; the cross between any of the three European races and a Jew is a Jew."[7] Scientific racism had triumphed, leaving unresolved Americans' longstanding conflicts over the civic and ethnic foundations of their nation.

The Empire Strikes Back, 1915–45

The USA was scarcely alone in restricting immigration in the 1920s. World Wars I and II, the rise of welfare states promising economic security to their citizens, and the great depression of the 1930s encouraged most industrial countries around the world to increase surveillance of their borders and of their resident populations in the twentieth century. Like most other nations in a century of war and international conflict, the USA increasingly imagined itself restricting immigration in order to promote national unity, national security, and economic prosperity.

While draconian, American immigration restriction was also surprisingly uneven. Congressmen representing southwestern agribusinessmen, along with senators concerned about repercussions on American diplomacy in the Americas, had succeeded in exempting the western hemisphere from significant restrictions. In addition, Congress allowed free entry of immigrants who were reunifying families; women and children took advantage of these provisions in considerable numbers, buoying immigration totals even for sharply restricted groups such as Italians and Poles.

Thus immigration restriction did not reduce all international migration. Ever more immigrants, including Arnulfo Caballero, now crossed international borders within the American hemisphere. Furthermore, the restriction of immigration did not effect the domestic liberty to move. Growing numbers of migrants left the rural south or Great Plains but remained within the USA. Still others came from offshore territories of the USA, such as the Philippines and Puerto Rico. The results of restriction could not have been pleasing to scientific racists. True, the total numbers of immigrants diminished (see Figure I.1) and as they declined, women and children made up half of the newcomers. But while immigration from southern Europe and Asia declined significantly, the representation of darker skinned peoples, many of them Catholic, and from the Caribbean, Philippines, and Mexico also grew among newcomers (see Table 6.1.)

Already during World War I, American industries had gone looking for workers to replace European immigrant workers. They found them in existing small migrations of Negro southerners toward West Virginia mines and toward Detroit, Pittsburgh, Chicago, and Philadelphia. Thus began the great migration of black southerners sparked largely by

Table 6.1 The impact of restriction on American immigration

Originating in	*Percent of total immigration between 1900 and 1910*	*Percent of total immigration between 1924 and 1946*
Northern and western Europe	21.7	43.1
Southern and eastern Europe	70.8	18.9
Canada	2.0	21.5
Mexico	0.6	11.5
Other	4.9	5.0

Source: Calculated from figures in Thomas J. Archdeacon, *Becoming American: An Ethnic History* (New York: The Free Press, 1983), p. 183.

word-of-mouth reports about jobs and by hopes that the industrial cities of the north offered an escape from Jim Crow laws and from southern white violence. That, at least, is what Henry Owens, a farmer in a small cotton town near Decatur, Alabama hoped for.

Like many frugal, hardworking sharecroppers, the illiterate Owens ended each agricultural year in debt. When he finally realized a substantial profit growing cotton during World War I, his employer demanded a new contract that would deliver Owens a smaller share in the following year. Over 40 years old, and concerned about the future of his children (who included the future Olympic sprinter Jesse), Owens followed neighbors to Cleveland.[8] As cotton prices fell, a million other Negro southerners also transferred north before 1940. Among them were the grandmothers and great-aunts of the Black feminist Barbara Smith; they found work as cooks and servants for Cleveland's wealthier white women.[9]

The northward migration of Negro southerners in the 1920s did nothing to satisfy the demands for agricultural labor in the southwest, however; Mexicans such as Ignacio Reveles migrated to take those jobs. Along the long industrialized northern border stretching from New England to Detroit and Minneapolis, English- and French-speaking Canadians also migrated in large numbers. And, in the east, immigrants from the British colonies of the Caribbean replaced immigrants from Europe. Some had initially worked for American companies in the Panama Canal Zone; others became migrant harvesters in Florida's orange fields or New England's apple orchards. Arnold Crawford had worked in Cuba before coming to the USA from Jamaica in 1924 at age 26. Like many Jamaicans, Crawford tried to escape New York's discriminatory job market by opening a small trucking business. He later found a better living in the furniture business and moved to Brooklyn from Harlem, where Jamaicans initially clustered.[10]

With the onset of a worldwide depression in the 1930s, President Roosevelt moved the new Immigration and Naturalization Service into the Department of Justice, confirming an important transition in the country's view of immigrants. Once perceived largely as laborers, they seemed a threat to national security in a world increasingly divided between fascists and communists. Consuls soon received orders to review visa applications from Mexicans and from Jewish refugees from Germany – neither subject to highly restrictive quotas – with special caution. Inspections at entry points also became more thorough, as the country sought to exclude those who might become "public charges" (by accepting charity). And, as fears of job competition from illegal immigrants again rose, border police patrolled even the boundaries with Canada and Mexico more rigorously. Increasingly, too, American employers refused to hire aliens and most New Deal, local, and state welfare programs limited public assistance strictly to citizens.

In Austria, the prosperous and well-educated Jewish convert to Protestantism, Frank Steiner, struggled to convince American officials he would not become a public charge or a dangerous radical. A cousin in the Bronx helped him to enter the USA in 1939. Steiner soon discovered he had more than 50 second and third cousins there – "an unexpected asset" in coping with Nazi terror, immigration bureaucracy, a depression, and American anti-semitism.[11] Not all immigrants had such assets, however. In the east, Italians voluntarily leaving the USA almost equaled the sharply reduced numbers of newcomers. Rates of naturalization also rose among impoverished Greek and Italian immigrants who had showed limited past interest in citizenship, and by 1940, over two-thirds of the foreign-born residents of the USA were again naturalized citizens. While Mexican government representatives and even Mexican–American organizations urged voluntary repatriation of immigrants from that country, the city of Los Angeles summarily deported unemployed Mexican workers along with their citizen children. Pressures on Mexicans and on 50,000 Filipinos to leave the west coast only intensified as California growers found several hundred thousand American citizens suddenly eager to replace them.

They drove, walked, and hitchhiked from the rural dustbelt of lower midwest states, such as Arkansas and Oklahoma, in the 1930s, looking for work as harvesters. Most of these California-bound migrants were old-stock Americans, many of them with roots in the rural south. Among them was the family of Walter Tatham, a self-described "tumbleweed" who had already moved a dozen times in his life. Tatham left Sallisaw, Oklahoma, in the flatbed truck belonging to his son Oca and Oca's pregnant wife Ruby. The truck also carried Walter's Cherokee wife, Cora, three teenage children, two grandchildren, Ruby's half-brother, and six neighbors sharing the cost of the gas. Cora Tatham had been known locally as a religiously inspired "prayer warrior" and her children shared her pentecostal faith. In 1934 the Tathams arrived in Kern County, California, eager to pick cotton or harvest oranges – work Mexicans had previously done.[12] Only the Tatham women picked potatoes, grapes, and oranges for long, however. Son Oca Tatham was soon fixing cars and trading in used goods.

As the USA became the industrial arsenal for democracy during World War II, migrant whites like the Tathams quickly moved from the California fields to west-coast war production jobs, while east-coast war plants and shipyards hired Negro southerners under federal contracts and guaranteed them equal wages and fair treatment for the first time. As many as nine million additional southerners – the majority of them white – also took to the roads during the war years. For the first time, too, significant numbers of American Indians left their reservations – for jobs as metalworkers in the construction trades and war industries. By 1950, 20 percent of Indians in the USA lived in cities. And the country that had pushed Mexicans out now called them back temporarily as braceros.

In the east, Spanish-speakers from the island of Puerto Rico – a territory of the USA since 1898 – also came looking for jobs. Among the Puerto Rican migrants was Maria Concepcion DeJesus. Born in rural Rio Piedras in 1914, she had married at 16 after a stint in an urban tobacco mill. DeJesus's sister Rosa had left in 1940; in 1943 Concepcion joined her sister in New York, hoping to escape her deteriorating marriage. Leaving her three children with their father, she took a job in New York's garment industry, then sent for the children, who flew into the USA.[13] Although not technically immigrants, Puerto Ricans like DeJesus would share the experiences of earlier unskilled Catholic newcomers with limited facility in the English language.

Because immigration declined after 1914, large numbers of Negro and white southerners and much smaller numbers of American Indians had quickly replaced foreigners as workers in both the northeast and southwest. More immigrants than in the past now also came from the racially mixed areas of Mexico, the Caribbean, and Latin America that scientific racists viewed as destined to subordination to the USA. Far more than in the past, the mobile newcomers were already familiar with the USA and with its racial prejudices before they moved. Both the new migrations and the new immigrations of the interwar years thus helped to fulfill W. E. B. DuBois's early prediction that the twentieth century would become the "century of the color line."[14]

Contact across the Color Line

Awareness of color shaped almost all new cross-cultural encounters from World War I through World War II. When they left the south for the north during these years, American Negroes – unlike many foreign-born migrants from Mexico or Jamaica – expected to find the equality promised by American civic nationalism. Yet the Americans they met in American cities were often earlier immigrants and their children, not the old-stock white Americans they had known in the south; few of these natives of American cities had found easy economic or social acceptance, and the triumph of scientific racism in the form of immigration restriction left many feeling themselves like outsiders to the American nation. But while predictably violent in some ways, relations between the newest newcomers and the natives of recent immigrant origins also produced new forms of cooperation.

Certainly Negro newcomers to cities and urban natives with origins in Europe had every reason to approach their meetings with trepidation. Native blacks and newly arrived immigrants had been competing for urban jobs at least since the 1830s. Each new immigrant group from Europe had with time learned the privileges of whiteness by winning that competition. For their part, many American and Protestant Negroes had adopted nativist arguments against immigrants as wage depressors, as foreign Catholics or Jews, and as dangerous radicals. Culturally homogeneous clusters of immigrants had also long been a prominent feature of northern urban life but their understanding of racial segregation was fundamentally different from that of black southerners. No Jim Crow laws created immigrant neighborhoods; at most wealthier homebuyers had signed real estate covenants, promising not to sell to a few upwardly mobile Jews or Italians seeking to leave low-income areas. For the majority of immigrant renters and home-owners, residential segregation was a choice, and competition for symbolic control of local streets or playgrounds a source of occasional violence at most. White immigrants in American cities had every reason to expect that Negro newcomers would want to live among "their own kind" while newcomers from the south dreamed of integration as a reward for their move northward.

As a result, the sites of urban violence shifted dramatically with the great migration of Negro southerners. Tensions between natives and Negro newcomers were apparent already during World War I as dark-skinned renters looked for ing where white immigrants and their children already Race riots resulted in the deaths and injuries of scor Negro newcomers in East St. Louis, Tulsa, and Chicago in 1919. The Chicago riot began not in the meatpacking plants, as a competition over jobs, but with the stoning death of a Negro boy swimming off a beach claimed by white swimmers for themselves. Again in 1943, a Detroit race riot began when whites barred black teenagers from a local amusement park. Throughout these years, the Catholic Church that had provided moral guidance for so many urban immigrants from Europe wrestled with the consequences of its toleration of nationality parishes. Would parishes, and their Catholic neighborhoods, reject the few black Catholics among the migrants? Increasingly, Catholic liberals called for the integration of parish neighborhoods; parishioners instead sought to protect their parishes as segregated neighborhoods for "their own kind." Competition for housing and recreational space seemed about to eclipse competition for jobs as the main source of inter-racial urban violence.

While racial tensions scarcely disappeared from American workplaces during these years, they often took surprising turns. In California in 1936 and 1937, for example, Filipinos, Mexicans, and other foreign-born strikers were the attackers and white migrants from Oklahoma and Arkansas were the scabs under attack. In the ILGWU, in New York, however, older immigrants proud of their separate locals soon learned that Negro co-workers viewed segregation within Jewish or Italian locals as a northern version of Jim Crow and believed ethnic locals functioned mainly to exclude them.

In the 1930s the new Congress of Industrial Organizations (CIO), with its industrial unions in steel, meatpacking, and autos, nevertheless provided an important new site of cross-racial cooperation. Departing sharply from AF of L traditions, and with slogans such as "Negro and White – Unite and Fight," the CIO seemed determined to become a multi-racial, multi-ethnic, and yet also thoroughly patriotic and American bastion of collective bargaining. If immigrants such as Nicola

Sacco had been punished for their radicalism, their children could at least embrace a working-class Americanism in the CIO. The CIO openly embraced a role in the American political mainstream as an active partner in the Democratic Party's New Deal political coalition. And it openly embraced Negro members, along with white industrial workers from a wide variety of backgrounds.

While union seniority rules frustrated the initial advances of Negro workers into wartime industrial jobs, unions of the CIO, such as the United Auto Workers (UAW), continued to emphasize cross-racial solidarity and fair employment practices into the postwar era. Negro membership in the CIO grew, and articulate and popular Negro labor leaders of multi-racial unions emerged. In fact, CIO unions initially enjoyed greater success in organizing Negro and Mexican than white rural southerners. In California, men such as Oca Tatham shared the anti-radical and nativist views of many Anglo employers that "Communist Generalissimos" ran CIO cannery and agricultural workers' unions. A federal official working with southerners noted that "Our campers .. shy away from the idea" of joining unions.[15] UAW officials in Detroit during World War II also distinguished good Negro activists from hostile, individualistic white southerners. Only in the 1950s did significant numbers of white southerners embrace union activism in the north.

Like unions, urban political machines also still functioned as meeting places for natives and newcomers, especially in eastern cities. For earlier immigrants, urban machines remained an important expression of opposition to prohibition in the 1920s and a way to support urban, "wet," and sometimes Catholic candidates for national office, such as Al Smith in 1928. Unlike earlier immigrants, Negro newcomers to the city needed no help with naturalization but they nevertheless learned the art of ward heeling quickly. Negro voters had elected their first representatives in Chicago already before World War I; they became municipal employees in large numbers after World War II. Many of New York's first Negro machine politicians were West Indians, but southern Negroes soon joined them.

Mayors of culturally diverse cities also still mediated group conflicts by distributing city services, public housing, and jobs. For example, New York's Mayor Fiorello LaGuardia shifted resources toward Harlem as Negro newcomers boycotted and picketed Italian- and Jewish-owned stores that – preferring to employ "their own kind" – refused to employ Negro newcomers in the 1930s. "Don't buy where you can't work" the protestors' signs read. In response, Italian renters protested their own limited access to new public housing projects designed for lower-income Puerto Ricans and Negroes. The construction of large public housing complexes further reduced the supply of available housing for communities in transition from first- to second-generation majorities, encouraging many Catholic families otherwise committed to remaining within their neighborhood nationality parishes to look for housing elsewhere.

With the rise of federal activism during Franklin Roosevelt's depression-era New Deal, both urban machines and social settlement houses also lost some of their importance as sites of peaceful interaction between natives and newcomers. City welfare departments using bureaucratic procedures increasingly replaced old-stock American women reformers such as Jane Addams with largely female case workers, charged with investigating their clients to determine whether they qualified for support. In Leonard Covello's East Harlem, settlement houses working with Negroes often discovered that European immigrants boycotted their programs. By contrast, in the southwest, new settlement houses emerged to work with Mexicans who, as immigrants, seemed more like the Europeans of an earlier era. But when the Tathams in California ran out of food, they obtained it from a New Deal or a California state relief worker, not from a ward-heeler or social settlement house.

With the migration of so many Protestant southerners, the Catholic Church also lost considerable importance as a site of intercultural contact. To the dismay of many of its immigrant faithful, it increasingly resisted the formation of new nationality parishes and instead insisted on racial and ethnic integration everywhere from the neighborhood parish school through the priesthood. There would be no new Negro, Mexican, or Puerto Rican parishes created for the newest immigrants after World War II. Nevertheless the prominent physical presence of the Catholic Church in urban residential neighborhoods in the northeast actually allowed it to attract Negro converts among this overwhelmingly Protestant great migration. Much like the Puerto Rican migrant Maria Concepcion DeJesus – who struggled as a poorly paid garment worker to give her children a Catholic education – ever more Protestant Negro newcomers believed Catholic schools provided the best education for their children.

By the onset of World War II, older immigrants from Europe and black newcomers appeared to have established an uneasy urban truce. The most violent and systematic expressions of racial prejudice during the sizeable wartime migrations did not result from encounters of older immigrants and Negro newcomers over housing or jobs. Instead violence erupted as soldiers or policemen battled Negro or Mexican civilians or when the US government itself treated its Asian subjects and citizens as a threat to national security. Los Angeles had its wartime riot in 1943. There, angry white soldiers and sailors enjoying leave in the town began harassing and then attacking elegantly clad "zoot-suit" Mexican teenagers on the pretext that they belonged to gangs. In New York later the same year, rioting and looting broke out in Harlem after a white policeman shot a black soldier.

The continued influence of scientific racism on government policy was still painfully obvious at the onset of World War II. Americans refused to trust the loyalty of immigrants from Japan as they did immigrants from Germany or Italy. After Pearl Harbor, FBI agents on the west coast interned leaders of all Japanese organizations as possible spies. And in early 1942 Executive Order No. 9066 required all persons of Japanese descent – whether aliens barred from citizenship or their citizen children – to leave the west coast for relocation camps farther inland.

The family of Kazuko Itoi, for example, was ordered to a

fairground assembly center, and then sent to Minidoka camp in southern Idaho. Itoi's brother Henry married his Seattle sweetheart while in camp. Meanwhile debates raged among his fellow citizens over whether or not to serve in the American army (eventually, some 23,000 served). Most *nisei* (immigrant) and *issei* (second-generation) Japanese sent to American "concentration camps" lost all their west-coast property. Released before war's end, Kazuko Itoi understandably did not want to return to Seattle. She settled in Chicago and then Indiana, while her brother Henry moved to St. Louis.

Surprisingly, the interactions of natives and newcomers had changed relatively little as native migrants became the "newcomers" in cities and older immigrants and their children the "natives." But after years of scientific racists raging about the threat of the alien "races of Europe," the migrations that followed immigration restriction again focused Americans' attention on cross-cultural exchange between persons of differing skin color. The result was a new round of group formation and the development of new critiques of scientific racism.

Cultural Diversity and Identity

Home, family, neighborhood, and church ties continued to be the most important sources of individual identity among the migrants of the interwar years. But like immigrants faced with the rising tide of scientific racism in the late nineteenth century, newcomers' identities also evolved as they became aware of how urban immigrants and old-stock northern whites defined them. To a considerable degree, cultural difference remained salient among blacks and whites even in an otherwise color-conscious era.

For the Tathams in California, family ties continued to link them to a home culture in the Protestant and religiously enthusiastic rural dustbowl of the midwest; Walter Tatham returned temporarily to Oklahoma, and his children and grandchildren visited relatives there occasionally. Moving frequently with the harvests, native white migrants like the Tathams did not form self-segregated communities in California. (In Detroit and Chicago observers did sometimes detect neighborhood clusters.) But their southern and rural roots nevertheless distinguished them from other westerners of European origin. In the 1930s, native whites called people such as the Tathams Okies or Arkies; in the 1940s, the children of immigrant parents in northern cities called their counterparts from Tennessee and Kentucky hillbillies. For their part, the Tathams referred to their Croatian immigrant neighbors in California as "sons of Vitches" (since many had names such as Radovic or Zaninovic).

The Tathams themselves drew their strongest sense of cultural identity from their rural religious practices. Baptist and Methodist churches abounded in the northern cities and in California, but rarely did they offer the type of worship or fellowship – complete with Wednesday-night suppers and enthusiastic worship services – that rural or southern Protestants preferred. Cleo Tatham, Oca's sister, found that even the local Assembly of God church her family initially attended in California was a "high polished" place where the pastor and Swedish- and German-American parishioners corrected her speaking in tongues as "out of order." Old-stock American supervisors of New Deal migrant camps were less gentle, referring to such practices as "crude negroisms," or as "chattering, jabbering and stuttering."[16] Already in 1936, Oca Tatham was building a church with other migrants in McFarland, California. "Did we need the church in the Depression?" he reflected. "You bet we did. We couldn't turn to our landlords . . . We didn't have everything, but we had peace and joy."[17]

For southern Negro newcomers to northern cities, too, a sense of cultural identity began at home, in their neighborhoods, and in their churches. Barbara Smith recalled that for her migrant aunts and grandmother in Cleveland, "Home meant Georgia," a place Smith had never visited. "One of the last to leave, my grandmother never considered Cleveland anything but a stopping place," yet "their loyalty to their origins . . . provided us with an essentially Southern upbringing, rooting us solidly in the past and at the same time preparing us to face the unknowable future."[18]

Family practices also marked northern and southern Negroes and black Jamaican immigrants as culturally distinctive. Northern Negroes and Jamaicans alike wrung their hands over the relaxed sexuality, drinking, street life, and broken marriages of the poorest southern migrants, while southern newcomers in turn made fun of northern and Jamaican families as Puritanical, Black Yankees, or even Black Jews. Such labels – applied by southerners to West Indian small businessmen such as Arnold Crawford – suggested praise and envy as well as resentment.

As this suggests, religion provided the clearest marker of cultural difference among mobile blacks. Storefront Holiness and Pentecostalist churches identified worshipers as southerners who demonstrated little interest in joining the native northern Negro churches they found stiff and cold. Immigrant Jamaicans' membership in Anglican or Presbyterian churches made them appear even more formal, status-conscious, or even culturally "white" to black southerners. Native northerners and Jamaicans alike complained about the shouting of southern preachers and the enthusiastic gospel singing of southern worshipers.

In American cities of the 1930s, a new religious group also offered Negroes the option of uniting religiously on a racial basis, ignoring their cultural differences. During the Great Depression, a southern migrant to Chicago, Elijah Mohammed, responding to a mysterious messenger from abroad, rejected Christianity, claiming it was the creation of white devils. Mohammed's new faith, called the Nation of Islam (NOI), differed dramatically from the multi-racial Islam faith but rapidly gained converts among the urban poor of the north. Among them was the young prisoner Malcolm Little (later Malcolm X), the son of a West Indian mother and black American father, who had migrated from the rural midwest to Boston, and into a life of crime, in the 1940s. NOI supporters argued that white racism had frustrated migrants' hopes for economic success and equality in the northern promised land. Elijah Mohammed's religious form of Black nationalism did not require a return to Africa, however; it promoted economic self-sufficiency and self-segregation to guarantee that Blacks would control their own ghetto communities.

In a nation increasingly focused on the color line separating whites from blacks, the European races that had been the focus of so many nineteenth-century scientific racists occupied an anomalous position. Beginning already in the 1920s, sociologists at the University of Chicago provided evidence that immigrants from Europe were assimilating and losing their distinctive cultural identities, which they termed "ethnic." Louis Wirth, author of *The Ghetto*, along with Robert E. Park and William I. Thomas (author, together with Florian Znaniecki, of *The Polish Peasant in Europe and America*) mainly studied immigrants from southern and eastern Europe while hinting at the future assimilation of rural Negroes to urban modernity. By the 1930s, sociologists described Jews, Catholics, and Protestants forming triple marital melting pots – a theory that featured religion as the most enduring form of cultural diversity.

Among newcomers, too, some groups seemed neither white nor black in American racial schema. Their Spanish language and Catholicism made even very dark Puerto Ricans and Mexicans seem so culturally distinctive that most white Americans could not think of them as black. By 1940, New Yorkers distinguished between a Negro ghetto in Harlem and an emerging East or Spanish Harlem, where Puerto Ricans were rapidly replacing Italians as renters. Puerto Ricans concurred in differentiating themselves and their neighborhoods from Americans , black or white, but they showed little aversion to living close to or among Negroes, since Puerto Ricans – like most racially mixed peoples from the Caribbean – were of many skin colors.

On the west coast, World War II also encouraged white Americans to abandon undifferentiated racial hostility against Orientals to distinguish instead among Chinese, Koreans, and Japanese as separate peoples. Koreans had initially fled to the USA as Japan invaded their homeland; Dora Kim, a Korean-American growing up in San Francisco's Chinatown remembered her parents "told stories about how the Japanese kidnapped and killed the beautiful Korean girls."[19] Chinese-Americans were horrified by the Japanese invasion of China in the 1930s, and Kim remembered some Japanese friends trying to "pass" as Chinese as a result. During the war years, American newspapers also "explained" to white San Franciscans how to distinguish physically between Chinese- and Japanese-Americans. In 1943, Congress even created a small immigrant quota for its new wartime ally, China, and it allowed Chinese immigrants in the USA to naturalize and acquire citizenship for the first time.

Voluntary Associations' Campaign Against Scientific Racism

In the interwar years, new voluntary associations organized by the newcomers reinforced the ties of family, neighborhood, and religion much as they had among earlier immigrant groups. They preserved cultural identities among whites, blacks, and recent immigrants from Latin America, Europe, and Asia. Increasingly, however, racial identities based on color bridged cultural differences among newcomers and became the foundation for voluntary association, making cultural difference a phenomenon more often of the domestic or private world. Rather than simply reflect the color line, furthermore, ever more voluntary associations also actively committed themselves to the campaign against scientific racism.

White migrants like the Tathams rarely formed any voluntary associations other than their churches. Although he had a Cherokee mother, Oca Tatham's racial identity as a white extended back to the voluntary citizenship of the early republic, as even immigrants in California seemed to recognize. Thus, when the Tathams and other white migrants worked briefly on the Sierra Vista Ranch, Giuseppe DiGiorgio – a Sicilian immigrant and one of the largest produce-growers in California – treated them as just another "racial group" and he built not a "white" but an "American" camp for them, much as he had provided separate housing and dining facilities for

"Japs," Filipinos, Portuguese, and Mexicans.[20] Migratory white natives disappeared quickly into culturally diverse southern California towns, where they generally lived apart from Mexicans but might have recent immigrants from Europe as neighbors. Even as poor migrants, the Tathams seemed uninterested in their own color; they understood themselves to be Americans, with no need of hyphens, modifiers, or racial identity.

While voluntary associations for the children of immigrants from Europe rarely promoted culture-bridging and white identities, only Jewish organizations regularly assailed immigration restriction as racially discriminatory, continuing their long campaign against scientific racism. With time, European immigrants' voluntary associations instead collapsed or changed with the rising numerical dominance of the second generation. Government programs put many of the earlier immigrant associations out of business as providers of insurance, funerals, or occasional charity. Foreign-language newspapers also now had to print bilingual or even all-English editions. Few second-generation Italians and Poles organized clubs along ethnic lines and when they did so they typically focused on recreation, sports programs, or language instruction, not the preservation of cultural differences or the promotion of whiteness.

The second generation remained interested in homeland problems, however. Many gave support to democratic causes in their parents' birthplace. The second generation provided important support for Irish and Chinese Republican causes before and during World War I, and to the newly independent Polish republic, to Zionist initiatives for a Jewish homeland in Palestine, and to Mussolini's Italy after the war. Such initiatives reflected, in part, a new way to preserve ethnic distinctiveness in the USA while simultaneously embracing Americans' national sense of mission to spread democracy beyond their own borders.

Forming in the 1920s and 1930s, Mexicans' voluntary associations emphasized cultural distinctiveness but chose names such as the "Sons of America" that emphasized the amalgamation of many peoples in the western hemisphere. The most successful Mexican society, founded in 1929, was the League of United Latin American Citizens (LULAC), which focused on teaching English and encouraging American citizenship. LULAC also took up the fight against racial discrimination, much as did the NAACP. Similarly, while Japanese, Korean, and Chinese American voluntary associations remained separate, rejecting racial identities as Orientals, their associations nevertheless focused ever-greater attention on discriminatory practices.

Less hostile to racial identities but equally concerned with discrimination were American Indians. Indians had become citizens by decree in 1924; in 1934 the Wheeler–Howard Indian Reorganization Act reversed federal policies that encouraged the parceling of reservations into privately owned plots, and allowed some tribes such as the Menominee to revive sovereignty, communal ownership of lands, and tribal governance and identities. Throughout the interwar years, the Native American Church and various peyote religious revivals on the southern plains encouraged an explicitly Native and pan-tribal identity. At the same time, secular organizations such as the National Council of American Indians continued to focus on ending racial discrimination against Indian citizens.

The growing importance of organizing in pursuit of the full rights of citizenship was particularly obvious among those of African descent. True, natives and newcomers also formed voluntary associations that reinforced their cultural differences. State associations for migrants from Georgia or Alabama "did what had to be done" to provide sociability, mutual aid, and economic support for the poor. Jamaican and Barbadian newcomers organized rotating credit associations that provided small cash payments useful for buying a house or opening a business, or supported scholarship competitions for the education of promising students. But these cultural differences usually did not prevent the two groups of migrants from recognizing the shared discrimination they faced as a result of their dark skins.

Already in the 1920s, the large and diverse population of Negroes in northern urban ghettoes supported a flowering of self-consciously Black cultural creativity, much as it had for Yiddish-speaking Jews on the Lower East Side in 1900. Life in the bi-racial American south, with its distinctive history of interracial violence, and in the Black-dominated colonies of the British Empire had already produced high levels of race consciousness among southern and West Indian migrants. In the north, the writers, performers, and cultural entrepreneurs of the Harlem Renaissance – Claude McKay, Zora Neale Hurston, Jean Toomer, and Langston Hughes – helped to form a distinctive Black literary culture rooted in Africa, in the experiences of slavery, in discrimination throughout an African diaspora, and in Negroes' common struggle against racial discrimination. Musical and written interpretations of life and human experience on the black side of the American color line also drew increasing numbers of white readers and listeners.

Through the interwar years, New Negroes nevertheless divided into competing voluntary associations with different visions of the future; while some groups promoted Black nationalism, others still sought integration into a color-blind, American, and civic nation. Influenced by campaigns against British imperialism worldwide, West Indians such as Arnold Crawford easily thought of American Negroes as part of an African diaspora or a Pan-African world. In New York, Crawford joined the United Negro Improvement Association (UNIA) founded by Black nationalist and fellow Jamaican immigrant, Marcus Garvey. Promoting Black economic independence, Garvey encouraged Negroes to purchase shares in his Black Star shipping company, and called for a return to Africa, where Negro Americans could more effectively "civilize and Christianize" the continent than white imperialists had been able to do.

Garvey dismissed as careerists the American New Negroes who sought a color-blind America or integration through urban political machines. Of the editors of the prominent Negro newspaper, *The Chicago Defender*, Garvey insisted, "The primary motive of newspaper promoters was to make quick and easy money, even publish the gravest falsehoods, the worst crime and libel against the race, if it pays in circulation and advertisement." NAACP official Robert W. Bagnall thought much the same of Garvey, describing him as "A Jamaican of unmixed stock, squat, stocky, fat and sleek . . . Boastful, egotistic, tyrannical, shifty, adept as a cuttle fish in beclouding an issue . . . A sheer opportunistic and demogogic charlatan." Still, Crawford – along with many migrants from the American south – admired Garvey's idealism and the pride he obviously took in both his origins and skin color. Like many an alien radical before him, however, Garvey landed in prison and was deported.[21]

For the Negro leaders of the NAACP, Urban League, and other groups founded during the rising tide of scientific racism at the turn of the century, events of the interwar years merely strengthened their demands for racial equality at home. The militarism, anti-semitism, and authoritarianism of German Nazis and Japanese and Italian fascists were so obviously twentieth-century expressions of scientific racism that even white southerners and supporters of Jim Crow sometimes paused to reflect on the discriminatory public policies of the USA. As Roy Wilkins of the NAACP trenchantly observed, "You can't be against park benches marked 'Jude' in Berlin and be for benches marked 'Colored' in Jacksonville."[22]

During the 1930s and 1940s, the NAACP persisted in its calls for a color-blind civic America. As the federal government tackled the problems of the depression, civil rights activist Ralph Bunch and labor leader A. Philip Randolph pressured the Democratic Party to guarantee Negroes a New Deal, too, gaining an outspoken advocate in First Lady Eleanor Roosevelt. Threatening to march on Washington, Negro labor leader and sleeping-car porter A. Philip Randolph requested, and obtained, a presidential promise of equal employment opportunities in wartime industries.

By the onset of World War II, then, toleration of cultural diversity and criticisms of scientific racism had expanded even if discriminatory policies remained the rule in domestic and immigration law. W. E. B. DuBois had surprised his colleagues in the NAACP in the 1930s by embracing cultural pluralism and socialism and by urging Negro consumers and producers to create "an economic nation within a nation." In wartime San Francisco, the teenaged Dora Kim proudly marched in a contingent of Koreans in a parade of American patriots. Wartime advocates of cultural diversity – who portrayed the USA as Yugoslav immigrant Louis Adamic did in 1944 as a "nation of nations" that included Negro Americans – also demanded the end of racial discrimination.[23] But in the wildly popular Hollywood combat movies of the era, army buddy heroes bonding during combat usually included only Catholic and Jewish city boys fighting alongside rural but exclusively white southerners and midwesterners, not American Negroes. At war's end Americans still had to confront what Swedish author Gunnar Myrdal in 1944 termed the American dilemma of race.

Further Reading

Elliott Robert Barkan, *And Still They Come: Immigrants and American Society, 1920 to the 1990s* (Wheeling: Harlan Davidson, 1996).

Lizabeth Cohen, *Making a New Deal: Industrial Workers in Chicago, 1919–1939* (New York: Cambridge University Press, 1990).

Hasia Diner, *In the Almost Promised Land: American Jews and Blacks, 1915–1935* (Baltimore: Johns Hopkins University Press, 1977).

Gary Gerstle, *Working-class Americanism: The Politics of Labor in a Textile City, 1914–1960* (New York: Cambridge University Press, 1989).

James N. Gregory, *American Exodus: The Dust Bowl Migration and Okie Culture in California* (New York: Oxford University Press, 1989).

David Gutierrez, *Walls and Mirrors: Mexican Americans, Mexican Immigrants, and the Politics of Ethnicity* (Berkeley: University of California Press, 1995).

John T. McGreevy, *Parish Boundaries: The Catholic Encounter with Race in the Twentieth-century Urban North* (Chicago: University of Chicago Press, 1996).

Carole Marks, *Farewell, We're Good and Gone: The Great Black Migration* (Bloomington: Indiana University Press, 1989).

Clara Rodriguez, *Puerto Ricans: Born in the U.S.A.* (Boulder: Westview Press, 1991).

Irma Watkins-Owens, *Blood Relations: Caribbean Immigrants and the Harlem Community, 1900–1930* (Bloomington: Indiana University Press, 1996).

7

The Postwar USA: Nation of Immigrants or Multicultural Nation?

By 1980, Dora Yum Kim may have been the most prominent woman in San Francisco's Korean-American community. But very little in her early life had pointed in that direction. Although her father had encouraged her to be proud of her Korean origins, Kim as a young woman had been concerned mainly with doing well in high school, finding a Korean-American husband, and holding onto her job while raising children.[1]

Born in 1921, Dora Yum lived for over 30 years in San Francisco's Chinatown. She remembered, "I grew up with discrimination . . . I just took it for granted and did what I could . . . I never thought of Chinatown as a ghetto. We just couldn't live anywhere else."[2] Her parents helped her continue her education even after her marriage to a Korean-American man from Hawaii, Tom Kim, who was a ship's officer and marine engineer. And her mother, in particular, told her to work. In 1953, after false starts as a nurse and clerk-typist and disappointments with employers refusing to hire Oriental women, Kim began a job with the California Department of Employment counseling job seekers.

After her parents' death, and along with their five children, Dora and Tom Kim left Chinatown in 1958. Through her job in the employment office, Kim hired a young American Indian woman as baby-sitter and applied for a supervisory position at work. When she failed to receive her promotion, she filed a written complaint and was surprised when the "head of the California State Employees Association, who happened to be a black guy, came over to me and said, 'Since your name is down as being the one who protested it, you will never get promoted.'" Asian-Americans became supervisors only after Kim retired.[3]

By 1970, Kim's children were leaving home. Since she still spoke Korean, Kim began counseling new immigrants, many of them well-educated professionals, and the experience reawakened her interest in her ethnicity. "It was really my son's influence," she admitted. "My son Tommy was really active in the Asian American movement at San Francisco State."[4] Many of these young activists regarded themselves as radicals, and critics of the USA, and they were harshly critical of the racial discrimination Kim had accepted without questioning. In 1975, after teaching English to newcomers at San Francisco's International Institute, Kim, along with her son, opened a storefront office, the Korean Community Service Center, the first Korean organization of its kind, funded by the Vanguard Foundation and the mayor's Community Development Fund. As a volunteer worker, Dora Kim developed hot meal and recreational programs for elderly Korean-Americans.

Kim remembered one of the young activists at the center in the 1970s telling her, "'You have to tell the Koreans how bad the United States is.' I said 'Are you kidding? The Koreans came to America to escape communism. And you're going to tell them that America is bad?'" But mainly she remembered the constant struggle for funding for the center as the federal activism of the 1960s and 1970s gave way to the fiscal conservatism of the 1980s. Still, when she celebrated her "hwan'gap" festival on her 65th birthday in 1986, Dora Kim felt moved by her community's expression of gratitude.

The America in which Dora Yum Kim became an ethnic activist clearly differed from the America her parents had known. During her lifetime, opponents of scientific racism finally succeeded in eliminating racial discrimination from American law, including immigration policy, allowing more

Koreans to enter the USA as immigrants. Once unthinkable, a woman now led a Korean ethnic organization, and the American government even supported its activities. As a second-generation immigrant, a woman and a member of a racial minority, Dora Kim's options had expanded in the second half of the century. Kim along with many Americans now wanted a nation without racial prejudice. But they still disagreed about what kind of nation the USA should become.

Migrants and Immigrants in Cold War America

By 1945 the global economy that encouraged the mass international migrations of the nineteenth century had been demolished by a worldwide depression and two world wars. After 1945, Europe's empires shattered into dozens of new nations in Africa and Asia while a worldwide "cold war" between the USA and the USSR limited prospects for a new era of economic globalization. Never before had the power of nations to limit and to shape human mobility seemed so great.

The borders around the USA remained firmly guarded, and harsh restrictions, including discriminatory immigration quotas, firmly in place. During World War II, the US Congress had proved itself willing at most to loosen a few restrictions in the interests of foreign policy. It had, for example, created the bracero program and introduced a quota for Chinese immigrants but it had also approved deportation, without hearing, for any alien believed to belong to organizations advocating the overthrow of government. At war's end millions driven by fascism, military conflict, and communism from their homelands in Europe and in Asia, had found refuge in American military zones. Thousands of American servicemen had married and wanted to return home with Japanese and European wives. Rather than revise existing law, Congress merely passed new acts to admit carefully limited numbers of "Displaced Persons" and "war brides."

The Cold War created further pressures on Congress to act, however. Racially restrictive quotas, like the country's segregated military, were an obvious embarrassment to a country that had advocated the four freedoms in its campaigns against Nazi Germany. Scholars such as Franz Boas had collectively declared scientific racism a myth in 1940. Seeking re-election, Truman ordered the integration of the American Army in 1948. Competing with the USSR for global influence, both he and Republican President Dwight Eisenhower wanted Congress to eliminate discriminatory immigration quotas. But Congress continued to privilege national security over presidents' demands and over employers' calls for more laborers.

Passed in 1952, the McCarran–Walter Act created tiny Asian quotas and left discriminatory European quotas intact. The American hemisphere remained exempt from quotas but migrants from the Americas still faced intense border scrutiny. The 1952 act prohibited entry to suspected communists, and gave priority as immigrants to professional and highly skilled workers. To mollify critics, the law also gave high visa priority to relatives of naturalized citizens and it allotted additional visas to refugees fleeing communism. President Eisenhower also acted to allow additional refugees fleeing from communist revolts in Hungary and Cuba to enter the USA in 1954 and 1959.

Immigration thus remained restricted while the demand for labor escalated with a booming economy, encouraging the migrations of southerners from within and outside the USA. New arrivals from Puerto Rico soon made up almost 5 percent of the population of New York City. And even larger migrations continued out of the American south. Between 1940 and 1960 16 million white and 4 million Negro farmers headed for northern and western centers of first war production and then postwar industrial development. White southerners from the mountain regions of Appalachia and from declining mining towns of the upper south and Piedmont traveled highway 75 to Ohio and Michigan industries. Negro southerners moved north on the east coast or west to Los Angeles, San Francisco, and Seattle. Some were poor men much like Henry Owens. Others were women like Ruby Lee Daniels who arrived in

Chicago in 1946 from Clarksdale, Mississippi, where she had worked in the fields, as a WPA laborer, and as a cook in a white household. Daniels's first marriage had gone sour, and a new but married lover seemed unlikely to provide much support for the son they had together. And southern landowners' introduction of a new mechanical cotton picker had eliminated her chances even to work as a seasonal harvester.[5] Ruby Daniels went to Chicago expecting to find work there. With a strong postwar economy, new workers also arrived from abroad. Over half of immigrants arriving between 1951 and 1965 still came from Europe and over 6 percent from both the Caribbean and from Asia and the Middle East. Among immigrants from the Americas, Mexicans remained the largest group. So badly was their labor needed that the USA again negotiated with Mexico during the Korean War to recruit braceros for temporary work.

First examined and selected in Chihuahua, 300 miles from home, José Reveles followed in his father's footsteps and sought work in the USA. As a bracero, he first traveled with hundreds of other young men to the Texas border, where American agents waiting in an El Paso stadium selected Reveles to go to Carlsbad, New Mexico. There he worked as a harvester for an American cotton-grower. When his work contract expired he returned to Mexico to marry and become a father. Unhappy with work in Durango, Reveles went again to Guadalajara and then to Chihuahua to gain a three-month bracero contract harvesting cotton and grapes in California. This time he returned to Guadalajara in a cattle car, with only meager savings.

With visas hard to get, many Mexican men crossed into the USA without visas; border patrol agents called them wetbacks. But Reveles was lucky to obtain a green card and he relocated his family to El Paso, where he worked for a roofing company. There, a US Border Patrol agent stopped him on the street one day in 1954 and – unimpressed by Reveles's "green card" (which he shredded) deported him to the border town of Juarez. Reveles's wife and two children in El Paso had no idea where he was. But his green card was, in fact, legitimate and after obtaining a replacement, Reveles returned yet again.

In the early 1960s, hearing of better work opportunities, the Reveles family relocated to Colusa, California, where José's father had worked 40 years earlier.[6] Only in 1962 did the USA decide to terminate the bracero program that had introduced so many young Mexican men such as Reveles to work opportunities north of the border.

While important, work was not the only motive driving immigration in the postwar era. Women and children continued to enter the USA from Europe and Asia to unify families. The numbers of refugees also climbed. Between 1959 and 1961, 100,000 political refugees fled Castro's revolution in Cuba. Many were business and political leaders in the reactionary American-supported regime of Cuban dictator, Fulgencio Batista. Growing up in a wealthy family, Sylvia Gonzalez later admitted, "I didn't know that there was poverty in Cuba." Describing herself as a debutante, she was initially attracted to Castro's revolution, but soon followed her family to Miami.[7] Among the refugees were also a smaller number of humble workers. Miguel Taboada, for example, had been chauffeur to Batista. He traveled farther, to settle in Los Angeles, where he worked as a taxi driver.

Escaping Jim Crow also remained important to American Negroes, but the ones who followed Ruby Daniels to Chicago in the 1950s and 1960s entered cities that were beginning to lose the industrial jobs that had made them magnets for migrants for over a century. American industry itself was relocating– to the suburbs, to the south, and to the southwest. Responding to American reformers – who had long advocated the dispersal of urban industry and workers – much government-funded New Deal public works and wartime and cold war defense industry had been constructed outside the urban northeast. Ironically, manufacturing plants (for example in the textile industry) moved to the same southern states migrants abandoned. Once again (see p. 138) businessman investors and migrants seemed to cross paths as they traveled in opposite directions.

Furthermore, while Ruby Daniels and other black southerners poured into northern cities, postwar prosperity allowed million of long-time urban dwellers to follow the path preferred by upwardly mobile Americans-to better housing in suburban districts. In the 1940s and 1950s federal government policies facilitated large-scale suburban migration by funding veterans' education, preparing them for middle-class jobs, and by providing them with loans for house purchases. In the northeast, Jewish and Protestant city-dwellers moved quickly, in part because of their superior education and income, in part because their religious institutions – organized as congregations – could easily be reorganized in the suburbs. Catholics, with their territorial parishes, more often remained in cities until urban projects to "renew" or replace slums with highways, the construction of public housing, and the arrival of fresh waves of rural black migrants caused them, too, to consider the attractions of suburban life.

Many residents of new, postwar suburban "Levittowns" – with their many, low-cost, and identical ranch houses – were the children and grandchildren of earlier immigrants. In the west, Chinese- and Korean-Americans such as Tom and Dora Kim were among them. Even more numerous were the rural whites who – like Oca Tatham and his six children – had escaped migrant labor and poverty during the war. Moving constantly during the 1930s, according to his children, Oca Tatham, "used to buy low and sell high." He remained in business for himself and after World War II he developed a suburban subdivision "Tatham Country Homes" near Fresno.[8]

By 1960, immigration restriction had reduced the representation of foreigners to only 5 percent of the American population, lower than it had been at any time since the 1820s. But with so many people moving about within the USA, the America population remained impressively diverse. Contacts across cultural lines also continued in the postwar era, at first with few obvious changes from the past.

Postwar Contacts

If anything, postwar encounters of natives and newcomers in American cities of the northeast and west made the color line ever more salient. In particular, the postwar great migration of black southerners ended whatever uneasy truce had developed in American cities prior to World War II. By war's end, older European immigrants and their children and Negro newcomers all sought to improve their housing with wartime savings as new arrivals from the south crowded into existing, and already overcrowded, Negro neighborhoods.

Between 1945 and 1965, disturbing numbers of urban ethnic whites threw firebombs or garbage at the homes of their new Negro neighbors. But even more moved to the suburbs. As a result, racial and socioeconomic segregation soared well beyond levels typical of immigrant-dominated cities in 1900. As newcomers from the south poured into New York's Harlem or Chicago's south side, urban renewal diminished available housing, and observers increasingly commented on the emergence of packed black ghettoes – a term borrowed from New York's Jewish Lower East Side – in most northern cities.

Not all whites and blacks experienced difficulties sharing neighborhood turf, however. Growing up in Cleveland in the 1950s, Barbara Smith portrayed a local scene little different from Ernesto Galarza's Sacramento at the turn of the century. "The white people, mostly Italians and Jews, quickly exited from our immediate neighborhood but some remained in the schools," she reported. "Most of our white classmates, however, were Polish, Czech, Yugoslavian or Hungarian. Their families had emigrated from eastern Europe following the World War. Despite the definite racial tensions between us, we had certain things in common. Cleveland was new to their people as it was to ours . . ."[9]

Despite these contacts, marriage across the color line remained extraordinarily rare in the north, even where not generally prohibited by law (as it still was in the south and parts of the west). This marital segregation contrasted sharply with increasing intermarriage among children of older immigrants, who after World War II still respected religious but less often ethnic divisions among whites. In California, immigrant men from India did marry Mexican women, while in the east, Puerto Ricans – like many Latin Americans – saw nothing wrong with love across the color line and intermarried frequently.

As suburbs and cities segregated along racial lines, so did their public schools. De facto segregation in the schools of the northeast rarely reached the levels found in the Jim Crow south, but it was nevertheless increasingly problematic, especially when funding for urban schools dropped as more prosperous parents moved to the suburbs. Teachers – many of them the children of Jewish, Italian, and Irish immigrants – struggled to teach curricula designed to transform the language and living habits of immigrant newcomers; many could not understand why their students failed to respect them as Mary Antin had her teachers at the turn of the century. As natives, Negro southerners had good reason to view civics courses' glorification of American national greatness and democracy with some skepticism, and southern whites scarcely felt they needed such lessons.

With federal, state, and city government programs increasingly providing economic assistance – job training, unemployment benefits, welfare relief, and even civil service jobs – and advice about employment, naturalization, and voting, urban institutions also evolved as sites of cross-cultural encounter. Social settlement houses in urban ghettoes closed or moved with their older immigrant clients, often ignoring Negro newcomers who were English-speaking American natives. In the early 1950s, the family of Ruby Daniels in Chicago experienced this change in a very personal way, as city case workers came into her home to check if Luther Haynes – the father of two of her children and the man she would later marry – was living with her. When a razor was found in her bathroom, Daniels lost financial assistance through the federally funded program Aid to Dependent Children (ADC).

Urban politics diverged somewhat in northern and western cities, however. As late as the 1960s, the authors of *Beyond the Melting Pot* pointed to the persistence of Negro, Puerto Rican,

Italian, Irish, and Jewish voting blocs and of ethnic appeals as features of New York City elections. In Chicago Ruby Daniels Haynes supported the Democratic machine by getting out the vote each election day. Her loyalty to the machine eventually allowed Haynes to obtain a spot in public housing in 1957, a move she regarded as a big step upward toward financial stability. In the west, by contrast, low rates of naturalization among Mexican immigrants and the absence of machines left city governments in the hands of the Anglo-American elite, joined by the 1960s by earlier immigrants from Europe and by conservative white southerners such as Oca Tatham, who became a Republican supporter of Barry Goldwater in 1964.

Changes like these did little to alter the longstanding importance of family, neighborhood, church, or a few urban institutions as foundations for migrants' identities. But at the same time, the cold war seemed to force natives and newcomers into an uncomfortable paradox that heightened racial identities while erasing cultural and ethnic loyalties. The expanding role of the USA in world politics had local consequences everywhere migrants settled in the 1940s and 1950s.

Cold War Identities

Perhaps inevitably, the cold war between Soviet communism and American democracy focused worldwide attention on the national qualities that had produced the competing economic and political systems of the USSR and the USA. On the one hand, official and informal racial discrimination persisted and was widely tolerated in the USA, as was a sharpening and increasingly national color line between white and black. On the other hand, the USA advocated throughout the world an "American way" – a revised version of its older civic religion and one that promised equality, economic liberty, material prosperity, consumer choice, and representative government to all, regardless of race or religion. It was in this paradoxical context that celebrations of the USA as a nation of immigrants first emerged.

In the 1950s, wartime images of the USA as a culturally diverse nation of nations gave way to cold war visions of a nation of immigrants transformed by exposure to American prosperity and values. Marcus Lee Hansen had in 1940 already described immigrants from northern Europe as builders of nineteenth-century America. Ten years later, in *The Uprooted: The Epic Story of the Great Migrations that Made the American People*, historian Oscar Handlin described later American history, too, as a product of Europe's immigrants. But unlike Hansen, who had studied immigrants' connections to their homelands and who believed immigrants' grandchildren (the "third generation") recovered interest in their origins, Handlin instead described a transition from painfully alienated rural immigrants, adrift in a strange urban and industrialized land, to the confusion of the second generation and then to the full Americanization of the third generation.

Many cold war intellectuals associated this "straight-line" assimilation into the American mainstream with the acquisition of a distinctive national American "character." Any remaining doubts that anti-capitalist radicals could be good and loyal Americans had disappeared over the previous two decades. Already in the late 1930s, the Congress's House Un-American Activities Committee (HUAC) searched for evidence of such disloyalty among labor leaders; active throughout the 1950s, its investigations drove NAACP founder W. E. B. DuBois out of the USA while preventing critics of American foreign policies from entering. Once the sharpest critic of Marcus Garvey's Black nationalist campaign to return to Africa, DuBois died in Ghana, a supporter of socialism and pan-Africanism. In the tense cold war years, FBI agents watched even 1950s' NAACP and labor reformers for signs of disloyalty.

Proclaiming the USA a nation of immigrants did little to diminish awareness of color as an element of individual and group identity. Abandoning Social Darwinist categories, Americans now described all whites, regardless of origins, as Caucasians. In 1950, the US Census Bureau – which for 50 years had recorded race or color as Social Darwinists advocated – decided that race and color – and at least for whites and black – were the same. So long as immigration from Europe continued, some of the children of white and black immigrants remained bilingual and bicultural, living in urban ethnic neighborhoods and participating in ethnic immigrant organizations. Many more – including many of the native and second-generation veterans of World War II – insisted, on the contrary, they were fully American and indistinguishable from whites of different origins. In the suburbs of the 1950s, observers noticed that children of European immigrants identified themselves mainly as Catholics or Jews, not by their national origins. Their encounters with newer migrants – whether Mexicans in the west, Puerto Ricans in New York, or Negroes in cities everywhere – had driven home the point that immigrants from Europe became not just Americans, but white Americans, and that immigrants from the Caribbean became not just Americans, but black ones.

In reshuffling people in its census, the USA also continued to identify, as separate races, American Indians, Japanese, Chinese, Filipinos, and "other race – spell out." (For "other race," the 1960 census suggested "Hawaiian, Part Hawaiian, Aleut, Eskimo.") Beginning in 1950, under a commissioner of Indian Affairs who had earlier directed the Japanese War Relocation Authority, the federal government also announced its intention to terminate gradually its special relationship with individual Indian tribes. By 1960, almost half of all Indians already lived off their reservations. Intermarriage with whites had also increased, so that the numbers of Indians dropped in US census listings. Presumably, many of their children, too, had become white.

Veterans descended from immigrants from Asia considered themselves patriotic Americans, as did Dora Kim. But the experience of racial discrimination continued to shape even Kim's identity, reminding her of her origins. For Chinese immigrants, cold war concerns about security and loyalty also remained troubling and reinforced ethnic identities. Like the Jewish Anti-Defamation League, Chinese-American organizations began a long, defensive campaign against American stereotypes of

Orientals as sneaky or inscrutable lawbreakers who had entered the country illegally as false "paper sons." The campaign was a difficult one. Even the FBI regarded the loyalties of the most recent arrivals from China with suspicion after the communist revolution there in 1949.

Avoiding troubling issues of racial identity and racial divisions, cold war intellectuals focused attention on faith in God as a unifier of all Americans and as an essential component of American national character. In 1953 the words "under God" were added to the pledge of allegiance students repeated daily to the American flag; soon thereafter the new motto "In God We Trust" appeared on the currency of the USA. Attendance at churches and synagogues indeed soared in the 1950s. It was also widely believed that religious diversity "inoculated" Americans against totalitarianism, although Americans also described their nation as unified around newly imagined "Judeo-Christian" values. American Jews pointed to Israel as an important anti-communist force in the Middle East while, for American Catholics, communism became the focus for critiques – of modernity, materialism, freethinking, and weak families – once aimed at American Protestants.

The domestic migrations of the previous decades had also fundamentally altered American regionalism. The south remained distinctive for its officially imposed segregation of blacks from whites and both rural south and rural midwest remained senders rather than receivers of domestic migrants. White Protestants in both places still saw their rural homes as the true heartland of America precisely because they had attracted so few foreigner residents. Migrations from Mexico and Asia also gave the southwest a unique regional identity. While the cities of northeast focused almost exclusively on the color line between blacks and whites, in the southwest, migrant white Americans and earlier immigrants from Europe worried as much – or more – about browns and yellows.

Nevertheless, the USA was less regionally diverse by 1960 than it had been in 1900. Rural southerners and midwesterners now had extensive family ties to residents of the west and the northeast. Catholics lived in large numbers everywhere except the rural south, and small numbers of Jewish-Americans lived in cities throughout the country. The religious enthusiasms of the rural south and midwest had spread nationwide with Negro and white migrants. The USA was now also a single, national marketplace for consumer goods, linked by a large new interstate highway system and a popular, mass culture that extended beyond Hollywood movies to include music and entertainment first developed by immigrant and black entrepreneurs in places such as Harlem, Los Angeles, and the Lower East Side. Large corporations had introduced chili to the midwest and Cuban mambo to the south. A taste for country music had traveled with families like the Tathams, as did Negro blues and jazz with listeners like Ruby Daniels Haynes. Worse, however, the violence Negro migrants had encountered in northern cities persuaded them that whites – whether native or foreign-born, and whether northern or southern – were universally prejudiced against them. By 1965, Americans could no longer portray the color line as a southern problem; as Myrdal had recognized, it was truly a national dilemma.

The Demise of Scientific Racism

Ironically, a color line divided opponents of scientific racism even to the eve of their final successes. In 1954, a Supreme Court decision (*Brown* vs. *The Board of Education of Topeka, Kansas*) long pursued by the NAACP and Urban League generated a new nationwide mass Civil Rights Movement to end racial discrimination. It drew its strength less from the migrants to the north than from the Negroes who remained in the south. The leaders of the southern movement – men such as Martin Luther King, who had been inspired by the Indian nationalist Gandhi's example of non-violent protest – emerged from the segregated black churches of southern cities to challenge Jim Crow laws. Beginning with boycotts of a segregated bus system in Montgomery, Alabama, the Civil Rights Movement supported sit-ins, freedom rides, campaigns to register southern voters, enrollment in universities, and a march of a quarter of a million Negro Americans on Washington in August, 1963.

The century-long reign of officially sanctioned scientific racism seemed to collapse in the face of this new political movement in 1964 and 1965. The Civil Rights Act of 1964 and the Voting Rights Act of 1965 returned Americans in many respects to the ideals of the civic nation as they were understood just after the Civil War. The Civil Rights Act invalidated all state, local, and federal legislation that discriminated on the basis of race, sex, and national origin, and it provided for federal enforcement of the law. (A 1968 Civil Rights Act also extended for the first time the protection of the Bill of Rights to American Indian citizens.) Its passage encouraged the recently re-elected President Lyndon B. Johnson to announce his plans for a Great Society and a war on poverty even as he committed additional American troops to an escalating war between communists and anti-communists in Vietnam. New federal agencies heard complaints from Negroes and women about discrimination and encouraged progress toward racial and gender equality through Affirmative Action programs. In Chicago, three of Ruby Daniels Haynes's sons participated in the Job Corps training programs of Johnson's Great Society, and one, after serving in Vietnam, found stable employment with the Illinois Bell Telephone Company in the suburbs.

The Great Society was anything but color-blind, however. It measured progress toward integration quantitatively, encouraging employers, government programs, and educational institutions to categorize Americans once again by race. The Great Society revised rather than eliminated racial categories. In 1970, census takers distinguished among White, Negro or Black, and Indian (American), Japanese, Chinese, Filipino, Hawaiian, Korean, or "other Asian" races while classifying persons of Hispanic "origin or descent" (Mexicans, Puerto Ricans, Cubans, Central or South Americans, and "Other Spanish") as an ethnic group. Federal agencies thus generally recognized five racial and ethnic categories – a "racial pentagon" of white, black (or African-American), Asian-American,

American Indian (or Native American) and Hispanic.

Affirmative Action and War Against Poverty programs survived the transition to Republican Richard Nixon's presidency in 1968, and Dora Kim's Community Center was one beneficiary in the 1970s. Still, Civil Rights legislation and the Great Society had responded mainly to Negroes' century-long campaign for justice; they were not programs to end discrimination against immigrants. Advocates of immigration reform – Catholic, Jewish, Greek, and Italian-American groups, along with several CIO unions – had formed only a minor branch of the Civil Rights Movement and many white ethnic groups in the 1950s instead used the rhetoric of the USA as a nation of immigrants to demand reform only of immigration policy. When scientific racism collapsed, however, it did so not only on the streets of Montgomery, Alabama, but also at the borders that immigrants still crossed. The occasional debater in Congress noted that "just as we sought to eliminate discrimination in our land through the Civil Rights Act, today we seek by phasing out the national origins quota system to eliminate discrimination in immigration . . ."[10] Influenced by debates over Negro equality, Congressmen now also wanted to avoid selecting newcomers by race.

But in the Hart–Celler reform of immigration in 1965 Congress never promised restoration of the free liberty of movement that had existed in 1865. The new law raised the numbers of immigrants to be admitted only slightly. It phased out national origin quotas but introduced hemispheric quotas (170,000 for the eastern and 120,000 for the western) that imposed a numerical limit on the Americas for the first time. It created preferences to allot visas outside the Americas, giving priority to persons with close family ties to current US residents, to workers "in occupations for which labor is in short supply," and to refugees fleeing persecution in communist countries or the Middle East. In 1978, Congress modified the act (although not the numbers admitted), eliminating hemispheric divisions and creating a unified preference system with a limit of 20,000 newcomers from any country anywhere in the world.

Although it did not much increase foreigners' liberty of

movement, the 1965 Hart–Celler Act did aim to create a color-blind nation and it broadened access to American citizenship modestly. Its preference system privileged relatives of earlier immigrants along with skilled persons, not any particular race. Ironically, however, the collapse of scientific racism produced no new celebration of the American civic nation. Instead, fierce debates soon raged over the nation's future. Young "new ethnics" quickly took civic equality for granted. What they now demanded was a culturally democratic and "multi-cultural" America.

The New Ethnicity and the Multicultural Nation

The collapse of official scientific racism in the mid-1960s raised expectations for rapid change without immediately fulfilling them. The resulting transformation in Americans' identities, group affiliations, and sense of national belonging was dramatic. Race and ethnicity no longer excluded individuals from the civic nation, yet the children and grandchildren of the vast international and internal migrations of the twentieth century embraced racial and ethnic group identities with new fervor.

Eliminating Jim Crow laws in the south did not create jobs, end residential segregation, improve education in urban schools, or halt the transfer of industrial jobs out of northern cities. It did not eliminate the color line for poorly educated and unemployed children of Negro, Mexican, or Puerto Rican migrants. Already in 1964, discontent among urban youth erupted in collective violence in Watts, a black neighborhood of Los Angeles. It was the first of many violent ghetto riots to follow. In Chicago, Ruby Lee Daniels Haynes had realized that her son Kermit was in a gang and hiding from the police. Conflicts between other alienated young men and white police officers ignited most urban riots in the mid-1960s. As one young black man reported, "I've had it with equality and all these lies about opportunity."[11] For Ruby Haynes, the four-day Chicago riot seemed just one more episode of violence in an already-violent urban world where she lived surrounded by poor and often angry, frustrated, and poorly educated young black men.

Quickly, a new generation of Black nationalists emerged to speak for these angry young men. Former Nation of Islam leader Malcolm X had long challenged the leadership of the Civil Rights Movement. After X's assassination in 1965, younger men such as Huey P. Newton, founder of the Black Panther Party, argued for urban Black Power, including a UN-supervised plebiscite allowing Blacks to choose national autonomy. Others likened integration to genocide. Fearing white violence, Black Panthers carried guns, and – disturbed by what they saw as Black females' dependency on white welfare workers – urged Black men to reclaim masculine prerogatives of leadership in their communities. Stokely Carmichael of the Student Non-Violent Coordinating Committee (SNCC) may have been joking but he nevertheless horrified female activists in the Civil Rights Movement by telling them that the proper position for women in SNCC was "prone."

Even radical Black nationalists mainly focused on community service, however. Black Panthers provided free breakfast programs, medical clinics, and legal assistance in Oakland. In New York, the Nation of Islam supported small business ventures. Black activists demanded community control over New York City schools, bypassing the centralized Board of Education. Panthers like Bobby Seale and Elaine Brown began seeking, and occasionally gaining, municipal political office. In this respect, they were not so different from early community activists as horrified white observers may have feared.

As new spokesmen for the largest racial minority in the USA, Black nationalists also created a blueprint for a new ethnicity for the young Americans who now began to call themselves "peoples of color." The upwardly mobile children of migrants from Mexico, Asia, and Indian reservations – many the first in their families to attend college – had been welcomed belatedly into the civic nation, but most had experienced formal or informal racial prejudice in integrating schools and neighborhoods during the 1950s and 1960s. Soon, they formed an important element in a larger and self-consciously radical student movement that objected to university politics and requirements, to male patriarchy, to the Vietnam War, and to the corrupting impact of corporate power on American democracy.

Oddly, a generation that fomented the sexual revolution and popularized the individualistic slogan, "Do your own thing" nevertheless created new identities for themselves based on dreams of racial and ethnic solidarity. The Negro college student Barbara Smith (granddaughter of Georgian domestic servants migrated to Cleveland) soon thought of herself as a Black, African-American feminist. Wilma Mankiller (whose Cherokee father had moved her from Oklahoma to San Francisco in 1956) became a Native American advocate of red power. Dora Kim's son Tommy became an Asian-American and bracero Arnulfo Caballero's son Cesar Caballero became a Chicano.

By the time Barbara Smith graduated from the all-female Mount Holyoke College in 1969, the era of ghetto riots was nearly over. Believing that "Black is Beautiful," Smith wore her hair in an "Afro." She had also heard white feminists pronounce that "Sisterhood is Powerful." Forming the Combahee River Collective in the early 1970s, Smith chose instead to build an autonomous Black feminist movement; she also later "came out" as a Black lesbian. After founding Brooklyn's "Kitchen Table: Women of Color Press," Smith reflected on her choices. "I learned about Black feminism from the women in my family . . ." she remembered, ". . . witnessing daily how they were humiliated and crushed because they had made the 'mistake' of being Black and female in a white man's country." She admitted her upset with "what Black men . . . were saying about the irrelevance of 'women's lib' to women of color" but she had found little in common with white feminists rebelling against privileged, middle-class America's cult of female domesticity.[12]

Wilma Mankiller instead wanted to rebuild an autonomous Cherokee nation. Mankiller had hated leaving Oklahoma at age 11; she was particularly upset when new San Francisco schoolmates made fun of her name. When her family moved to the racially mixed suburbs, she became a fan of black music and suffered an identity crisis so severe she ran away to live with her unmarried white grandmother. Mankiller later married an immigrant from South America and had two daughters but, increasingly unhappy with domesticity, she subsequently enrolled as a student at San Francisco State. Then, encouraged by her brother, Mankiller helped to occupy Alcatraz Island in 1969. Throughout the west, activists in a new American Indian Movement (AIM) occupied federal lands, demanding fulfillment of forgotten treaties. In 1970, Indian nations also began electing their own leaders and Mankiller returned to Oklahoma to promote Cherokee economic development. At first distrusted as a "hippie woman from California," she was elected the Cherokee Nation's first female chief in 1985.[13]

The new ethnicity of radicals such as these provoked sharp generational conflict among immigrants from Asia and Mexico, in part because many of their parents had embraced, at least in part, the image of the USA as a welcoming nation of immigrants. In Texas, the former bracero Arnulfo Caballero had found work in El Paso in the 1950s while his wife and son César remained in Juarez. In 1958 the entire family transferred across the border. Growing his hair long in the 1960s, César upset his fiercely patriotic father – who had naturalized as soon as possible – by dropping out of ROTC at the University of Texas at El Paso (UTEP). Caballero then joined MECHA – the nationalist Chicano Student Movement of Aztlán – that demanded an independent homeland for Chicanos in the southwest.

Like the senior Caballero, Dora Kim had little patience with young radicals in the 1960s. Self-consciously following the example of Black Americans, San Francisco State students organized a series of Third World Strikes against the Vietnam War in 1968 and 1969 and then built a pan-ethnic Asian-American movement to protest racial oppression. Some advocated revolution, or yellow power, and, modeling themselves on the Black Panthers, called themselves Red Guards. Others sought to create Asian-American studies programs ". . . to educate and inform about how Amerika [their term for a racist America] screwed us."[14]

Nevertheless, older Americans also responded positively to some radical appeals. In 1974, the Japanese American Citizens League (JACL), which had been founded in 1929 as a civic and patriotic group, created a National Committee seeking redress for their World War II internment and relocation. Before gaining both a presidential apology and financial compensation for their losses, participants in the JACL's yearly "Days of Remembrance" followed younger activists in discussing the painful consequences of discrimination. As one internee concluded, "We felt we were raped by our own country [and] . . . a rape victim feels guilt and shame . . . And so it is with us . . . the camp experience had a very negative psychological effect on us . . . Our self-esteem, our self-regard were shattered."[15]

Within a few years, many children and grandchildren of European groups subjected to immigration restriction also remembered experiences with discrimination and rejected celebrations of the USA as a nation of European immigrants. The most prominent public spokesmen of "white ethnicity," Italian-American Catholic priest Gino Barone and Slovak-American university professor Michael Novak, also promoted new identities for the children and grandchildren of European immigrants. Barone wrote of PIGs (the descendants of Polish, Italian, and Greek immigrants), while Novak called Catholic, Orthodox Christian and predominantly working-class whites the unmeltable ethnics. Most observers instead called them the "white ethnics,"contrasting them to peoples of color such as Smith, Mankiller, Kim, and Caballero.

Both of these white ethnic spokesmen were considerably older than the young radicals, and as uncomfortable with their radicalism as Dora Kim or Arnulfo Caballero. (For a biography of a white peer of the peoples of color, see the student exercise.) Born in the early 1930s to the children of Slovak immigrants, Michael Novak had moved early to the suburbs, studied for the priesthood, written about the Second Vatican Council, and become a Catholic critic of the Vietnam War.

Novak argued that unmeltable ethnics' slow economic progress and the patriotism nurtured in their industrial unions and in tight-knit families and communities made them distrustful of the radicals – who were instead destined for lives as well-educated and highly paid intellectuals and professionals.

The new ethnicity's attention to history, cultural preservation, and individual self-esteem were widely shared by Americans by the 1970s. Few remembered immigration historian Marcus Lee Hansen's predictions of third-generation cultural revivalism when African-American journalist Alex Haley (the biographer of Malcolm X) described new ethnics as searching for their "roots." As roots seekers, white ethnics and peoples of color both revamped family holidays and meals (inventing the new African-American holiday of Kwanzaa, for example), joined older ethnic organizations or formed new ones, and taped the memories of elderly relatives, healing the familial rifts student radicalism had sometimes opened.

Their focus on individual ethnic identity in turn survived the end of the Vietnam War and even the decline of student radicalism. By the end of the 1970s, the new ethnicity seemed less a product of exclusion from the nation than a way for full citizens to recognize exclusion as a thing of the past while still remembering and pondering its long-term consequences. Gradually, supporters of the new ethnicity shifted their focus from protest to educational, cultural, and political reform, although their interest in personal transformation also remained strong. By the late 1970s, new textbooks began appearing that celebrated American diversity and portrayed the USA as a mosaic, salad bowl, or kaleidoscope of distinctive racial groups. Such accounts generally portrayed race – not religion or national origins – as the most important source of American diversity. Unconsciously differentiating themselves from earlier thinkers about the relationship of culture and democracy, such as Horace Kallen, new ethnics increasingly called themselves not cultural pluralists but multiculturalists.

For those who embraced it, multiculturalism became a new way to imagine an inclusive American nation in which hyphenated Asian-, African-, Native-, Hispanic-, and

Euro-Americans could be culturally equal and equally worthy to the American nation. It accepted that the country's many immigrant and ethnic minorities had quite different histories and that those histories were likely to support distinctive identities for quite some time. It provided the foundation for Jesse Jackson's political efforts to transform the Civil Rights Movement into a "rainbow coalition" to solve the problems of the poorest Americans. And in 1980, it often seemed completely uncontroversial and perfectly compatible with mainstream, middle-class life in the USA.

No longer an angry young man when interviewed in the 1980s, César Caballero called himself a Chuppie (a Chicano, Urban Professional). Living in an integrated upper-middle-class suburb of El Paso and working as a University of Texas library director, Caballero's community activism now encouraged Mexican-American children to remain in school and to value their heritage.[16] In San Francisco, Tommy Kim had received a stipend from city government to work at the community center while completing his M.A. in social welfare at San Francisco State University. Like many young Asian-American activists, including Warren Furutani – elected to the Los Angeles Board of Education in 1988 – Kim also now sought mainly to reform and educate the nation about its cultural diversity and Asian-Americans about their history and culture.

Multicultural nation-building was a common response to the collapse of scientific racism, not just in the USA but around the world. Between 1961 and 1967, Canada and Australia had also abandoned discriminatory immigration policies, and in Canada, multiculturalism and bilingualism aimed to unite French-speaking minority, English-speaking majority, and a large population of postwar immigrants from southern Europe, Asia, and the Caribbean. Nations that had abandoned racial discrimination much earlier generated no such multicultural movements, however. Instead, French observers criticized American multiculturalists for preserving racial categories, and perpetuating Social Darwinist thinking. Committed to a secular, color-blind civic nation, France even forbade Jewish and Moslem students from wearing distinctive headgear to school. Most Brazilians, too, saw no need for multiculturalism; they viewed their nation, even when ruled by military dictators, as a racial democracy of racially mixed people who were uninterested in anyone's color or origins.

American Nationalists in Conflict

Even before the 1970s ended, however, multiculturalism in the USA had its critics; by the 1980s "culture wars" raged over alternative national visions. For many, a color-blind civic nation still remained an attractive goal. For others, the challenge was instead to revive the moral values of rural America without embracing its racism. Still others called for a new civic nation that acknowledged the racially and culturally mixed identities of all individuals rather than celebrating or reproducing group difference.

Since the nineteenth century, public schools in the USA had been funded in large part to educate children for citizenship. Perhaps inevitably, reformers and radicals among multiculturalists disagreed with each other and with their critics about what citizenship education now required. Radical or "hard" multiculturalists often promoted separate education and curricula for African-, Native-, and Euro-Americans. As Black nationalists, Afro-centrists in the 1980s argued that only Black teachers educating Black children in Black schools about Black life and history could solve the problems of the poorest ghetto dwellers. At reservation schools and colleges, Native-American educators already enjoyed that autonomy.

The majority of multiculturalists were instead reformers who promoted a single, "soft" multicultural curriculum for all. Their agenda included study of the country's many ethnic groups, Black History and Women's History months, and support for public celebrations of diversity in the form of food, dance, literature, and music. Reformers believed that respect and recognition for cultural difference enriched all Americans and kept them in harmony as a nation. In the 1980s and early 1990s, radicals and reformers fought intense fights over how to write and implement multicultural school curricula in both New York State and California.

Reviving the civic nation

Not a few Americans flatly rejected multiculturalism, and its impact on education, wanting teachers to celebrate a civic America purged of its racism and expecting government to perfect the practice of equality. To liberal intellectuals such as historian Arthur Schlesinger, Jr., multiculturalism promoted only national disunity and ethnic separation. Others feared the multicultural curricula focused too much on the failures of American democracy, hindering the USA in its global competition with communism. Still others argued that classifying Americans by race, rather than treating them as individuals, was a dangerous mistake. Many were reluctant to abandon completely Martin Luther King's image of an integrated nation. Michael Novak, for example, was proud that working-class descendants of immigrants from Europe had supported the Civil Rights Movement and he rejected portrayals of "Euro-Americans" and immigrants as oppressors of peoples of color.

Defenders of the civic nation also included religious minorities troubled by the use of racial categories to measure progress toward equality. Catholic and Jewish Americans were well aware of their own under-representation in national political offices, notably as presidents. As late as 1999, controversy arose when the House of Representatives – which had never had a Catholic Chaplain – again passed over a Catholic finalist. Yet to guarantee religious liberty, the USA had rigorously refrained from categorizing individuals by religion. No data could easily measure the progress of once-disparaged religious minorities, and many felt this was the proper precedent for a color-blind nation, too. For many Jewish Americans, racial "check boxes" on census forms or job applications raised especially alarming parallels to Nazi Germany.

By the 1990s, supporters of a color-blind nation could also point to encouraging signs that official scientific racism was, in fact, dead. In 2000, the nomination of an Orthodox Jew, Joseph Lieberman, for the vice presidency was followed by an opinion poll showing 92 percent of Americans would vote for a Jewish president. Roughly the same percentages would choose a Catholic, female, or black presidential candidate. But voters were more skeptical of other forms of diversity ignored by multiculturalism. Only 80 percent would choose a Mormon president, and even fewer – 59 percent – a gay one. Most significantly, less than half would choose an atheist seeking the presidency.[17]

Seeking common values

Apparently, too, many Americans still desired shared national values and knew which ones they wanted educators and government to promote. Beginning in 1968, Richard Nixon's Republican Party had attracted many traditionally Democratic voters, including those in Michael Novak's EMPAC (Ethnic Millions Political Action Committee), who were critical of radicals' attacks on traditional family and gender relations. Explaining how he became a critic of federal activism and a supporter of Republican Barry Goldwater in 1964, the former Oklahoman and Democrat Oca Tatham also spoke of moral values. He reported himself to have been particularly upset by a 1957 Supreme Court decision to ban school prayer. He told his interviewer, "When we see . . . the extent they'll go to stop God's work and stop prayer, then we know what some of them will do. We'll finally be like the Communist nations where no one will be allowed to pray."[18]

Fears like Tatham's grew during a new round of religious revivals that began quietly in the 1960s and attracted nationwide attention by 1980. Once again, born-again Protestants influenced by American Evangelical, fundamentalist, Pentecostalist (or charismatic) preachers embraced moral renewal, sought new converts, and feared the influence of atheists they called "secular humanists." From 1944 until 1956 Oca Tatham and his family had attended Calvary Tabernacle in Fresno; by the 1960s they were attending the large, new People's Church, and were hearing new evangelical voices in a grand Crystal Cathedral. There, former hippies who became "Jesus Freaks" eventually joined the children and grandchildren of Oca Tatham. Like Oca Tatham, younger converts sought to protect their children from urban secular culture, with its drinking, dancing, and open sexuality.

Children and grandchildren of the Catholic and Orthodox Christian unmeltable ethnics sometimes joined in the religious revivals of the decade. Having watched the Catholic hierarchy introduce radical changes in rituals like the mass and customs such as abstinence from meat-eating on Fridays, white ethnic Catholics seemed more willing to consider conversion to Protestantism than in the past. American Judaism also changed as young people raised in Reform and Conservative traditions rediscovered more emotionally exuberant or communitarian forms of Orthodoxy. By the early 1980s, a pan-religious and morally conservative "Moral Majority" of Protestants , Catholics, and Jewish Americans had joined older and often corporate and wealthy critics of federal activism in a broad new alliance, generally called the "new right" of the Republican Party. Together, they worked to outline the shared values that might define a racially inclusive but more homogeneous American nation.

Whether they were Protestants, Catholics, or Jews, members of the Moral Majority feared that governmental policies permitting abortion and divorce, substituting equality for protection of women and children, and removing religious symbols from public places encouraged immorality. African-American woman such as Ruby Daniels Haynes, with her many husbands, lovers, and pregnancies, often symbolized the Moral Majority's worst fears of moral decay. Academicians and government officials had been debating the origins of problems in urban black families – female-headed households, welfare dependency, and teenage pregnancies – since the 1960s. In the 1970s and 1980s, vicious stereotypes of "welfare queens" provoked particularly powerful emotions among upwardly mobile white ethnics who believed they had, however slowly, "pulled themselves up by their own bootstraps," with the powerful work ethics and family solidarity that African-Americans supposedly lacked. The New Right soon supported a simple solution to a national threat: end federal support for welfare. During the economic boom of the 1990s the US Congress eliminated the programs that had provided Ruby Daniels Haynes with intermittent income as she struggled to raise her children and hold low-wage jobs in Chicago hospitals.

The stigmatization of African-American women made it difficult for African-Americans, unlike many Hasidic Jews or white urban ethnics, to feel at home in the otherwise culturally and religiously diverse Moral Majority. In fact, many African-Americans shared some of the values of Oca Tatham and of Michael Novak. Like many urban white ethnics, Barbara Smith remembered that "the women in my family, and their friends, worked harder than any people I have known before or since," and like many rural southerners, she added "my grandmother believed in Jesus and in sin . . . ; my mother believed in education and books . . ." Like all in the Moral Majority, furthermore, "they believed in each other . . . and also seemed to believe that Beverly [her sister] and I could have a future beyond theirs."[19] Nor did the Catholic intellectual Michael Novak share all the values of other members of the Moral Majority, some of whom displayed the Confederate battle flag on their pickup trucks and praised the morality of individualism, voluntarism, and small-town life. As a fellow at the conservative American Enterprise Institute, Novak remained concerned with economic justice, sought meaning in tightly knit urban communities, and pondered the morality of wealth, modern business practices, and of corporate capitalism. Yet Novak, and not Smith, was widely considered part of the Moral Majority.

Thus a color line remained, not just in the Moral Majority but in the broader New Right coalition as well. While many in the Moral Majority opposed multiculturalism, even more opposed federal support of it. Historically, federal activism had been African-Americans' only guarantee of inclusion in the civic nation and by the 1980s, that inclusion again seemed under threat. By then, a few white men had argued successfully that Affirmative Action programs resulted in reverse discrimination against them. And in the late 1990s, New Right initiatives forbade governments and universities in Texas and California from using racial categories to pursue Affirmative Action. By the time of the presidential election of 2000, multiculturalism seemed on the verge of total defeat.

Return to the melting pot?

Nevertheless, the culture wars of the 1990s had also hidden a growing movement of quieter voices that proposed alternatives to a multicultural America, a morally renewed America, and a color-blind civic America alike. Proposals for a "post-ethnic," "mestizo" or even "cosmopolitan" nation looked as much to Hawaii and to Latin America – where racial and cultural amalgamation were the rule – as to the white-only marital melting pots described by Crèvecoeur in the 1780s and by Zangwill in 1909. Rather than revive the metaphor of the melting pot, however, such proposals usually suggested new American symbols of biological and cultural mixing more appropriate for the twenty-first century. New critics especially emphasized the degree to which identity had become a matter of choice, and how often American identities failed to conform to the "racial pentagon" introduced by government programs in the aftermath of the civil rights legislation of the mid-1960s.

Already under pressure from white ethnics unhappy with the racial pentagon, such as Gino Barone in the 1970s, the Census Bureau began to enumerate Americans' understandings of their own ethnic identities. In 1980 Americans were asked to choose the "ancestry group" with which they identified. Anticipating confusion, instructions specified, "Ancestry (or origin or descent) may be viewed as the nationality group, the lineage, or the country in which the person or the person's parents or ancestors were born before their arrival in the United States" but noted that "A religious group should not be reported as a person's ancestry." Again in 1990, census takers recorded the "ancestry or ethnic origin" of every American, taking into account that "ancestry refers to the person's ethnic origin or descent, 'roots,' or heritage." Individuals could list multiple ancestries but not multiple races.

Crunching data with newly powerful computers, social scientists discovered that large groups of Americans considered themselves simply Black or White or American (identifying with no particular ancestry or origin at all). Many others embraced a single ethnic or cultural identity as multiculturalists believed. Even the products of mixed marriages among whites tended to identify with one ancestry group thus exercising some choice over their ethnicity. Similar choices were not, however, open to a man such as Alex Haley, the author of *Roots*, who also had an Irish grandfather but did not search there for his roots in Europe.

While more white Americans were choosing their ethnic identities, color still imposed racial identities on Americans like Haley with even "one drop" of "black blood." Had multiculturalism reinforced rather than challenged the color line? Scholar David Hollinger suggested that a post-ethnic society would be achieved only when all Americans, regardless of skin color, could freely choose their cultural identities. Others pointed to the Caribbean, to Latin America, and to Hawaii, where centuries of mixing had produced in-between racial identities, and a different linkage of color – to class, rather than to skin color. They argued that Americans were just as mixed in descent as Hawaiians or Latin Americans but that public policy and public rhetoric had too long, and too consistently, encouraged them to choose identities that matched the ones in official, governmental use.

Paradoxically, interracial marriages had actually increased during the era of multiculturalism and with the end of laws prohibiting it after 1967, opening questions about racial as well as ethnic identities. About a third of Native American men and women were marrying white spouses already in 1970 and among Asian-Americans the proportions were even higher. By 1980 about two percent of Black women marrying each year were choosing white spouses, as were many more Black men. By the 1990s prominent Americans, such as the young golfer Tiger Woods, who had both African-American and Asian-American parents, wanted to be able to "check all that apply" even on census listings of race. They wanted to embrace all elements of their identity, not just one.

But fear of racial amalgamation was too longstanding an American tradition to disappear quietly or suddenly. In 2000, invoking the color line yet again, Michael Lind, senior fellow with the conservative New American Foundation, even blamed Black Americans for most resisting change, proclaiming himself "disgusted with the whole thing. This census should have been the first one not to identify people by race. Mexico got rid of its racial classifications in the 1820s. We keep ours basically because of the black civil rights lobby, which has lobbied in favor of the one drop rule."[20] Many civil rights organizations in fact rightly feared that discrimination patterns could not be monitored if identities could be freely chosen, blended, or mixed and matched at will. By imposing racial identities on Black Americans, whites had, since the seventeenth century, created the foundation for African-American solidarity. More than one observer noted that – unlike the USA – Brazil, with its national mythology of racial amalgamation, had never generated a strong movement to challenge the persistent poverty of most Afro-Brazilians.

By the time of the 2000 census, only 35 years had passed since the USA as a nation finally distanced itself from scientific racism. Not unsurprisingly, the future of the nation remained unresolved. Can equality and pluralism co-exist in the nation, as they clearly did in the life of Dora Yum Kim? The debate still rages. And even as Americans struggle to redefine diversity and the American nation, new voices are entering the debate. In rejecting official scientific racism, the USA had also opened the door to a new wave of immigrants. They, too, would have something to say about the future.

Further Reading

Molefi K. Asante, *The Afrocentric Idea* (Philadelphia: Temple University Press, 1987).

Chad Berry, *Southern Migrants, Northern Exiles* (Urbana: University of Illinois Press, 2000).

Dee Alexander Brown, *Bury my Heart at Wounded Knee: An Indian History of the American West* (New York: Holt, Rinehart, & Winston, 1971).

Yen Espiritu, *Asian American Panethnicity: Bridging Institutions and Identities* (Philadelphia: Temple University Press, 1992).

Nathan Glazer, *We are All Multiculturalists Now* (Cambridge, MA: Harvard University Press, 1997).

David A. Hollinger, *Postethnic America: Beyond Multiculturalism* (New York: Basic Books, 1995).

Gary Nash, "The Hidden History of Mestizo America," in Martha Hodes, ed., *Sex, Love, Race: Crossing Boundaries in North American History* (New York: New York University Press, 1999).

Arthur Meier Schlesinger, Jr., *The Disuniting of America: Reflections on a Multicultural Society*, rev. and enlarged ed. (New York: W. W. Norton, 1998).

Mary C. Waters, *Ethnic Options: Choosing Identities in America* (Berkeley: University of California Press, 1990).

Student Exercise
Ethnicity, Authors, and their Books

You have already read the story of another grandchild of immigrants from Europe. See the author's statement in "American Diversity – and Me; American Diversity – and You," pp. 12–17. Obviously, my life, too, was shaped by the events described in this chapter.

Questions for Discussion

Re-read my statement now and then consider the following questions.

1. What are the main similarities and differences you see between "white ethnics" and the "peoples of color" described in this chapter?
2. Would you label me a "white ethnic?" Why or why not? What does my biography share with the white ethnics? Does it share anything with the peoples of color?
3. Many people believe that an author's life influences her work. Do you think this book could be considered a product of the new ethnicity? Of white ethnicity? Or of Americans' recent enthusiasm for multiculturalism? What does it share with multicultural points of view, as you now understand them? How is it different? Which of these models of the American nation do you prefer? Why?

8

Today's Immigrants; Tomorrow's Nation

The first thing most Americans probably noted when they met Tesfay Sebahtu or Mrs. Rosalyn Morris was that each was black. Perhaps they also heard the accents that marked Sebahtu and Morris as recent immigrants. Aside from their dark skin and foreign birth, Sebahtu and Morris had very little in common, however. With their shared color and differing cultures, this man from Africa and woman from Jamaica introduce us to the new immigrants who will reshape the American nation in the twenty-first century.

Mrs. Morris was born poor. When she came to Yonkers, New York, in 1968 as a 40-year-old single mother, she had already been working in the kitchens of richer women for 27 years. Fifteen years later, she had relocated to Brooklyn but was still working, as a housecleaner at a Hilton Hotel. Belonging to no ethnic organizations, not even to a church, Mrs. Morris had become a citizen. And she expressed a quiet satisfaction with her life in the USA. When her daughter complained about Americans who "have this big thing about color," she acknowledged the problem: "She says there's a color line. She's right." But she then reminded her daughter that there would have been no chance for her to go to college in Jamaica. And she reserved special criticism for welfare recipients among her African-American neighbors. ". . . These young mothers with children," she insisted, "they should be put to work. That's where I would be – always have been. When I was young with several children and no husband to take care of us, I didn't get welfare. I worked for what I could get. . . ."[1] At least at this moment, Mrs. Morris seemed a candidate for membership in the Moral Majority.

Tesfay Sebahtu's story could not be more different. In 1981, he came to the USA as a 14-year old refugee from civil war in Africa. There, his deceased father had been a wealthy businessman in Eritrea – a part of Ethiopia once colonized by Italy. When Catholic refugee services sent the young Sebahtu to the USA, his mother and sisters fled to nearby Sudan. Placed in a foster home near Washington, DC, Sebahtu located his mother and sisters, and a Catholic VOLAG (voluntary agency) helped him reunite with them in this country.

During the 1980s, Sebahtu graduated from high school and community college and received an electrical engineering degree while doing odd jobs and driving a taxi. His mother – once a wealthy woman herself – found work as a dishwasher in a hotel. When interviewed in the early 1990s, Sebahtu was experiencing difficulties finding work in his profession, and was considering returning to the University of Maryland for a graduate degree. Still, his family had succeeded in purchasing a house, in part because he and his mothers and sisters had pooled their incomes. Unlike his mother, Sebahtu did not contemplate returning to Eritrea but he did spend considerable time at the Eritrean Cultural and Civic Center in Washington. There he ate Italian and Ethiopian foods, and enjoyed the company of other refugees from his homeland. According to his interviewer, Sanford Ungar, Sebahtu dreamed of marrying an Eritrean woman and working for an American company abroad for a time before settling permanently in the USA.[2]

As a refugee with an elite childhood, and expectations of a life of border-crossing as a professional worker, Sebahtu seemed a sharp departure from the huddled masses of immigrants at the beginning of the twentieth century. Nor was he alone. Since 1965, about a third of the immigrants who entered the USA were middle-class and well-educated professionals, many from the elites of their far-flung homelands in what was once called the Third World. Mrs. Morris, on the other hand, was a reminder of how attractive the USA remained to unskilled and poorly educated people looking to improve prospects for their children by working long hours at low wages for most of their own lives.

Without changes in US immigration policies since 1965, Sebahtu might not have gotten a visa to enter the USA so easily for he did not flee either a communist government or religious tensions in the Middle East; only in 1980 had the USA accepted the United Nation's definition of refugee as part of its own immigration policies. But changes in American policies since 1965 had also made it more difficult for the poorest, and unskilled migrants from the Americas – those most like Mrs. Morris – to enter the country. All immigrants, regardless of class or background, also continued to face numerical restrictions and confusing bureaucratic requirements before obtaining a green card that allowed them to live and work permanently in the USA.

Once they entered the USA, whether as refugees, unskilled workers, or highly educated professionals, immigrants faced many familiar issues. Would they embrace or reject racial or ethnic identities? Would they participate in ethnic group affairs or ignore them? How would natives define the ethnic differences between themselves and the newcomers? In some respects, the biggest change from the past was not in the newcomers but in the country that received them. For the first time in the history of the USA, substantial numbers of Americans now celebrated cultural diversity. At the same time, the fact that white Americans almost universally perceived both Mrs. Morris and Tesfay Sebahtu as black raised concerns about how far the nation had moved toward eliminating its color line.

New Migrations

The 1965 Hart–Celler Immigration Reform Act had an immediate impact on immigration into the USA. The great internal migrations from south to north ceased. Not only did the numbers of immigrants increase during the economically troubled 1970s (see Figure I.1) but the geographic origins, class backgrounds, and motives of immigrants also changed. In the 1970s and 1980s, new domestic migrations reversed those of the past, moving from the northern "rust-" or "snowbelt" toward a southern and southwestern "sunbelt." Changes in immigration law and the economic boom of the 1990s allowed large numbers of aliens to adjust their status and "become immigrants" while large numbers of newcomers continued to cross American borders. Between 1965 and 1998 the USA counted almost 20 million new immigrants with green cards making immigrants 10 percent of the population in 2000.

For most Americans, the changing origins of immigrants after 1965 were particularly striking. "The Third World Comes to America," headlines shrieked in the 1980s. In fact, most migrants came from the developing regions of the poorer parts of the world, much as they had also in the past. Migration from Europe had not ceased: well over 2 million immigrants arrived from traditional sending areas in Great Britain, Germany, and southern and eastern Europe between 1966 and 1993. But Europeans no longer dominated international migrations to the USA as they once had. Between 1966 and 1993, more than 7 million newcomers arrived from other countries in the American hemisphere, with by far the largest group (more than 5 million) coming from Latin America (notably Mexico) and the Caribbean (with the largest numbers from the Dominican Republic, Cuba, and Haiti). During the same years, more than 5 million arrived in the USA from countries in Asia (with especially large numbers originating in China, Vietnam, Korea, and India) and the Pacific (especially the Philippines). Immigration into the USA was now truly global. What mattered most to some observers, however, was that so many newcomers had dark skin. Sometime in the twenty-first century, demographers reported, racial minorities would become the new American majority.

While the 1965 elimination of racial discrimination made these changes possible, policy alone could not explain why immigrants now came from around the globe. Human mobility had again increased rapidly throughout the world since

World War II. The collapse of European empires and the creation of new nations in Africa and Asia generated much violent conflict, producing millions of refugees. From the 1960s through the 1980s, local wars between communists and anti-communists had the same effect in southeast Asia and parts of Latin America. The collapse of communism also allowed residents of the former USSR and its allies in central and eastern Europe to move more freely after 1989.

A new round of economic globalization also increased migration rates worldwide. More than a catchphrase, globalization accurately described the expanding and intensifying commercial and cultural exchanges between First (richer and more developed) and Third (poorer or developing) World countries. Beginning already in the 1950s, multinational corporations exported American consumer goods to Latin America and Asia; after 1970 they also transferred industrial production there, and after 1990, to former communist countries, too. Rapidly growing industries in eastern Asia and in the Middle East attracted migrants from abroad. Rapid and relatively cheap jet transport, and new forms of communication – telephones, satellites, and computers – linked the scattered regions of the world, facilitating migration in multiple directions.

While the USA received larger numbers of immigrants and refugees from a wider range of backgrounds than most other countries, few countries remained untouched by these international migrations. In fact, the impact of new immigration on the USA was less pronounced than in many parts of Europe, Canada, Australia, Africa, and the Middle East. The largest numbers of refugees from African countries had fled to other African countries. And the country with the highest representation of foreign laborers in the world in the 1990s was the oil-rich United Arab Emirates.

As the largest migration of the American hemisphere, Mexicans particularly felt the impact of numerical quotas imposed on them for the first time by immigration reform in the USA. While most migrants from Mexico were still poorly educated rural men, much like José Reveles and his father, women, and urban workers also now found American industrial, agricultural, and service jobs attractive. Overwhelmingly blue-collar, they were nevertheless more highly skilled, more prosperous, and better educated than workers who remained in Mexico. Migrants left from all over Mexico, although many had worked temporarily in developing areas of northern Mexico before transferring across the border. Whereas 90 percent of Mexican immigrants once headed for the southwest of the USA, many more now relocated to American cities throughout the country, to New York, and even, for the first time, to the southeast. Mexican men found work in construction, restaurants, and landscaping, while Mexican women worked in food processing, in the garment industry, and as domestic servants.

American immigration policy's explicitly stated preference for highly skilled and well-educated workers created very high hurdles for unskilled job-seekers from the Americas. Luisa Rojas, a woman who left Guatemala for the USA in 1968, remembered her fruitless efforts to get a visa from the American consul and her decision to seek help from "a friend of a friend of a friend" in the consul's office. "He say to me, if I give some money to him I can have the visa. And I'm scared because I think maybe he's mean, you know, because sometimes they lie. I paid him before I have the visa . . . I think was a hundred dollars, and later this man have the visa for me for only one month . . ."[3] Remaining after her tourist visa expired, Rojas joined an expanding group or workers without the necessary legal documents allowing them to live in the USA.

Following quickly on the elimination of the bracero program, the 1965 reforms frustrated Mexicans who knew jobs awaited them but who could not obtain visas easily or quickly. Unlike Rojas, large numbers simply walked or waded across the border into Texas, California, or Arizona. Even in the midst of the stagflation of the 1970s and the economic recession of the 1980s, and even in cities like New York, which lost jobs and population in the 1970s, foreigners like Rojas perceived economic opportunities Americans seemed unable to see. They thought of themselves as immigrants not as "over-stays" or "wetbacks"; Americans usually called them "illegals."

By 1985, the US Census Bureau had to put to rest wild charges that 12 million illegals lived in the USA and that the country had lost control of its borders. Even when the Census Bureau instead estimated a smaller group of 3 million foreigners lacking proper documents, Congress took action under pressure from disturbed citizens. The 1986 Immigration Reform and Control Act granted amnesty to a large number of illegals, allowing them to become immigrants and to obtain the green cards necessary to live legally in the USA. More than 2 million became immigrants. The advantages were obvious. Working without documents had forced illegals into informal, low-wage, and dangerous jobs. Luisa Rojas's husband, a truck driver in Guatemala, for example, worked in a foundry where he suffered frequent burns. Unable to exchange a tourist visa for a student visa, his son had moved out of the family house and lost his job in a plastics factory because he feared "the Immigration" (or "la Migra") would discover him. A green card gave former illegals access to better jobs, greater security, and considerably enhanced peace of mind. It also removed the stigma of appearing a law-breaker in the eyes of natives still concerned with national security.

While immigration reform had created higher hurdles for unskilled immigrants from the Americas, it opened relatively more visas to highly skilled immigrants and for persons from Asia and Europe. Europeans showed less interest in emigrating than in the past; their economically revived homelands, including even Italy, were beginning to attract immigrants from Asia and Africa themselves. Even highly educated Europeans sometimes faced long waits before they could obtain visas, however. And new Italian and Irish immigrants remained a visible presence in an east-coast city like New York well after 1965. At the same time, immigration to the USA from Asia rose sharply. Although poorer Chinese and Koreans also worked in factories and opened small stores, restaurants, and other businesses on the west and east coasts, large numbers of better educated immigrants like the Korean Hwangbo family enjoyed a middle-class life from the moment they arrived in the USA.

The father of Kay Hwangbo came to the USA intending to

study at the University of Connecticut. Postwar universities in the USA enjoyed a worldwide reputation for high-quality advanced training, especially in scientific and technical fields, and large numbers of foreign students entered the USA on student visas and then – once exposed to American life and occupational opportunities – gained green cards as permanent immigrants. Students pioneered new migrations from places like Vietnam and Cambodia, the Dominican Republic and Guyana, Brazil, Ethiopia, Iran, Yemen, Pakistan, and India. These "brain drain" migrations were initially controversial, for critics suggested they retarded development of the Third World. With globalization, and the obvious development of some regions within Asia, Latin America, and the Middle East such fears seemed somewhat exaggerated by the 1990s.

Hwangbo soon moved his young family from Korea to suburban Maryland, where he worked as an aerospace engineer. There, daughter Kay Hwangbo described herself as "the one who studied all the time, the nerdy Asian." She graduated from Harvard in 1983, noting, "Koreans see things in a very stratified way . . . they like Harvard. They like it more than Yale or Princeton."[4] But not all middle-class immigrants made such an immediate or easy adjustment as the Hwangbo's, as the story of Tesfay Sebahtu's mother, who instead experienced downward mobility from "mistress to maid," suggests.

As a refugee, Mrs. Sebahtu and her children had relatively little control over when they left Eritrea or where they were able to seek asylum. Although US policy provided preferences for visas each year, refugees tended to enter the USA in distinctive waves. In the 1970s and 1980s, both the president and Congress created special programs for admitting additional refugees in response to specific foreign crises. Although offered special assistance, refugees also faced special problems in the USA. Rates of welfare dependency were much higher among refugees, especially those from southeast Asia in the 1980s, than for other immigrants, largely because refugees more often had no relatives in the USA and had not been motivated to come to USA by the search for work.

The role of the USA as the leading anti-communist nation

of the world continued to make it a particularly attractive destination for refugees from communism . They came from nearby Cuba in the 1960s, 1980s, and 1990s, from Vietnam in 1975, from southeast Asia in the early 1980s, and from the USSR and its east bloc allies in the 1990s. Shoua Vang and his family were among 80,000 Hmong farmers who fled the highlands of Laos after serving as American allies during the Vietnam War. Sent by a voluntary agency (VOLAG) to a sponsor – Saint Paul's Lutheran Church in Menominee, Wisconsin had promised to hire Vang as a janitor and help the family adjust to American life – Vang quickly lost his job. He then moved with his family to St. Paul, Minnesota, where he first worked as a translator in a Model City Health Clinic serving the black and refugee poor, and later opened a store for his fellow Hmong in the Twin Cities.[5]

Attracting much less attention than refugees such as Vang or Mrs. Tesfay were the many women immigrants who – in sharp contrast to the past – entered the USA in numbers roughly equal to men after 1965. In fact, two-thirds of new immigrants were women and children, sparking some critics to worry about the declining "quality" of immigrants, comparing the USA to countries that privileged working-age, highly skilled, male job-seekers. The 1965 immigration reform created few visa preferences in traditionally female professions, excepting only nurses from the Philippines and Caribbean, whose entry was facilitated with high priority visas in the 1980s. Many women instead entered the USA with visas for reunifying families separated by male migration.

Thus for example, the mother of Lila Shah remained behind with two small daughters in India while her husband, sponsored by an aunt, moved by himself for a year to Syracuse, New York and began working there. Although she remembered feeling very resentful about having to follow him, Lila Shah was a small child who dutifully accompanied her mother and was quickly fascinated with her new apartment home, where she remembered waking in the middle of the night to check that, indeed, water continuously ran through the taps, as it did not in her home in India.[6]

Although Lila's mother settled into life as a middle-class housewife in Syracuse, most women who entered the USA to unify their families spent the better part of their lives as part of the female workforce. The mother of Kay Hwangbo, for example, not only worked for the US Food and Drug Administration but chose to remain in Washington when her husband took a job in Korea's new satellite development program, and began to commute between the two countries.

Rates of employment among foreign-born and native-born women in the USA had converged as opportunities for female wage-earning broadened across the twentieth century. Whereas once Americans had celebrated a female cult of domesticity, more now admired highly educated female natives who worked during marriage and motherhood, as only poorer women once had. Female newcomers from Latin America and from the Caribbean – many of them lacking proper immigration documents and some of themselves professionals – often took jobs as domestic servants and child-minders for American women entering high-pay, traditionally male professions for the first time in the 1970s and 1980s. They also worked in service industries, like health care, building maintenance, and food service. Working for low wages, women immigrants from Asia, Africa, Latin America, and the Caribbean revived the American garment industry – and also experienced the old abuses of sweatshop employment – in Los Angeles, Miami, and New York alike. At the same time more highly educated women, like Arati Prabhakar, the director of the National Institute of Standards and Technology, more often than natives entered male-dominated scientific and technical professions; Prabhakar was an electrical engineer.[7]

With newcomers coming from around the world, the immigrant population of the USA also became more religiously diverse. Buddhist and Hindu temples and Moslem mosques now confronted a nation that understood itself as Judeo-Christian. Still, the work of Protestant evangelical missionaries in Latin America and Asia had left their mark on immigration. Oca Tatham, for example, had transformed a 1970s vacation to Mexico into evangelical work when – musing on the poverty he saw around him, he thought, "How pleased the people in a place like this would be to have a church." Through his Assembly of God contacts, Tatham found a local Pentecostalist, a Chinese-Mexican woman, and helped her to build a chapel and school in Mexico.[8] As many as a third of immigrants from traditionally Catholic Latin America, along with many Koreans and Filipinos, became Protestants before entering the USA.

The newest immigration also contributed to a geographical shift in the American economy as urban jobs transferred from the northeast toward a broad band of southern states, from South Carolina to California, characterized as the sunbelt or "new" south. In the 1970s, immigrants from the Caribbean still preferred east-coast cities but now settled from Florida to New York. Cuban refugee businessmen and industrial workers made Miami the northernmost city of Latin America. Immigrants from Asia divided more evenly between east and west-coast cities, and the sunbelt, while sunbelt agriculture and industry attracted workers from Mexico and Central America. Refugee programs self-consciously tried to scatter their clients throughout the country, but the Vangs were unusual in deciding not to relocate subsequently to California, where many Hmong lineage groups tried to reunite in a more hospitable climate. By 1980, two-thirds of all immigrants lived in just four states – California, New York, Florida, and Texas; many of the remainder lived in the southwest or in a few Illinois cities, including Chicago.

Nor did the rise of international migration in any way discourage natives from moving about. In the stagnating economy of the 1970s and 1980s, small towns in the rural midwest and on the Great Plains lost their native farmers and the aging and declining urban industries of Detroit and New York lost their native workers, exacerbating high unemployment rates in urban ghettos. Among discouraged residents leaving the midwest and northeast for the sunbelt were large numbers of African-Americans. Ruby Daniels Haynes, for example, returned to her hometown in Clarksdale to retire; there she lived in public housing and finally escaped the violence of the Chicago ghetto.

Beginning in the 1980s, more immigrants also began to follow America's migrants toward the booming economy of the southeast. Many black migrants to the southeast, unlike Ruby Daniels Haynes, followed the lure of white-collar jobs in banking, financial services, and corporate centers relocating to the cheaper cities of the sunbelt. And in the 1980s and 1990s young and wealthy urban professionals, both black and white ("Yuppies" and "Buppies"), reclaimed older urban residential neighborhoods, "gentrifying" the cities of the west, northeast, and south.

Demographers are now busy studying whether domestic and international migrants prefer different cities or parts of the USA, or even different parts of the sunbelt. We must also await explanations for why some rustbelt cities attracted gentrifiers and new immigrants as working-class natives deserted them and why the economically troubled city of New York in the 1970s still seemed so attractive to newcomers. Still, it seems obvious that a few large, American cities and their suburbs, along with the sunbelt, had become the most important destinations for newcomers and mobile natives alike. They in turn became the most important sites for the new cross-cultural encounters that accompanied these newest migrations.

New Points of Contact

Because a few large cities and their suburbs – Miami, Los Angeles, San Francisco, New York, Chicago, and Washington – and the sunbelt were their preferred destinations, new immigrants after 1965 interacted far more frequently and extensively with middle-class Americans and with white and black southerners than they had in the past. Encounters of natives and newcomers had been a predictable dimension of urban life since the 1830s but for some Americans in the southeastern portions of the sunbelt, encountering immigrants from abroad was a new experience. Whether in neighborhoods and jobs, or in schools, local politics, and churches, the consequences for immigrants of Americans' ban on official racism, battles over multiculturalism, and persisting color prejudices were complex. Poorer and middle-class immigrants often had very different experiences, in part because poorer immigrants interacted more frequently with black Americans while middle-class immigrants more often worked and lived largely among whites.

Once again, immigrants and African-Americans lived in close proximity in American cities, but after 1965 African-Americans were more often the natives and foreigners again the newcomers. In Los Angeles, with its relatively small native black population, those newcomers included Mexicans, Filipinos, Koreans, Salvadorans, and Iranians; in San Francisco, it was Chinese, Filipinos, Salvadorans, and Vietnamese. Miami had a large native black population; it received a multiracial Caribbean mix of immigrants from Cuba, Haiti, Jamaica, Colombia, and Santo Domingo. In Chicago, with its very large native population of blacks, new immigrants typically revitalized aging neighborhoods abandoned by earlier white immigrants.

For middle-class immigrants such as Lila Shah or Kay Hwangbo, life in the suburbs introduced them instead to middle-class, white Americans as neighbors. And in El Paso, in the sunbelt, in the 1980s, self-described Chuppie César Caballero got to know neighbors who were white natives of the north; they had moved to Texas to supervise and manage new maquiladora assembly plants opening on the Mexican side of the border, reversing the commute Caballero's father had made daily in the 1950s. Commuter bedroom communities in both California and New York attracted nationwide attention as multi-ethnic suburbs, much like parts of Hawaii, where no one ethnic or racial group dominated. In the rural south, native blacks frequently met prosperous relocated black professionals who might be their own relatives.

Quite unlike the past, after 1965, both poorer and middle-class immigrants worked in multi-ethnic settings. In the southeast, African-Americans, Laotians, whites, and Mexicans all worked in significant numbers in chicken-processing plants and textile mills. In restaurants in San Francisco and New

York, the cooks and waiters in Chinese restaurants spoke Chinese but kitchen workers spoke Spanish. Especially in the economically stagnant 1970s and 1980s, African-Americans in cities feared recently arrived immigrants from the Caribbean would push them out of domestic service, office cleaning, home health care, and food service. Sociologists also sometimes confirmed what African-Americans feared – that employers preferred immigrant employees in low-wage jobs, citing their willingness to accept long hours, and low wages, without complaint. Economic competition among immigrant and native black small business owners was also intense. In New York, for example, Dominican and Korean owners of hair and nail salons competed with African-Americans; each claimed to offer special services and expertise to diverse clienteles.[9]

Fears of competition emerged in professional workplaces, too. As American medical care reorganized, foreign-born doctors became the norm in many inner-city hospitals. Doctors and nurses with a wide variety of accents and medical degrees worked alongside Americans, serving both middle-class and poorer clients in clinics like the one that employed Shoua Vang. In engineering and computing, American-born engineers were even sometimes the minority, working not only alongside but also under the supervision of men such as Kay Hwangbo's father or women like Arati Prabhakar. Southern students in math and science classes in Charlotte, North Carolina, complained about fast-talking northern professors and insisted they could not understand the accented English of public school teachers from China, India, or South America. The newest immigrations clearly challenged white middle-class Americans' deep assumptions that it was natives who held positions of authority and who gave orders to subordinated newcomers as workers or clients. But upwardly mobile and professional black Americans expressed similar discomforts. When African-American men objected to difficulties hailing taxis on urban streets, their complaints were aimed largely at taxi-driving newcomers such as Tesfay Sebahtu.

Thirty years of debate about the color line, multiculturalism, and federal activism had also altered the labor movements, schools, churches, and local political organizations where newcomers and natives had long met. Faced with declining industries and the collapse of the New Deal activism that had legitimated its power, the American labor movement lost some of its impetus to bring immigrants together into a multi-ethnic coalition to curb corporate power. In many cities and in the sunbelt, however, new immigrants also gave unions new life.

Latin American workers in hotels, meatpacking, and poultry processing plants brought with them lively traditions of labor protest, saw labor activism as an important form of democratic expression, and quickly learned to work with native English-speaking organizers and with co-workers from Africa and Asia. Much like farm-workers in California in the 1930s, newcomers sometimes complained that their native co-workers in the sunbelt – especially southern whites – lacked their commitment to economic justice and cared mainly about getting ahead as individuals.[10] In New York and Los Angeles, garment workers' unions continued to work with immigrants from Asia and Latin America to raise wages and improve working conditions in the sweatshops of the revived industry. But in many of these sweatshops the employers, too, were newcomers from Cuba, Korea, or China.

Despite occasional cooperation in labor initiatives, competition among the poorest natives and newcomers also provoked violence in American cities, much as they had in the past. The economic stagnation of the 1970s and 1980s heightened tensions between black natives and new immigrants. In Miami, scene of four major riots between 1980 and 1989, native African-Americans particularly resented refugee programs they believed had helped the Cuban community to expand, residentially and economically, at their expense. Cuban landlords and employers, African-Americans claimed, preferred hiring their fellow countrymen, and even Haitians and Jamaicans, over native blacks. Haitians, for their part, believed that native blacks were as prejudiced against them as whites were. In Los Angeles in 1992, disillusioned young African-American and Latin American immigrants, including many without documents, looted and burned local businesses in the nation's first multi-ethnic riot. In New York and Los Angeles, Koreans, Chinese, Iranians, and Indians operating small businesses in poor ghetto communities also sometimes saw everyday conflicts over petty theft and cultural miscommunication escalate into name-calling and even gunfire.

As bastions of multicultural reform, the schools and colleges where immigrants and their children studied in large numbers saw it as their task to prevent just such hostility and hate crimes. Multiculturalists often incorrectly assumed initially that new immigrants from Asia, Latin America, and Africa were peoples of color who shared the cultures of African-Americans, Asian-Americans, and Hispanics. But compared to the Americanizers of the turn of the century, educators in the 1970s and 1980s seemed determined to respect the languages, cultures, and feelings of the new immigrant children in their classrooms. And many still seemed convinced that bilingual instruction for the recently arrived would lower drop-out rates and allow children to make a less painful cultural transition to English (see p. 151).

Richer and poorer immigrants encountered very different schools and school programs, however. Many Chinese, Spanish-speakers, and Caribbean immigrants like Mrs. Morris's daughter attended under-funded, crowded, old, and poorly staffed urban schools dominated by the poorest African-Americans, whose lives had not improved significantly with the end of official racial segregation. Maintaining order was often a higher priority than teaching in neighborhood schools where many students had unemployed, absent, addicted, or dead parents and where drug use and gang warfare soared among alienated students. Financially strapped urban schools struggled to provide help to immigrant students. Few could find teachers qualified in the dozen or more native languages typically found in Los Angeles or New York school districts in the 1980s, so offered bilingual instruction mainly in Spanish and Chinese. In such schools, multicultural textbooks, curricula, and assemblies could do little to reverse the high levels of cynicism and despair found among teachers and students alike.

In sharp contrast, in the suburbs, middle-class immigrants could choose between well-funded public schools and private school education. Fewer children of English-speaking professional parents either needed or wanted bilingual education. While Lila Shah in Syracuse reported becoming "as American as fast I could be" at school, she also participated in community-sponsored "Festivals of Nations," where immigrants sold food and clothing from their homelands. On the west coast, schools sponsored International or Multicultural Day events that encouraged Native- and African-American students, along with immigrants, to represent their cultures to each other in entertaining fashion.

American politics had also changed significantly from the days when urban ward heelers and machine politicians traded municipal services for votes. Throughout the 1970s and 1980s, Americans themselves expressed increasing pessimism that political action by anyone, regardless of background or culture, could solve the nation's problems. Voting rates dropped throughout the country. After the Watergate scandal, and the loss of the war in Vietnam, hostility to federal activism also rose in both political parties and throughout the country, fueled by religious revivals and by conservative hostility to feminism, the Civil Rights Movement, the sexual revolution, and urban violence.

African-Americans became mayors of many troubled American cities – New York, Chicago, Washington, and Philadelphia – with growing immigrant populations in the 1970s and 1980s. Many probably also expected to incorporate newcomers into rainbow coalitions of peoples of color within the Democratic Party. Multiculturalism encouraged all local officials and office-seekers to view immigrants as potential block voters who would support candidates of their own backgrounds as parts of the rainbow. Nor did newcomers completely disappoint such expectations. Cubans in Miami elected fellow Cubans to the mayor's office and to the state legislature, and Dominicans in New York also soon had their own representatives in city government.

But local politics also produced such complex coalitions that neither Republican nor Democratic Party could be certain of immigrant voters' future impact on local or national politics. Unlike earlier working-class Cuban immigrants in Tampa, for example, the anti-communist Cuban refugees of Miami consistently voted Republican. Many Mexicans, along with some Caribbean immigrants such as Mrs. Morris, shared the social conservatism of the Moral Majority. But many other Mexicans – like unionized white ethnics, too – preferred the economic policies of the Democratic Party and many West Indians hesitated to abandon the Democratic Party's commitment to Affirmative Action. In Charlotte, North Carolina, native whites and blacks seemed equally shocked when white newcomers from the north brought suit against the local public school system, trying to overturn a landmark Supreme Court busing decision that had integrated the city's schools 30 years before.

As journalist Gustav Niebuhr observed at the end of the 1990s, American houses of worship even more than local political parties had become "multilingual zones."[11] Refugees received help from Jewish, Catholic, and Protestant VOLAGs (voluntary agencies). Tesfay Sebahtu came to the USA with the help of Catholic Refugee Services and Shoua Vang with the help of a Protestant church. As a young child, Vladimir Sinayuk and his parents left Chernovtzi, USSR, with the help of the Hebrew Immigrant Aid Society (HIAS). HIAS helped the family learn English, find a place to live, and secure green cards. The Sinyuks spoke Yiddish to their Jewish neighbors in the Bronx, and Vladimir soon began studying at a yeshiva so that he – unlike his father raised in the USSR – could make his Bar Mitzvah when he turned 13.[12]

Meanwhile Catholic parishes sought Spanish-speaking priests to try again to bridge the growing cultural distance between older and wealthier parishioners and poorer laborers arriving from Santo Domingo, Haiti, Mexico, the Philippines, and Brazil. Latin American immigrants placed increased demands on urban Catholic Social Services and they swelled the numbers of children enrolling in parochial schools at a time when the female sisterhoods that had provided such services were shrinking and the numbers of priests available to serve in parishes were also diminishing.

Generally peaceful, almost always stressful, and sometimes violent, immigrants' encounters with natives did not depart totally from past patterns. Still, the end of official racial discrimination and the rise of multiculturalism had changed the political and institutional context for many cross-cultural contacts. Class differences were as important as they had been in the years around 1900, but the cleavage of class now cut through both native and immigrant populations. As newcomers reacted to their encounters with natives, forming new ethnic groups, they also often responded to class-specific experiences on opposite sides of the still intact American color line.

New Ethnic Groups

The newest immigrants to the USA after 1965 appeared to be creating ethnic groups on the same foundations – family and neighborhood solidarity – and in many of the same forms – religious and ethnic voluntary associations – as the immigrants of the past. Reacting to a more multicultural America and living in an increasingly interconnected world did, however, make their transformations somewhat different from earlier immigrants'.

Much like the immigrants of the past, poorer and wealthier immigrants alike believed that their expectations of family solidarity differentiated them from Americans, and especially from poorer black Americans. Newcomers still focused on transmitting their distinctive values to their children through family ties. Teaching children to work and to obey in order to do well in school were common themes in immigrant families from both Asia and the Caribbean. Shoua Vang described teaching his youngest children to take responsibility for each other while his wife worked the afternoon shift in a factory job. His oldest, teenaged son admitted to being a "workaholic," highly motivated at school, concerned about his younger brothers and sisters, and committed to helping his family succeed with a farm they had purchased along with

10 of his fathers' cousins. While he recognized his younger siblings resented their father's instructions to stay inside and do school work rather than play with friends, he concluded it was "for their own good."[13] Studies showed that parental pressure often worked and that even very poor foreign-born students from Asia, the Caribbean, and Latin America initially did better in school than their native black and white counterparts.

Immigrant parents such as Vang were often shocked by noisy public schools, by students' casual relations with their teachers, and by American teenagers' obsession with material possessions such as sneakers and computer games. Even the daughters of middle-class Asian families, Kay Hwangbo and Lila Shah, who both received outstanding education for professional careers, heard regular parental objections to American values as expressed in youth culture. Much like parents of Mexican- and Cuban-American families, the Shahs were determined that the well-educated and career-oriented Lila respect Indian sexual morality and remain close to her family. Lila Shah respected her parents' complex attitudes, writing that they were "staunchly Indian in their beliefs and in the way they lead their lives. My family is decidedly patriarchal, and though my father is not domineering, he does have the power in the family . . . All my parents' friends are Indian and neither of my parents feels deprived because of this. They find the morals of this country generally lacking . . . Perhaps this may sound as if my parents do not like Americans, but this is not true . . . They simply do not agree with some of the aspects of American culture like drinking, dating, divorce, and the style of American individualism that stresses the 'me' over anyone else – including parents."[14]

Even when middle-class immigrants encountered youthful anti-authoritarianism, consumerism, and low academic expectations among white students in prosperous, suburban schools or in the sunbelt, they – along with poorer immigrants such as Mrs. Morris – nevertheless associated those values with young African-Americans. Parents worried when children seemed attracted to the consumer goods and popular culture (symbolized by rap and hip-hop music) that celebrated the sexual expression, cynicism, and violence of ghetto youths. Poorer immigrant parents assumed that American education would guarantee their children financial security, regardless of their skin color, and even highly educated immigrants interpreted their sometimes severe financial reverses as the temporary consequences of migration, not the product of racial discrimination. Mrs. Morris's daughter disagreed, of course, and studies in the 1980s and 1990s revealed declining educational achievement among many second-generation children educated, as she had been, in poor, demoralized, urban schools.

While family solidarity remained an important marker of ethnic identity for richer and poorer immigrants alike, neighborhood solidarity was of greatest importance to the poorest immigrants. As in the past, new immigrants formed their own urban neighborhoods in multi-ethnic cities. Los Angeles's impoverished Latin Barrio and South Central had an east-coast counterpart in the more prosperous Little Cuba of Miami, while New York's oldest Chinatown in Manhattan expanded to encompass much of what was once Little Italy; poorer immigrants gravitated toward this old, downtown Chinatown. But in New York, and elsewhere, new Chinese, Indian, Jamaican, Dominican, and Haitian neighborhoods emerged not only in downtown districts but also in the more suburban boroughs of Queens, Brooklyn, and the Bronx. Nor was clustering limited to new immigrants; in the new south city of Charlotte, North Carolina, natives complained about emerging "Yankee suburbs" where newcomers from the north dominated recently built subdivisions.

As in the past, religious organization by immigrants gave formal expression to family and neighborhood solidarity. The congregational organization of Protestantism encouraged immigrant evangelicals to organize their own small Spanish-speaking storefront churches rather than join those of white or black natives. Korean Presbyterian and Methodist Churches appeared throughout the sunbelt and in most large cities. Without the nationality parishes of the past, immigrant Catholics nevertheless found support from parish priests to introduce their familiar devotions and life-cycle rituals, such as girls' fifteenth-birthday parties, to the cycle of multi-ethnic parish events. For many who left the USSR and were of Jewish descent, many practices of Judaism were actually first learned only after entering the USA.

For immigrants whose faiths fell outside the Judeo-Christian tradition, furthermore, building religious centers had special significance. Hindu temples appeared throughout the USA in the 1980s as did Buddhist monks and nuns in their distinctive garb. Islam became the fastest-growing religion in the USA after 1965. Newly arrived Moslems found little familiar in the Black Nation of Islam. Concerned about rising tensions between the US government and the Moslem fundamentalists of Iraq, Iran, Afghanistan, and Pakistan in the 1980s and 1990s, immigrant Moslems struggled to educate Americans about their religious requirements of frequent prayer, gender segregation, and fasting and rest during Ramadan. And many feared that anti-Islamicism had replaced anti-Catholicism and anti-semitism as the latest religious expression of American hostility to newcomers.

While most Americans were at least vaguely familiar with major world religions such as Buddhism and Islam, few appreciated the religious practices of immigrants such as Shoua Vang who had vowed to rebuild his clan's "sacred drum" if he succeeded in entering the USA. Along with fellow clansmen, Vang helped to build a Hmong cultural center on his rural farm near White Bear Lake, in Minnesota, so they could play their drum. Still, he worried, "we don't want to disturb our neighbors with music or many people praying."[15] In Florida and in New York, immigrants from the Caribbean who sacrificed animals, chanted and danced and beat drums as part of the ceremonies of santería and voudou – spiritual practices that blended elements of Catholicism with African native religions – were even more aware of natives' disapproval.

Immigrants after 1965 arrived in a country debating the new ethnicity and multicultural visions of the American nation. Regardless of their background, they found existing groups – from radical Chicano, Asian-American, and Black nationalist associations to Dora Kim's Korean Community Service Center and Michael Novak's EMPAC – prepared to welcome them. In most cases, however, newcomers quickly elected to form their own ethnic organizations. As Dora Kim had noted, few newcomers from Korea shared radicals' critiques of American representative democracy or capitalism. But neither were they completely comfortable working with her multicultural program of cultural preservation and community service to the poorer and older Korean-Americans of San Francisco.

Dora Kim believed that most tensions between older and newer Korean immigrants originated in class differences. "The post-1965 Korean immigrants were pretty well off because you had to be relatively rich to be able to afford to pay the cost of application and relocation," she observed. Like Kay Hwangbo, she also perceived the newcomers as "really status-conscious . . . They're trying to get ahead; earlier immigrants were just trying to survive." By the mid-1980s, Kim's center served older members of the second generation of the earlier migration, who were often working-class and considerably less sophisticated than the newcomers. Newcomers had opened their own centers, which Kim criticized peevishly, noting "many of them are run like businesses. . . . It seems that the new immigrant Korean community just isn't that big on volunteerism or service . . . I don't know if that's because they're immigrants struggling, or if it's because they just don't know how important it is to support social causes here in America."[16] Kim seemed disappointed that newcomers cared so little about creating a multicultural America or honoring earlier immigrants from Korea. And yet soon after Kim spoke about her frustrations with the newer immigrants, Kay Hwangbo, a Harvard graduate who could have found work as a journalist almost anywhere, chose to take a job with the Los Angeles newspaper *Korea Times*, suggesting that the newest immigrants, too, had developed loyalties to an ethnic community and that some were eager to serve it.

Similar tensions characterized group formation for other immigrants, too. In New York, new arrivals from the Caribbean respected the agenda and activism of existing civil rights organizations but rarely joined them, preferring to form their own societies. These promoted economic mobility through rotating credit, provided sociability for former residents of St. Lucia or Barbados, and celebrated Caribbean holidays. New York's late summer "Carnival" became a particularly visible expression of West Indian immigrants' insistence that their ethnic groups would celebrate multiculturalism in their own ways and represent themselves culturally, rather than submerging their identities in those of African-Americans.

Nor did new ethnic voluntary associations appear only among immigrants who might, had they wished, joined the multicultural panoply or American racial pentagon as peoples of color. In the south, newcomers from the north – labeled Yankees by their southern neighbors – complained of southerners' aggressive evangelical Protestantism and eagerness to "refight" the Civil War. But they rarely formed "New Jersey," "Ohio," or even "Union" or "Northern" clubs when they transferred to the sunbelt. Instead, they celebrated their ethnic roots as descendants of immigrants. In Charlotte, North Carolina, for example, the Christopher Columbus Club for Italian-Americans was made up almost exclusively of displaced northerners, along with a few Italian-speaking newcomers from Italy, Canada, and South America.

The product of a new era of globalization, the new technologies of the late twentieth century also left their mark on ethnic group formation in the USA. Unlike earlier immigrants, newcomers who arrived in the USA after 1965 traveled home easily for visits, talked frequently on the telephone with relatives, and viewed videos in their native languages imported from Hong Kong or from India's "Bollywood." Although rates of return to the homeland were lower than in the past (undocumented workers from Mexico representing the single possible and almost unmeasureable exception), many immigrants nevertheless participated in transnational organizations that bridged old and new homes. Refugees in the USA had long organized to send money and assistance to their native countries; Cuban refugees in Miami remained particularly focused on change at home. Immigrant job-seekers from

Mexico more often participated in self-help or religious organizations with branches in two countries. The Mexican government's decision to allow emigrated, and even naturalized Mexican-Americans to retain their Mexican nationality even when they became American citizens indicated a growing interest among many states to maintain contact with those who emigrated. Recent candidates for office in the Dominican Republic campaigned in New York City, and both Mexican and Italian citizens living in the USA both gained the right to vote by absentee ballot in their homelands in the late 1990s.

Ethnic Identities, the American Nation and a New Century

As had every international migration of the past, the newest immigration after 1965 reshaped the regional cultures of the USA and its impact has differed significantly from place to place. (See the student exercise at the end of the chapter.) The most recent immigration has also sparked new nativist movements that assess the new immigration and the newest immigrants in negative ways. In addition, newcomers struggling to create ethnic identities in the late twentieth century did so in the midst of heated battles about multiculturalism, complicating an already complex transformation. In this way, at least, the mutual adjustment of newcomer and native was fundamentally different from that of the past.

As in the past, American cities – whether in the sunbelt, the southwest, or the northeast – generated new, culturally mixed cultures, that struck rural and small-town Americans as bizarre if not downright dangerous. Yuppies, Buppies, Chuppies, angry youthful rappers, drug use, fusion restaurants, and the extravagantly materialistic lifestyles of the wealthiest urbanites became new icons of this urban culture in the 1980s. All contrasted sharply with the Moral Majority's evocation of the church-oriented family values, home-cooked meals, and conservative sexuality morality of America's small towns or its old working-class ethnic neighborhoods.

Cities even generated their own new forms of American spiritualism and these, too, contrasted sharply with that of the Moral Majority. Moslem immigrants from Indonesia, Pakistan, and north and east Africa seemed poised to make of Islam the newest American melting pot religion. At the same time, native "New Agers" eclectically blended elements of Christianity, Buddhism, European paganism, and Native American religions. Neither seemed to promise the moral revival the Moral Majority had in mind, however. And some of the most conservative Protestants even viewed the expansion of New Age and "heathen" religious practices as the work of the Devil.

Despite such tensions, calls for immigration restriction never reached the fever pitch or widespread popularity that they did at the turn of the century. In the 1970s and 1980s, many black Americans feared the new immigrants imperiled their jobs and incomes but even these concerns dwindled somewhat during the economic boom of the 1990s. To discourage more permanent migrations of well-educated persons who could compete with natives, some members of Congress in the late 1990s also supported the creation of special work visa programs, comparable to those already available to agricultural workers, for highly trained and educated migrants in computer and other technical fields.

More persistent debates centered on worries over the numbers of illegals living in the USA. Americans viewed workers without documents as potential criminals who had already violated American laws by entering the country or overstaying their visas. Fears that the USA had lost control of its borders led to steadily increasing surveillance of the southern border by INS employees in the 1980s and 1990s. With easily traversed routes blocked, more migrants seeking to enter without papers depended on "coyotes" (guides, who charged steep fees) and died walking through the mountains and deserts of the southwest. In negotiating with its Mexican and Canadian neighbors to create NAFTA in the late 1980s, negotiators for the USA also hoped to move mainly goods and products; they did not address their restrictive immigration policies or attempt to revive this dimension of liberal ideology. When newly elected Mexican president Vicente Fox suggested in August 2001 that people, too, should enjoy greater liberty to cross borders, most American commentators quickly expressed their preference for existing restrictions.

Like past nativists concerned with mongrelization, some Americans after 1965 also worried openly about the "browning" of America as immigration from Asia, Africa, and Latin America increased. Computers even generated images of what Americans of the twenty-first century would "look like." These images struck many observers as reassuringly white. Despite a rise in white supremacist groups in the 1980s, along with the hate crimes their followers committed against Jewish, Asian, Mexican, and Black Americans, most nativists after 1965, like Americans generally, eschewed racial discrimination when expressing their concerns about immigration. Most denied they were nativists at all.

Instead, most who opposed immigration or focused on the problems immigrants caused once in the USA saw themselves first and foremost as fiscal conservatives or environmentalists. Those determined to achieve "zero population growth" argued that newcomers placed further pressure on the country's already threatened supplies of clean water and air. Voters in California especially feared impoverished newcomers' claims on welfare, healthcare, and schools. Despite evidence that immigrants were less likely than natives to apply for welfare, and that even illegals paid more in taxes than they withdrew in payments for healthcare and education, California voters attempted with Proposition 187 to deny these services even to the citizen children of illegal immigrants. The same did not happen in New York, where city mayor Rudolph Giuliani instead proclaimed the state willing to welcome any immigrants who felt chased out of the west. Differing attitudes toward governmental activism and issues of economic justice among white ethnics and former southerners like Oca Tatham may explain this regional difference in the reception newcomers received.

By far the most emotional objections to immigration came

from Americans who feared multiculturalism had so divided the nation that it could no longer effectively incorporate newcomers. But the legacy of celebrations of the USA as a nation of immigrants lingered and the fears expressed focused almost exclusively on bilingual education. Opponents claimed it hindered immigrants' incorporation and segregated children – especially Spanish-speaking ones – from their peers. Some immigrant parents, too, wondered whether all-immigrant classes were the best places for their children and worried that Americans educators' sensitivity to cultural preservation too easily marked their children as different from, or less capable than, their native peers. Demands for English-only instruction in schools rose in the 1980s, especially in the west and in Florida where English-speaking natives felt themselves outnumbered by Spanish speakers, and in the south, where many black and white Americans had little experience interacting with speakers with accents different from their own. In the northeast, again, conflicts over language use were somewhat more muted.

Debates over multiculturalism also focused special attention on the formation of new identities among immigrants. Immigrants certainly demonstrated a strong interest in becoming American in the most traditional sense. They acquired American citizenship more quickly and in higher proportions than immigrants earlier in the century, a positive sign of a civic connection to the American nation. Unsurprisingly, immigrants from Asia and Africa also naturalized at higher rates than those from nearby countries in the Americas such as Canada, Mexico, Jamaica, or the Dominican Republic, to which immigrants could easily return.

The most troubling unanswered questions about immigrants' evolving identities were not about citizenship but rather about their race and color, and thus about the large populations of immigrants from Asia, Africa, and the Caribbean. Beginning in the 1970s, white Americans pointed to immigrants from Asia, and to a lesser degree those from the West Indies, as "model minorities," praising their middle-class aspirations, and comparing them implicitly, and negatively, to African-Americans. Youth culture, meanwhile, often celebrated black ghetto men as the only remaining rebels against white, American, and middle-class conformity. The children of immigrants and of upwardly mobile black natives alike often worried about becoming what Kay Hwangbo called "nerds," or what some of her peers more harshly termed "twinkies" (yellow skin, internalized "white" culture) or "oreos" (black skin, internalized "white" culture). At the same time, intense pressures pushed immigrants from Africa and the West Indies to identify with African- or Black-Americans, and thereby to acquire American racial identities. Equally intense pressures seemed also to be pushing immigrants from Asia to identify with white and middle-class Americans.

By contrast, newer Spanish-speaking immigrants, like Puerto Ricans before them, seemed disinclined to accept Americans' racial and ethnic categories. Many preferred hyphenated identities more like those of Polish-, German- or Greek-Americans in the past. Others adopted Latino identities that emphasized their racially mixed backgrounds and American roots, not their national origins. And while multiculturalists typically divided Americans into separate ethnic categories, high rates of intermarriage among all recent immigrants suggested that many immigrants' children, too, might ultimately prefer a place in a mestizo or cosmopolitan nation. Thirty percent of Chinese, almost one-half of Japanese, and 19 percent of Korean immigrants married outside their national group in the 1970s and 1980s. Among Spanish-speaking immigrants, intermarriage ranged from 29 percent of Puerto Ricans and 37 percent of Dominicans to 63 percent of Cubans. In the southwest and northeast, where immigrants intermarried in large numbers, so did black immigrants and natives. By contrast, in the southeast and midwest, where fewer immigrants lived, African-Americans infrequently chose partners outside their racial group. At the time of the the 2000 census, when Americans for the first time had the opportunity to describe themselves as having more than one race, nearly 7 million did so – 5 percent of blacks, 6 percent of Hispanics, 14 percent of Asians, and 2.5 percent of white. Most Americans claiming multiracial identities were young, and increasing rates of interracial marriage suggest their numbers will only grow in the future.

Whether you, the reader, are an immigrant, immigrant's child, or longtime native, and whatever ethnic or racial identity you have developed while growing up, you too face questions about the future of America. Will multicultural diversity characterize the future and will all Americans continue to be, or to become African-Americans, Asian-Americans, Hispanics, and Euro- or white Americans? Will Americans again insist on a color-blind nation and abandon their hyphenated identities? Or will they divide themselves more starkly than ever before as blacks and as whites? Will they instead prefer the vision of a cosmopolitan nation of intermarried people with complex, culturally and racially diverse origins? You too will have important choices to make in this new century and you too will help to provide answers to those questions.

Further Reading

Jean Leslie Bacon, *Lifelines: Community, Family and Assimilation among Asian Indian Immigrants* (New York: Oxford University Press, 1996).

Elliott Robert Barkan, *And Still They Come: Immigrants and American Society 1920 to the 1990s* (Wheeling: Harlan Davidson, 1996).

Linda G. Basch, Nina Glick Schiller, and Cristina Szanton Blanc, eds., *Nations Unbound: Transnational Projects, Postcolonial Predicaments, and Deterritorialized Nation-states* (Langhorne: Gordon and Breach, 1994).

Pierrette Hondagneu-Sotelo, *Gendered Transitions: Mexican Experiences of Immigration* (Berkeley: University of California Press, 1994).

Nazli Kibria, *Family Tightrope: The Changing Lives of Vietnamese Americans* (Princeton: Princeton University Press, 1993).

Gil Loescher and John A. Scanlan, *Calculated Kindness: Refugees and America's Half-Open Door, 1945 to the Present* (New York: The Free Press, 1986).

David M. Reimers, *Still the Golden Door: The Third World Comes to America* (New York: Columbia University Press, 1985).

Leland T. Saito, *Race and Politics: Asian Americans, Latinos, and*

Whites in a Los Angeles Suburb (Urbana: University of Illinois Press, 1998).

Carol B. Stack, *Call to Home: African Americans Reclaim the Rural South* (New York: Basic Books, 1996).

Reed Ueda, *Postwar Immigrant America: A Social History* (Boston: Bedford Books, 1994).

Roger Waldinger and Mehdi Bozorgmehr, eds., *Ethnic Los Angeles* (New York: Russell Sage Foundation, 1996).

Mary C. Waters, *Black Identities: West Indian Immigrant Dreams and American Realities* (New York: Russell Sage Foundation, 1999).

Student Exercise

This Week's Headlines: An Oral Report on Immigration's Impact on Local Communities

Throughout the USA for the past 30 years, immigration has often been in the headlines. Yet the many regions of the USA have been affected very differently by that immigration.

In some areas of the countries, few immigrants have settled, and few natives meet foreigners as part of their everyday life. In other communities, newcomers form sizeable minorities, or even absolute majorities.

In some areas, most immigrants are from Asia, or from Latin America, or from the Caribbean. In other communities, immigrants of many groups are well represented, and have created a new mosaic of ethnic community institutions.

In some places, natives argue that immigration is good for the broader community. In other areas, nativist voices loudly protest the negative impact newcomers are having on their quality of life and local institutions.

Think about the impact of immigration on your local

community in each of these respects. Has your home town experienced much immigration in recent years? Why or why not? Where do immigrants in your hometown originate? Do they come predominantly from one place, or from many? Would you classify them as working-class, middle-class, or a mixture of classes? Do they live together, and apart from natives? How have your neighbors viewed the influx of immigrants in the USA or into their home community? As something positive? Or as a negative development?

Read your local newspaper for the next two weeks, looking for news articles that report on issues related to immigration. Choose one article that best represents the impact of immigration on your community or that best reflects your own viewpoint on immigration. Then explain to the class why you chose this article.

Conclusion: Immigration and American Diversity

The USA is far from unique in being a diverse nation but the nature of its diversity is nevertheless uniquely American. The connection between immigration and American diversity is long, deep, and complex but despite this fact immigration is not its only source. The natives of America have always been diverse and they have remained diverse. Yet whatever they called the newcomers, natives have consistently distinguished themselves from the newly arrived. Newcomers repeatedly replenished American diversity, were transformed by their contacts with their diverse American neighbors, and remained diverse as they became Americans. With each new round of interactions, natives changed, too, as did their understanding of what made the American nation different from others.

For over 10,000 years, migrations to North America have created distinctive racial, religious, ethnic, and regional groups there. In 1500, natives spoke multiple languages; newcomers guaranteed that the American population remained multilingual even if their children rather quickly abandoned the languages of their parents. Newcomers introduced from the far-flung corners of the world not only new religions and political ideals – from monarchy and republicanism to anarchism and communism – but also a host of mundane habits, foodways, and family practices. Over the centuries, skin color, religious beliefs, and gender relations have provided the most popular and persistent markers of diversity within the USA.

In seventeenth- and eighteenth-century British North

America, newcomers from Europe met slaves from Africa and the natives whose lands they wanted. They drew color lines between black, red, and white and excluded nonwhites from citizenship. White Americans added a new color line with the arrival of workers from Asia in the nineteenth century. Subsequent immigrations have complicated color lines without eliminating them. First the "tawny" colonials from Germany, then the "black Irish" and later the "swarthy" Greeks became white Americans. The children and grandchildren of Jamaicans became black Americans. The children and grandchildren of Japanese, Korean, and Chinese immigrants in the 1960s called for yellow power even as the ancestors of the first natives of America demanded red power. Some studies now suggest that in the future successful immigrants from Asia and Latin America may also become white, as may those Native Americans who abandon reservation life and customs, leaving a color line to separate only white from black.

Religion has proved an equally durable element of American diversity. Newcomers brought first Catholicism, Protestantism, and Judaism to American shores and later added Islam, Buddhism, and Hinduism. Every world religion is now also an American religion; every world religion also has American practitioners. As they gained citizenship and formed pan-ethnic political alliances, Native Americans' distinctive religious beliefs and practices became increasingly important as a focus of national and individual identity. Similarly, for the children and grandchildren of immigrants who abandoned the languages and ethnic voluntary associations of their forebears, churches and synagogues replaced interaction with an older national homeland as the most common basis for group solidarity.

Gender and family relations have also provided persistent markers of cultural difference in the USA. Every significant ethnic interaction in America has highlighted how gender roles differed among groups; each has made women's behavior the object of intense scrutiny by natives and newcomers alike. In the seventeenth century, the English criticized the child-rearing practices of natives, while natives laughed at

European men doing women's work in the fields. Later, first German, and then Italian, Catholics warned their daughters against emulating the lazy, frivolous, morally lax, feminist, or spendthrift ways of American women while American reformers instead sought to educate immigrants' daughters to abandon wage-earning so that fathers became breadwinners and mothers respected the American cult of female domesticity. Today, by contrast, as parents from India seek to arrange their daughters' marriages, many American feminists hope they will instead prefer individual autonomy and feel they can choose their own partners and family lifestyles. The children of immigrants are often acutely aware of differences between American and immigrant ideologies about gender and family roles; some experience considerable stress in adapting elements from both, feeling they must choose one or the other.

As a source of diversity, migration from abroad has usually sparked controversy and hostility, and sometimes even violence. Seventeenth-century migrations of Europeans to the Americas were migrations of conquerors and the slaves they transported had often been taken by force from Africa. Each wave of immigration generated its own nativist movement, beginning in the eighteenth century when indigenous peoples began to unite to drive out the newcomers and when the new citizens of the USA questioned the loyalties of still newer arrivals from Britain, Ireland, and France. Violence marked early eighteenth-century encounters between black and white jobseekers and between Protestant and Catholic urban dwellers. Migrations of conquerors continued after the USA became an independent nation, convinced its manifest destiny was to expand westward as the expense of Mexican and Indian natives alike. Later, new immigrations from southern and eastern Europe created an urban working-class that attacked factory owners' property and beat off scabs, whatever their backgrounds. Even today, violence between natives and newcomers can occur in immigrant stores in urban ghettoes, when white workers blame Asian immigrants for their unemployment or when black Americans resent the competition of the newly arrived.

Still, conflicts between natives – between white slave-owners and their slaves, during the USA–Mexico war, during the Civil War, during the wars between soldiers of the USA and the western Indians – have also been very violent. National unity was achieved with considerable difficulty in the USA as it was in most nations that have emerged from Europe's global empires. Immigration provided no clear or obvious foundation for unity as descriptions of the nation of immigrants sometimes implied. If anything, newcomers to American shores have tended to intensify regional and racial conflicts among natives.

Migrants to America created many regional differences simply by choosing their destinations. In the eighteenth century, French, Spanish, Dutch, and British carved out competing empires. In the early nineteenth century, foreigners avoided the south, fueled the industrialization of the north, and repopulated the west, exacerbating sectional conflicts over slavery and the future of the west. Throughout the nineteenth century, they brought the high arts and culture of first Europe and later Asia to the urban north and east, helping to create the cultural divide between urban and rural America, between "mainstream" and evangelical Protestants, and between "wets" and "drys." Bypassed by immigrants, first the south and more recently the rural midwest could claim to be the heartland of an older, more homogeneous America. Today's differences between New Right and multiculturalists and between the politics of nativism in Los Angeles and New York also reflect, in part, differing histories of migration into and out of these regions.

Immigration has often highlighted the color line between whites and blacks. With disturbing persistence, elite natives have privileged newcomers over native racial minorities. The British Empire first empowered Protestant newcomers from Europe over natives with red skins and enslaved Africans. The American constitution and federal law institutionalized much the same choice. In nineteenth-century America, employers preferred Asian and European over black workers, while the federal government relocated American Indians to make way for white settlers. Even in today's multicultural America, one sometimes hears arguments that newcomers from Jamaica, Korea, or Cuba are better students or better workers than native African-Americans.

It was only after the liberty to move freely over national boundaries had been revoked, and immigration restricted, that Americans began to celebrate immigrants as makers of America and as forgers of national unity. And even then, a narrow definition of immigrants guaranteed that large numbers of natives descended from the migrants of an earlier age – notably African- and Native-Americans – felt excluded by the celebration. The restoration of Ellis Island as a national monument celebrating immigrants and the economic and political liberty they enjoyed in the nation of immigrants drew especially sharp critical commentary from African-Americans. Symbols of immigrant incorporation reminded these critics of blacks' century-long exclusion from the nation; paeans to immigrants' economic success suggested that the poorest African-Americans had only themselves to blame.

In the 1970s and 1980s, multiculturalism offered a more inclusive vision of a diverse nation but it ignored, when it did not explicitly deny, the possibility that Americans also shared a common, national culture. Yet despite their diversity, Americans are not a random collection of individuals nor does all culture or all individual identity emerge from autonomous ethnic, religious, and racial groups. The USA could scarcely have become one of the most powerful nations in the world if its inhabitants were unable to forge common understandings allowing them to live and to work together. In fact, it is sometimes tempting to argue that by ignoring what they share, American citizens may seek to deny responsibility for the behavior of their nation as a world power.

Still, as the introduction demonstrated, most Americans currently believe that "being an American is a big part of who I am." In their encounters with immigrants, Americans have repeatedly revealed a few deeply held values that distinguish them from other nations. Both the most persistent and the more transitory expressions of American diversity point us to a few of those widely embraced national values.

Immigrants and foreign visitors alike are generally impressed by Americans' intense religiosity. Today, 95 percent of Americans claim to believe in God, a far higher proportion than in most other modern and industrialized countries. Nor is there an obvious color line in this religiosity; black Americans are only modestly more likely to be believers than white Americans. Most Americans assume without question that their neighbors possess religious affiliations. By contrast, atheists – today more often called "secular humanists" – are a small and distrusted minority; most Americans would not choose one as president.

Neither the persistence of religion as an element of American diversity nor of religiosity as a shared element of American culture is surprising. At least since the Pilgrims, white Americans associated their nation with moral greatness and with a special "mission" to the world. Established already in the Constitution's Bill of Rights, religious liberty was the most firmly protected form of American cultural diversity. Black Americans drew images of liberation from Old and New Testaments. And many immigrants adopted a religious faith in order to feel more comfortably American. Although they often chose the faith of their native homeland, their children and grandchildren were more often attracted to one of the many distinctively American evangelical Protestant sects that blend the religious practices and traditions of Britain with those of Africa. Nor are Protestant Americans alone in differing from their co-religionists in other countries. American Moslems, Catholics, and Jews do too.

Americans are by no means unique in their awareness of how gender and family relations vary across cultures. Nor are they unique among diverse and multi-ethnic nations in their quarrels over what constitutes proper gender relations or family roles. Still, it is probably no accident that when Americans placed harsh limits on citizens' religious liberty they did so in response to the unconventional marriage and family relations of nineteenth-century Mormons. To this day, the USA does not tolerate plural marriage, as any immigrant from a polygamous culture in Africa, the Middle East, or southeast Asia quickly learns.

Americans also share an intense and persistent awareness of differences in skin color – something they share with other English-speaking nations far more than with their neighbors in Latin American nations. First established in the British Empire of the seventeenth century, exclusionary color lines were institutionalized in American law and custom after 1776 and they have persisted in marking group boundaries and individual identities even after the abolition of formal racial discrimination in 1965. So powerful is the American color line that today – almost a full half-century after the death of officially sanctioned scientific racism – white Americans still sometimes worry about the future of the nation as the numbers of Americans of Asian and African descent sky-rocket with recent immigration.

Until very recently, the celebration of biological amalgamation or "race mixing" in the USA, along with the creation of in-between "colors" and identities, has seemed almost unimaginable to most black and white Americans. This was almost as true in a multicultural America obsessed with roots and hyphenated identities in the 1970s as it was in British North America in 1680 or during the reign of scientific racism in 1900. Yet such identities are common enough in other countries where people think of their nations as ethnic groups with a distinctive national culture and where it is the nation that reproduces distinctive physical and cultural characteristics in much the way that Americans imagine race does.

The fact that neither language nor political ideology have persisted as important markers of diversity among Americans also point to deeply held national values as sources of national unity. On these two points, the USA and its natives definitely expect conformity from the newcomers. Both demands originate in the American civic religion first proclaimed by the founding fathers of the late eighteenth century and then revised at the turn of the twentieth century as the USA grew to industrial and imperial strength and world leadership. The ideals of civic nationalism and of voluntary citizenship and the association of political and economic liberty are themselves cultural beliefs that distinguish Americans as a nation. They have influenced the thinking of each generation of American nationalists and of the main critics of American nationalism from Black nationalists in the 1840s through the "hard" multiculturalists of the 1970s.

Compared to our American neighbor to the north, Canada, or to nations such as the multilingual Swiss, Americans in the USA also firmly link the English language with membership in the nation. US census-takers have long tracked immigrants' progress toward English-language facility, and immigrants who arrive here as adults typically identify learning English as their biggest obstacle to feeling fully American. Bilingual education programs attracted the worse ire of the most recent nativist movement, even when they promised to transform students into English-speakers. Many Americans seem unable to believe solid evidence that most immigrants do in fact learn English; perhaps this is because so few natives of the USA know any language other than English themselves. Despite a globalizing economy, even many well-educated natives of the USA remain monolingual and doubtful they could learn a "foreign" language if they tried.

Americans' distinctive understanding of liberty also differentiates them in some ways from other nations. The result – as both new immigrants and foreign tourists often note – is a country that actually tolerates a narrower range of political expression than some other western democracies. There have been no monarchists, and few enough fascists or militarists in the USA, as there have been in many other nations. Requiring immigrants to swear an oath of loyalty to the Constitution when they naturalize, natives themselves seemed disinclined to criticize its principles, which embodied the ideals of the liberalism of the late eighteenth century.

Whether Federalists or Democratic Republicans, Whigs or Democrats, or Democrats or Republicans, Americans have believed fervently in the superiority of representative, republican, and limited government as the best means to protect individuals' rights to own property and to choose their own religious beliefs. While few proved willing to protect the liberty to move, Americans have instead fought long, bitterly and repeatedly over the relative powers of national and local governments in the federal system established by the Constitution. Hostility to centralized governmental power is much more evident and important a theme of political life in the USA than in most other modern industrial nations. Every group of Americans excluded from citizenship or from its full privileges – most notably African-American and American women – has protested its exclusion in the language of eighteenth-century liberalism. Even the Native-Americans who successfully demanded sovereignty over their own lands and a return to self-governance in the 1970s created representative governments and then proceeded to elect their own chiefs.

Similarly, Americans have not easily tolerated critics of capitalism, and they have preferred economic liberty to economic equality. Respect for private property and for its pursuit defined happiness in Jefferson's Declaration of American Independence. It was the foundation for Americans' later acceptance of the vast economic power of large corporations, even when they also regularly suspected businessmen of corrupting democratic politics. As immigration in the early twentieth century intensified class struggle in the USA, natives' deep respect for private property encouraged them to portray class struggle as "foreign" to American values. So too, socialism, anarchism, and communism – movements common in all industrializing societies – were portrayed as imports, and ultimately, during the Cold War, as un-American. In the USA, far more than in Europe, it is religious voices – from the Christian Socialists of the early twentieth century to Catholic bishops' critiques of the excesses of the free-market more recently – that make the most effective appeals for economic justice.

Foreign visitors are often surprised by Americans' tolerance for high levels of economic inequality. They may note the absence of Socialists, Communists, and even Social Democrats from the American two-party political system and search in vain for consistent or sharp ideological differences between Republicans and Democrats. And what do they make of surveys in which 90 percent or more of all Americans call themselves middle-class? Celebrating the USA as a nation of immigrants focuses on occasional immigrant tales of "rags to riches" that confirm the blessings of economic liberty as Americans understand it, while ignoring the many anti-capitalist and anarchist immigrant radicals, or their frequent deportations. Even racial and ethnic separatism becomes palatable to critics of multiculturalism when it takes the form of Nation of Islam businesses selling bean pies or Native-Americans opening gambling casinos on their reservation lands.

When members of other nations talk about an American national culture, however, they are not referring to Americans' monolingualism or their fervent faith in economic and political liberty and limited government. Most frequently they instead mean the commercial, popular culture that they see threatening cultural diversity on a global scale. Even to twenty-first century Americans, consumer choice in a free marketplace sometimes seems a more important – or at least a more commonly exercised – expression of personal liberty than does voting.

Ironically, the homogenizing American commercial culture that foreigners fear – whether in the form of American jeans, jazz, rock and roll, or fast food – is, to some considerable degree, a product of Americans' diversity, not their homogeneity. It is a product of newcomers and natives of many, and diverse, origins, and of their many encounters over the centuries. Most recently, immigrants played a disproportionate role in making Hollywood and even McDonald's hamburgers (marketing whiz Ray Kroc was the grandchild of Czech immigrants). The USA would not have jazz, hip-hop, gospel or – arguably – even tel-evangelists if there were no African-Americans.

Yet few articulate Americans today value American commercial and popular culture positively. Even fewer see it as foundation for national unity, let alone national greatness. Unable to envision commercial exports of popular culture as a moral mission to the wider world, Americans must fall back on older options when imagining the foundations for American national unity and greatness in the twenty-first century. Religiosity, acute awareness of skin color, facility in the

English language, and a commitment to the liberal and republic civil religion of the founding fathers are unlikely to disappear over the next century. Natives of today's USA imagine themselves part of a color-blind civic nation, a Judeo-Christian, multicultural, post-ethnic or mestizo America. But it is likely that today's newcomers will ultimately determine which visions of the American nation will prevail.

Notes

Notes to Introduction

1. John F. Kennedy, *A Nation of Immigrants* (New York: Anti-defamation League of B'nai B'rith, 1959?).
2. African-Americans and foreigners are rarely studied together as migrants, but see John E. Bodnar, Roger Simon, and Michael P. Weber, *Lives of their Own: Blacks, Italians, and Poles in Pittsburgh* (Urbana: University of Illinois Press, 1982).
3. A good starting place is Roger Daniels, *Coming to America: A History of Immigration and Ethnicity in American Life* (New York: HarperCollins, 1990).
4. See *Harvard Encyclopedia of American Ethnic Groups*, eds. Stephan Thernstrom, Ann Orlov, and Oscar Handlin (Cambridge, MA: Belknap Press of Harvard University Press, 1980); Elliott Barkan, ed., *A Nation of Peoples: A Sourcebook on America's Multicultural Heritage* (Westport, CT: Greenwood Press, 1999).
5. Hopefully, American students understand that categorizing people by race has no logical or scientific basis. Americans today nevertheless continue to talk about race – that is about skin color – and to distinguish races from national or ethnic groups.
6. Benedict R. Anderson, *Imagined Communities: Reflections on the Origin and Spread of Nationalism* (London: Verso, 1983).
7. *The New York Times Magazine*, May 7, 2000, p. 66.
8. Ibid.
9. See the editorial in London's centrist *Independent*, cited in Bruce Cumings, "The American Ascendancy: Imposing a New World Order," *The Nation*, May 8, 2000, p. 16.

10. David M. Potter, *People of Plenty; Economic Abundance and the American Character* (Chicago: University of Chicago Press, 1954); Daniel J. Boorstin, *The Americans* (New York: Random House, 1958–73), 3 vols.

Notes to Chapter 1

1. *A Cherokee Vision of Eloh'*, quoted in James Wilson, *The Earth Shall Weep: A History of Native America* (New York: Atlantic Monthly Press, 1998), p. 132.
2. John Noble Wilford, "New Answers to an Old Question: Who Got Here First?" *New York Times*, November 9, 1999, p. D1.
3. Venture Smith's story is told in Dale R. Steiner, *Of Thee We Sing: Immigrants and American History* (San Diego: Harcourt Brace Jovanovich, 1987), chapter 5.
4. Quoted material and the story of Kost are in Maxine Seller, *To Seek America: A History of Ethnic Life in the United States* revised edition (Englewood Cliffs, NJ: J. S. Ozer, 1988), pp. 18–19.
5. John Harrower's diary is excerpted in Thomas Dublin, ed., *Immigrant Voices: New Lives in America, 1773–1986* (Urbana: University of Illinois Press, 1993), p. 41.
6. Cited in Colin G. Calloway, ed., *The World Turned Upside Down: Indian Voices from Early America* (Boston: St. Martin's Press, 1994), p. 43.
7. Cited in Sarah E. Wilson, "Changing With the Times: A New Exhibition Shows How the Plateau Indians Incorporate Culture," *Humanities* 20, 5 (September/October, 1999), pp. 31–33.
8. Chrestien LeClerq, "A Micmac Responds to the French," quoted in Calloway, *The World Turned Upside Down*, p. 50.
9. Ibid., p. 38.
10. "Mahican Indians reply to William Burnet, Governor of New York 1722," ibid., p. 88.
11. Thomas Morton, *New England Canaan* (Boston: Prince Society Publications XIV, 1883), cited in Noble David Cook, *Born to Die: Disease and New World Conquest, 1492–1650* (Cambridge: Cambridge University Press, 1998), p. 171.
12. For Winthrop's story see Steiner, *Of Thee We Sing*, pp. 23–4.
13. Olaudah Equiano, *The Interesting Narrative and Other Writings*, ed. Vincent Carretta (New York: Penguin Books, 1995).

14. Steiner, *Of Thee We Sing*, pp. 70–1.
15. Winthrop D. Jordan, *White Over Black: American Attitudes Toward the Negro, 1550–1812* (Williamsburg: Published for the Institute of Early American History and Culture, 1968).
16. Dublin, *Immigrant Voices*, pp. 49, 57.
17. Ibid., p. 56.
18. "Letters from an American Farmer," excerpted in Gordon Hutner, ed., *Immigrant Voices: Twenty-Four Narratives on Becoming an American* (New York: Penguin, 1999), p. 6.
19. Quoted in William S. Simmons, "Cultural Bias in the New England Puritans' Perception of Indians," *William and Mary Quarterly* 3rd. series, 38 (January, 1981): 70, 62.
20. Quoted in Ronald T. Takaki, *A Different Mirror: A History of Multicultural America* (Boston: Little, Brown, 1993), p. 41.
21. "Reply of the Stung Serpent," quoted in Calloway, *The World Turned Upside Down*, p. 91.

Notes to Chapter 2

1. Crèvecoeur's story is in Hutner, *Immigrant Voices*, pp. 1–2. See also Daniels, *Coming to America*, pp. 101–102; Ned Landsman, "Pluralism, Protestantism, and Prosperity: Crèvecoeur's American Farmer and the Foundations of American Pluralism," in Wendy F. Katkin, Ned Landsman, and Andrea Tyree, *Beyond Pluralism: The Conception of Groups and Group Identities in America* (Urbana: University of Illinois Press, 1998), pp. 105–23.
2. Excerpted in Hutner, *Immigrant Voices*, p. 6.
3. Typescript in the Baker Library Special Collections, Dartmouth College, Hanover, New Hampshire, excerpted in Calloway, *The World Turned Upside Down*, pp. 56–9.
4. Anthony F. C. Wallace, *The Death and Rebirth of the Seneca* (New York: Alfred A. Knopf, 1970), p. 118.
5. Benjamin Franklin, *Observations Concerning the Increase of Mankind, Peopling of Countries, &c* (Tarrytown: William Abbatt, 1918), quoted in Jon Gjerde, *Major Problems in American Immigration and Ethnic History* (Boston: Houghton Mifflin, 1998), p. 70.
6. Robert Wallace, "A Dissertation on the Numbers of Mankind in Antient and Modern Times,"first published 1753, quoted

in Marilyn C. Baseler, *"Asylum for Mankind": America, 1607–1800* (Ithaca: Cornell University Press, 1998), p. 128.

7. *Pennsylvania Evening Post*, February 17, 1776, quoted in ibid. p. 128.
8. Quoted in Dublin, *Immigrant Voices*, p. 65.
9. The full story of John Hughes is in Steiner, *Of Thee We Sing*, chapter 7.
10. Pickering's story is in Hutner, *Immigrant Voices*, pp. 23–39.
11. The Hollingworth family's letters are in Dublin, *Immigrant Voices*, chapter 2.
12. Isaac Weld, Jr., *Travels through the States of North America, and the Provinces of Upper and Lower Canada*, 2 vols. (London: J. Stockdale, 1799); Jacques-Pierre Brissot de Warville, *Nouveau voyage dans les Etats-Unis de l'Amérique* (Paris: Buisson, 1791), quoted in David Hackett Fischer and James C. Kelly, *Bound Away: Virginia and the Westward Movement* (Charlottesville: University Press of Virginia, 2000), p. 135.
13. Takaki, *A Different Mirror*, pp. 84–8.
14. Richard Allen's story is in James T. Campbell, *Songs of Zion: The African Methodist Episcopal Church in the United States and South Africa* (New York: Oxford University Press, 1995), pp. 6–12, 33.
15. Quoted in Takaki, *A Different Mirror*, p. 79.

Notes to Chapter 3

1. My account of Haraszthy's life is based on Brian McGinty, *Strong Wine: The Life and Legend of Agoston Haraszthy* (Stanford: Stanford University Press, 1998).
2. Alexis de Tocqueville, *Democracy in America*, vol. 1 (New York: Alfred A. Knopf, 1966), pp. 292–3.
3. Assing's story is in Maria Diedrich, *Love Across Color Lines: Ottilie Assing and Frederick Douglass* (New York: Hill and Wang, 1999).
4. James M. Mangan, ed., *Robert Whyte's 1847 Famine Ship Diary: The Journey of an Irish Coffin Ship*, quoted in Gjerde, *Major Problems in American Immigration and Ethnic History*, p. 104.
5. Their letters are collected in Dublin, *Immigrant Voices*, chapter 3.

6. Tocqueville, *Democracy in America*, vol. 1, pp. 308, 191.
7. The stories of Delany and Douglass are in Takaki, *A Different Mirror*, pp. 122–31.
8. The story of Gro Svendsen's encounter with the Sioux is in Steiner, *Of Thee We Sing*, pp. 122–3.
9. Amy Bridges, *A City in the Republic: Antebellum New York and the Origins of Machine Politics* (New York: Cambridge University Press, 1984), p. 20.
10. Steiner, *Of Thee We Sing*, p. 106.
11. Tyler Anbinder, *Nativism and Slavery; The Northern Know-Nothings and the Politics of the 1850s* (New York: Oxford University Press, 1982).
12. Cited in Jon Gjerde, *The Minds of the West: Patterns of Ethnocultural Evolution in the Rural Middle West, 1830–1917* (Chapel Hill: University of North Carolina Press, 1997), p. 62.
13. "Speech at Peoria, Illinois," *The Collected Works of Abraham Lincoln*, ed. Roy P. Basler (New Brunswick: Rutgers University Press, 1953–55), vol. 2; "Seventh and Last Debate with Stephen A. Douglas at Alton, Illinois," *The Collected Works of Abraham Lincoln*, vol. 3.

Notes to Chapter 4

1. The story of her grandparents is in *Mormon Odyssey: The Story of Ida Hunt Udall, Plural Wife*, ed. Maria S. Ellsworth (Urbana: University of Illinois Press, 1992), pp. 3–4.
2. The story of Huie Kin is in Steiner, *Of Thee We Sing*, chapter 9.
3. See "The Making of an American," in Hutner, *Immigrant Voices*.
4. The story of Antonia Bergeron is in Tamara K. Hareven and Randolph Langenbach, *Amoskeag: Life and Work in an American Factory-city* (New York: Pantheon, 1978), pp. 58–64.
5. Quoted in Forrest G. Wood, *Black Scare; The Racist Response to Emancipation and Reconstruction* (Berkeley: University of California Press, 1968), p. 55.
6. Steiner, *Of Thee We Sing*, p. 145.
7. Quoted in Arnold Krupat, ed., *Native American Autobiography* (Madison: University of Wisconsin Press, 1994), p. 237.

8. Gertrude Bonnin's story is in "Impressions of an Indian Childhood," ibid., pp. 290–1.
9. Quoted in Dale T. Knobel, *America for the Americans: The Nativist Movement in the United States* (New York: Twayne Publishers, 1996), p. 199.
10. W. E. B. DuBois, *The Souls of Black Folk*, 1904, excerpted in Eric J. Sundquist, ed., *The Oxford W. E. B. DuBois Reader* (New York: Oxford University Press, 1996), p. 102.

Notes to Chapter 5

1. I summarize the story of Nicola Sacco as told by Paul Avrich, *Sacco and Vanzetti: The Anarchist Background* (Princeton: Princeton University Press, 1991), p. 27.
2. Thomas J. Archdeacon, *Becoming American: An Ethnic History* (New York: Free Press, 1983), Table V-3.
3. Marie Hall Ets, *Rosa: The Life of an Italian Immigrant* (Minneapolis: University of Minnesota Press, 1970).
4. For an introduction to Mary Antin, see Hutner, *Immigrant Voices*, pp. 158–67.
5. Sara Kindler, "The Family History of a Fourth-Generation Pole," in Thomas Dublin, ed., *Becoming American, Becoming Ethnic: College Students Explore Their Roots* (Philadelphia: Temple University Press, 1996), pp. 28–37.
6. Dublin, *Immigrant Voices*, pp. 234–59.
7. Jacob Riis, *How the Other Half Lives* (New York: Penguin Books, 1997), originally published 1890, p. 21.
8. Dublin, *Immigrant Voices*, p. 219.
9. Quoted in Harold C. Livesay, *Andrew Carnegie and the Rise of Big Business* (Boston: Little, Brown, 1975), p. 140.
10. Quoted in ibid., p. 144.
11. For his story, see Hutner, *Immigrant Voices*, pp. 234–45.
12. Riis, *How the Other Half Lives*, p. 21.
13. Quoted in Dublin, *Immigrant Voices*, p. 230.
14. Steiner, *Of Thee We Sing*, p. 185.
15. Dublin, *Immigrant Voices*, pp. 139–40.
16. Ibid., p. 170.
17. Paik's story is in Dublin, *Immigrant Voices*, pp. 181–3.
18. Riis, *How the Other Half Lives*, pp. 76–7.
19. Dublin, *Immigrant Voices*, p. 179.

20. Riis, *How the Other Half Lives*, p. 51.
21. Lillian Betts, "Italian Peasants in a New Law Tenement," *Harper's Bazaar* 28 (1904): 804.
22. Sara Kindler, "The Family History of a Fourth-Generation Pole," p. 34.
23. Dublin, *Immigrant Voices*, p. 219.
24. Quoted in Jack S. Blocker, Jr., *Retreat from Reform: The Prohibition Movement in the United States, 1890–1913* (Westport: Greenwood Press, 1976), p. 167.

Notes to Chapter 6

1. The story of Ignacio and José Reveles is in Steiner, *Of Thee We Sing*, chapter 13.
2. Quoted in Lawrence H. Fuchs, *The American Kaleidoscope: Race, Ethnicity, and the Civic Culture* (Hanover: University Press of New England, 1990), p. 151.
3. *Forward*, September 18, 1917, quoted in Hasia R. Diner, *In the Almost Promised Land: American Jews and Blacks, 1915–1935* (Baltimore: Johns Hopkins University Press, 1995), p. 52.
4. Quoted in Fuchs, *American Kaleidoscope*, p. 275.
5. Quoted materials from Roger Daniels, *Not Like Us: Immigrants and Minorities in America, 1890–1924* (Chicago: Ivan R. Dee, 1997), pp. 129, 139.
6. Quoted in Reed Ueda, *Postwar Immigrant America: A Social History* (Boston: Bedford Books of St. Martin's Press, 1994), p. 31.
7. Quoted matter from Gary Nash, "The Hidden History of Mestizo America," in Martha Hodes, ed., *Sex, Love, Race: Crossing Boundaries in North American History* (New York: New York University Press, 1999), pp. 23 and 24.
8. For Owens's story, see Kimberley L. Phillips, *AlabamaNorth: African-American Migrants, Community and Working-Class Activism in Cleveland, 1915–1945* (Urbana: University of Illinois Press, 1999), pp. 54–5.
9. Barbara Smith, ed., *Home Girls: A Black Feminist Anthology* (New York: Kitchen Table Women of Color Press, 1983), pp. xix–xx.
10. Jeannette Smith-Irvin, *Footsoldiers of the Universal Negro Improvement Association (Their Own Words)* (Trenton:

Africa World Press, 1989), pp. 56–8.

11. Steiner, *Of Thee We Sing*, chapter 12.
12. Dan Morgan, *Rising in the West: The True Story of an Okie Family from the Great Depression through the Reagan Years* (New York: Alfred A. Knopf, 1992).
13. Josephine Burgos, "East Side Story: What *West Side Story* Left Out," in Dublin, *Becoming American, Becoming Ethnic*, pp. 92–101.
14. DuBois, *The Souls of Black Folk*, 1904, excerpted in Sundquist, *The Oxford W. E. B. DuBois Reader*, p. 100.
15. Morgan, *Rising in the West*, p. 112.
16. Morgan, *Rising in the West*, pp. 72, 118, 127.
17. Morgan, *Rising in the West*, p. 133.
18. Smith, *Home Girls*, pp. xxi–xxii.
19. Soo-Young Chin, *Doing What Had to Be Done: The Life Narrative of Dora Yum Kim* (Philadelphia: Temple University Press, 1999), pp. 32–3.
20. Ibid., pp. 103–105.
21. Smith-Irvin, *Footsoldiers of the Universal Negro Improvement Association*, p. 7; for a short account of Garvey's life see Takaki, *A Different Mirror*, pp. 355–7.
22. Quoted in Quintard Taylor, Jr. "Postbellum African American Society and Culture," in *Encyclopedia of American Social History*, vol. 2, p. 849.
23. Quoted in Takaki, *A Different Mirror*, p. 368.

Notes to Chapter 7

1. Kim's story, introduced in chapter 6, is taken from Chin, *Doing What Had to Be Done.*
2. Ibid., p. 17.
3. Ibid., p. 114.
4. Ibid., pp. 112–13.
5. Daniels's story is in Nicholas Lemann, *The Promised Land: The Great Migration and How it Changed America* (New York: Vintage Books, 1992).
6. Steiner, *Of Thee We Sing*, pp. 216–31.
7. Oral histories of the Cuban refugees are collected in José Llanes, *Cuban Americans: Masters of Survival* (Cambridge, MA: Abt Books, 1982), pp. 13–28.

8. Morgan, *Rising in the West*, pp. 170, 201–2.
9. Smith, *Home Girls*, pp. xx–xxi.
10. *Congressional Record*, August 25, 1965, p. 217, quoted in David M. Reimers, *Still the Golden Door* (New York: Columbia University Press, 1985), p. 83.
11. Quoted in Fuchs, *The American Kaleidoscope*, p. 185.
12. Smith, *Home Girls*, quoted materials, pp. xxii, xxv, 272–82.
13. Wilma Mankiller and Michael Wallis, *Mankiller: A Chief and Her People* (New York: St. Martin's Press, 1993).
14. Epigram, quoted in William Wei, *The Asian American Movement* (Philadelphia: Temple University Press, 1993).
15. Quoted in Leslie T. Hatamiya, *Righting a Wrong: Japanese Americans and the Passage of the Civil Liberties Act of 1988* (Stanford: Stanford University Press, 1993), p. 133.
16. Caballero's story is in Al Santoli, *New Americans: An Oral History: Immigrants and Refugees in the U.S. Today* (New York: Viking, 1988), pp. 275–92.
17. "He's Just Red, White and Blue," *New York Times*, August 13, 2000, p. 4.
18. Morgan, *Rising in the West*, p. 223.
19. Smith, *Home Girls*, p. xxi.
20. "The Politics of Race and the Census," *New York Times*, March 19, 2000, News of the Week in Review, p. 3.

Notes to Chapter 8

1. The story of Mrs. Rosalyn Morris is in Thomas Kessner and Betty Boyd Caroli, *Today's Immigrants, their Stories* (New York: Oxford University Press, 1981), pp. 193–195, 198–202.
2. Sebahtu's story is in Sanford J. Ungar, *Fresh Blood: The New American Immigrants* (New York: Simon & Schuster, 1995), pp. 247–53.
3. Rojas's story is in Joan Morrison and Charlotte Fox Zabusky, eds., *American Mosaic: The Immigrant Experience in the Words of Those Who Lived It* (Pittsburgh: University of Pittsburgh Press, 1980), pp. 353–7.
4. Kay Hwangbo's story is in Ungar, *Fresh Blood*, pp. 288–90.
5. The story of the Vang family is in Al Santoli, *New Americans: An Oral History*, pp. 308–32.

6. Lila Shah tells her story in Thomas Dublin, ed., *Becoming American, Becoming Ethnic: College Students Explore Their Roots* (Philadelphia: Temple University Press, 1996), pp. 206–12.
7. See entry from Prabhakar in Hyung-chan Kim, ed., *Distinguished Asian Americans, A Biographical Dictionary* (Westport: Greenwood Press, 1999).
8. Morgan, *Rising in the West*, pp. 280–1.
9. Monte Williams, "Flak in the Great Hair War," *New York Times*, October 13, 1999, p. A20.
10. See, for example, Sam Howe Verhovek, "The New Language of American Labor," *New York Times*, June 26, 1999, p. A8.
11. Gustav Niebuhr, "Across America, Immigration is Changing the Face of Religion," *New York Times*, September 23, 1999, p. A16.
12. See Vladimir Sinayuk's short memoir in Dublin, *Becoming American, Becoming Ethnic*, pp. 213–16.
13. Santoli, *New Americans*, p. 329.
14. Dublin, *Becoming American, Becoming Ethnic*, p. 212.
15. Santoli, *New Americans*, p. 310.
16. Chin, *Doing What Had to Be Done*, pp. 119–20, 123.

Index

Breinigsville, PA USA
21 September 2009
224371BV00007B/5/A